DIRECT MARKETING DESIGN

THE GRAPHICS of Direct Mail and Direct Response Marketing

PBC International, Inc.
Telephone: (516) 676-2727

LOCUST VALLEY N Y

DIRECT MARKETING DESIGN

THE GRAPHICS of Direct Mail and Direct Response Marketing

By

THE DIRECT MARKETING CREATIVE GUILD

PBC International, Inc. • New York

Distributors to the trade in the United States:
PBC International, Inc.
P.O. Box 678.
Locust Valley, NY 11560

Distributors to the trade in Canada:
General Publishing Co. Ltd.
30 Lesmill Road
Don Mills, Ontario, Canada M3B 2T6

Distributed in Continental Europe by:
Fleetbooks, S.A.
Feffer and Simons, B.V.
170 Rijnkade
Weesp, Netherlands

Distributed throughout the rest of the world by:
Fleetbooks, S.A.
℅ Feffer and Simons, Inc.
100 Park Avenue
New York, NY 10017

Library of Congress Cataloging in Publication Data
Main entry under title:

Direct marketing design.

  Includes index.
  1. Direct marketing.   I. Direct Marketing
Creative Guild (New York, N.Y.)
HF5415.122.D58   1985   658.8′4   84-25502
ISBN 0-86636-006-9

Photography by K.Lin

Color Separation, printing, and binding by
Toppan Printing Co. (H.K.) Ltd., Hong Kong

Typesetting by Trufont Typographers, Inc.
Hicksville, New York

PRINTED IN HONG KONG

10   9   8   7   6   5   4   3   2   1

THE DIRECT MARKETING CREATIVE GUILD, INC.

publisher:	Herb Taylor
project director:	Cora S. Taylor
managing editor:	Steve Blount
editor:	Carol Denby
art director:	Richard Liu
art associates:	Charlene Sison
	Daniel Kouw
consultants:	Concepts in Design

Contents

Foreword

A True Story To Get You Started . . .

About ten years ago I was asked to speak on the subject of direct response advertising to the creative director of one of the most revered and respected consumer advertising agencies in New York.

I freely admit that I panicked.

Here were some of the most "creative" minds in the advertising business—visionaries who designed a page with showstopping graphics, molded elegant five-word turn-of-phrase headlines, and perfected terse, succinct, single-paragraph copy. Their ads were poems. Their television commercials were Pulitzer-prize winners. How would they receive the things I had to show?

Would they laugh at the length of my copy? Would they wince at the transparent come-on of my offers? Would they roll their eyes at my headlines? Or worse—would they sleep through my entire speech?

Faced with a room full of geniuses slumped in their seats, the essence of ennui, I announced that I was going to show them multiple tests—different ads we had split-run in the same media in order to let response identify our strongest communication. I challenged these admen and women to look at the tests and pick the winning ad.

Suddenly I had their attention. For 40 minutes, through ten different case histories, we played the "Which Ad Did Best" game. Nine out of ten times, they guessed wrong.

Finally one of them, who has since become a dear friend of mine, rose to tell me and the rest of the audience that he had discovered the "trick."

"It's simple," he said, "You look for *free, yours, new, now, or never before* in the headline. And when in doubt, bet on the ugliest one."

Free and Ugly!

Is that, in fact, what we direct marketing creative people do for a living? Compose ads that bark loudly, intrusive promises in a horsey, buckeye format?

No. What we do for a living is compose ads, direct mail packages, television commercials, and inserts that sell goods and services to the user on the spot. Communications so powerful that people leafing through a magazine or newspaper for information, going to a mailbox in hopes of finding a love letter or a check, or turning on the television to lose themselves in someone else's story will stop what they're doing and say to themselves, "I've got to have that product now!"

We do it without the help of a salesman, without the relevance, reputation, or ambiance of a store. We do it without an attractive point-of-purchase display, a pushy clerk, or even a product in hand to feel, touch, tinker with, or try on.

Direct response advertising has to be the medium, the message, the storefront, the sales clerk, and the product rolled into one.

The creative beauty of advertisements which achieve these objectives is what this book is all about.

And Now, for Something Completely Different . . .

Of course, the trouble with direct response advertising, or any kind of advertising for that matter, is that by the time you've really got a handle on what makes it work, what makes it work has changed.

This sure isn't the kind of advertising I was doing ten years ago.

I look back at the "free, yours, new, now, never-before" of yesterday with amused affection. I look back at the layouts, formats and designs of a decade past with the kind of detached interest I might feel upon seeing an old lover across a crowded street.

The book in your hands, therefore, bears no resemblance to the book we would have published a decade ago. This book reflects *today's* direct marketing. Powerful, effective, creative, and yes, often quite beautiful as well.

It is advertising that has earned the admiration of the direct marketing industry insofar as each piece was a finalist in the 1984 Caples Creative Awards. This is the only direct marketing award given for creative solutions to direct marketing challenges.

It is advertising that has arrested attention, manipulated behavior, and produced action. It's a coupon from a magazine clipped, completed, and sent. It's a response card from a direct mail appeal, filled out and dropped in the mailbox. It's a television program abandoned for the time it takes to make a telephone call.

This book is also completely different from other advertising anthologies because you can read it on so many different levels and learn from it in so many different ways.

You can look at the kind of copy and art treatments that are getting orders. You can identify the distinct tone of business-to-business communication as opposed to consumer appeals. You can discover the differences in communicating through various media—print, direct mail, catalogs, and collateral. You can see when a single medium is sufficient and when a multimedia integrated campaign is more effective.

You can use the book as a source for today's most innovative new formats and printing technologies: The pop-ups, pull-outs, peek-ins, die-cuts, and non-traditional envelopes. You can see the result of state-of-the-art laser and computer techniques that enable you to print, personalize, and use databases more creatively. You'll find inspiring new ways to carry a message to your prospect, not only on a page or in an envelope but in a box, a tube, a binder, a jigsaw puzzle, an egg carton, or on a hang tag.

You can judge these pieces scientifically too. How well did they achieve their stated objectives? How many sales were achieved, leads generated, or donations made? Here are the hard results. Not generalities. The numbers, dollars, percentages of return—the *pull* of the communications in this book.

. . . And Something Completely New!

The word "new" has been done to death in advertising. It is the ultimate, and perhaps the original, cliché. Its cuffs are frayed. Its pants are shiny with use. It has become seedy and dated. Today "new" is beginning to look a lot like "old."

Yet, with full confidence and good conscience I tell you this book is new.

It's not just newly collected, newly off the press, or newly bound. It's a *new* advertising resource. Because *never before* has there been such a collection of direct response advertising created by the top practitioners in the field—direct marketing advertising agencies, top direct marketing freelancers, catalog houses, companies who market their products directly, and companies whose business is direct marketing. It comes to *you* from the Direct Marketing Creative Guild, sponsors of the John Caples Awards.

It is not *free*. But the knowledge, inspiration, ideas, direct marketing acumen you stand to gain from it are beyond price.

Emily Soell, *President*
DIRECT MARKETING CREATIVE GUILD.

Introduction

Sixty years ago, this advertisement was created by a young copy cub named John Caples. It was an ad which became an incredibly successful classic, and its creator has had a profound influence on direct marketing.

This book is dedicated to John Caples.

A copywriter, research expert, educator, author, lecturer, business executive and, indeed, a legend, he is a very real part of advertising history.

The direct response advertising industry is in the midst of a virtual explosion.

Computerized databases are replacing old-fashioned mailing lists. Two-minute television commercials with toll-free telephone numbers yield millions of dollars' worth of purchases each month. Laser generated personalization is beginning to revolutionize direct mail. Interactive cable TV, tele-marketing, videotex, memory-capable video kiosks and several other innovative direct response technologies are pioneering their ways into the field right now.

The mainstays—direct mail and space advertisements—retain the prominence that has continued for generations. But at the core of *any* worthwhile direct marketing endeavor is creativity...the finest of which is selected and recognized each year by the John Caples Creative Awards program—sponsored, produced and presented by the Direct Marketing Creative Guild.

The first Caples Awards ceremony took place in 1978, at Rosoff's Restaurant in New York, during a regular monthly luncheon meeting of the Guild. The 200 entries covered only three categories—Direct Mail, Space and Broadcast—and anything produced during an entrant's entire career was eligible.

The judges for this milestone competition included Lester and Irving Wunderman, Maxwell Sackheim, Bob Stone, Tom Collins, and John Caples himself.

By 1984, the annual ceremony had moved to the Grand Ballroom of the Waldorf-Astoria Hotel in New York City, by all standards one of the most prestigious locations in the world. With a record-breaking 731 entries—nearly quadruple the scope of that first trailblazing luncheon a mere seven years ago—it was apparent that a trend had become a certainty.

The rapid growth of "The Caples" is signifi-cant enough in its own right. But it must also be viewed as a reflection of the remarkable rise of direct marketing within the advertising community as a whole.

In the past ten years, every major general advertising agency has embraced direct response. The Direct Marketing Creative Guild's membership has skyrocketed from 87 in 1975 to nearly 1,000 today.

Direct response creative work has become a major force in advertising design. In the eight chapters of this book you will see some of the finest ideas and executions to be found anywhere.

1

Business to Business

Pieces Mailed Directly to Businesses

The quality of business-to-business direct response mailing has improved markedly over the past five years. While there has always been a small body of classics produced each year, never has the ratio of superbly planned and executed packages to ordinary or mediocre ones been higher.

It appears that this upswing in creativity will continue, too. There are a number of reasons for this, including:

The high cost of personal sales calls. The average business/industrial sales call now costs over $250. To minimize that cost, the business-to-business marketer must not only produce leads, but produce leads from those who can make buying decisions. The mailings must not only get out, but get into the hands and ultimately the minds of decision makers.

Impatience with the slow payback and difficulty in measuring institutional advertising. Business and industrial marketers are putting more emphasis on direct response because the effect of those efforts can be measured. They can quantify the impact of their messages. And with the ability to measure and test, smart marketers can adjust their approach to improve the impact of each succeeding effort. They can also use the measured response to satisfy the demand for short-term paybacks from top management.

The rise of targeted or niche marketing. As companies have focused their resources on particular markets and on special segments within those markets, they turn to direct marketing. No other medium is so well suited to producing leads from a narrowly defined target group.

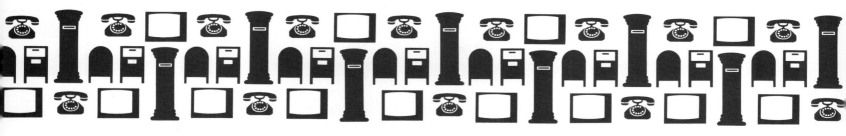

Increased competition. As the number of companies using direct response increases, the need to be outstanding increases. Today, packages have to be very special to get past assistants and secretaries, or perhaps even to get past the mailroom or receptionist. More than ever, packages are fighting for a share of the manager's time and attention. Once they have it, they won't succeed unless they can motivate action, either an order or a commitment to listen to a sales representative.

Bigger budgets. All of the factors above have led companies to allocate more of their advertising and promotion dollars to direct response. While that doesn't automatically mean the level of creativity in direct response will increase, it often does. This also forces small business-to-business marketers to find innovative ways to match the "sizzle" offered by their big-spending competitors.

Increased use of specialists. Most business and professional direct response efforts once emanated from the company's president or from the sales promotion department. Few of the people involved had any special knowledge of direct response techniques. Now clients are more frequently hiring direct response agencies or freelance creative teams. Both the agencies and the freelancers have increased their proficiency in efforts directed to business and have adapted techniques they have used successfully in consumer efforts. Larger marketers are hiring direct mail specialists to work for them full time, and are setting up direct response units separate from their traditional advertising or sales promotion departments.

Perception of the prospect. While it may be more difficult to get through to James Smith, chief financial officer, than to get through to Jim Smith, consumer, he's the same human being at home or at work, and needs to be wooed and motivated. The outstanding business-to-business creations reflect that.

It's often as daring, interesting, well-written and colorful as the mailings going to Jim Smith at home. That's not to say that a well-wrought letter, offset and inserted into a number 10 envelope, can no longer work. It can work—and, in some cases, may have to.

What are the hallmarks of today's top buiness-to-business creative efforts?

● **Mind-stopping ideas.** The "whimper" no longer suffices. Instead, many of today's most successful pieces create a big "bang." For example, a mailing promoting a medical device gives the practitioner an immediate and startling choice between detecting a disease by regular examination or by autopsy. A Chamber of Commerce mailing revolves around "Some Hot Air from Portland."

● **Outstanding graphics.** The look of mailings in the mid 1980s is a far cry from the industrial "dredge" that mucked up so many efforts in the past. Typefaces are modern and easy to read. Photographs—even of equipment—are compelling.

● **Imaginative use of direct mail's dimensional versatility.** In the past, business-to-business marketers seeking to stand out have enclosed mailings in cartons, tubes, even burlap sacks. Today's marketers have stretched the use of carriers and enclosures even further. An agency seeking new business leads sends out a promotion asking prospects if they want direct marketing programs that "cut the mustard" and encloses packets of mustard and relish along with baseball cards. A flooring manufacturer actually encloses a square foot of its new product (imagine how hard it is for the recipient to ignore it!) An airline encloses a duck caller.

Copy delivers the facts the business/professional recipient needs, yet tugs the heart-strings like a classic fund-raising appeal. Graphics enhance. Offers beckon the prospect. And the result is that business-to-business direct response mailings are every bit as creative—and as productive—as their consumer counterparts. With more and more creative talent harnessed in this area, and more at stake for business marketers, the quality of mailings is bound to increase even further in the years ahead.

They're OUT!

THE TOUGH BUNCH FROM PHILIPS

PM 3551
Maximum speed, minimum effort, swift, fast and sure footed

PM 6654/52
The gentle giants, powerful, easy

Title: They're Out
Art Director: Panorama Press
Copywriter: Len Milchuk, Jr.
Design Agency: PRMI Advertising/Public Relations
Client: Philips Test & Measuring Instruments, Inc.

PM 3256
...eful and versatile and knocks spots off the competition?

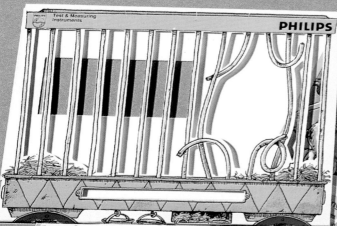

PHILIPS
Test & Measuring Instruments

...g and sharp, regal performance, supreme flexibility
PM 3305

Reply card
Philips Test and
Measuring Instruments

...contained in our records. If there are any errors or changes to be made, would you kindly insert your complete name and address in the appropriate area below. Thank you.

Have we got you in our sights?

I'm in hot pursuit of more information on Philips Test and Measuring instruments. Please send me details on the following products:

1 ☐ PM3305 — digital storage oscilloscope
2 ☐ PM3311 — digital storage oscilloscope
3 ☐ PM3267 — general purpose oscilloscope
4 ☐ PM6654/52 — timer/counter
5 ☐ PM6670 — timer/counter family
6 ☐ PM3256 — 75 MHz oscilloscope
7 ☐ PM3215/3217 — 50 MHz oscilloscopes
8 ☐ PM3551 — logic analyzer
9 ☐ PM3219 — 50 MHz storage oscilloscope
10 ☐ PM3310 — digital storage oscilloscope
11 ☐ PM3264 — 100 MHz oscilloscope
12 ☐ Philips Test & Measuring Catalog

Name _____

Title _____

Company _____

Address _____

City _____ State _____

Zip Code _____ Tel. No. _____

Studies showed that potential customers were not familiar with the breadth of Philips' instrument product line. This piece was designed to acquaint purchasers with the range of equipment manufactured by Philips.

Result:
The piece helped double monthly sales and created new interest among both old customers and future prospects.

Title:	Boston Ad Club
Art Directors:	Jory Sutton Mason, Dominic Farrell
Copywriter:	Paula Zargaj
Design Agency:	Ingalls Direct Response/Ingalls Associates, Inc.
Client:	Advertising Club of Greater Boston

This piece was mailed to businesses in the Boston area to solicit advertisers in the 1985 Directory of the Advertising Club of Greater Boston. The die-cut phone with the message "just pick up the phone", showed how easy it was to advertise by phone, or by returning the attached coupon.

Johnson & Johnson
PRODUCTS INC.
501 George Street
New Brunswick, N.J. 08903

Dear Surgeon:

The opportunity is now at hand to minimize the risks of drain o
collapse and breakage — major problems associated with clo
drainage designs.

The exclusive BLAKE Drain features a unique 4-flow channel c
which contains no holes for surrounding tissues to occlude an
tissue contact area. A maximum degree of collapse resistance
to the special fluted design.

The increased cross-sectional area makes the BLAKE Drain s
current, comparably sized silicone drains. The high tensile str
allows its use in virtually all surgical procedures where closed
is indicated.

A sample piece of the BLAKE Drain is enclosed for your review
the enclosed response card if you would like to evaluate the pe
the BLAKE Drain in your hospital.

Sincerely,
Johnson & Johnson
Patient Care Division

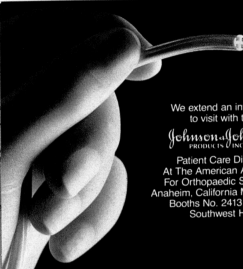

We extend an invitation
to visit with the

Johnson & Johnson
PRODUCTS INC.

Patient Care Division
At The American Academy
For Orthopaedic Surgeons
Anaheim, California March 10-14
Booths No. 2413 & 2415
Southwest Hall

Johnson & Johnson
PRODUCTS INC.
501 George Street
New Brunswick, NJ 08903

**Improved
Wound Drainage
Is Now At Hand**

Title: Exclusive Blake Silicone Drain
Art Director: William Beauchamp
Copywriter: Howard Galer
Design Agency: Simms & McIvor
Client: Johnson & Johnson Products, Inc.

To introduce a new incisions drain tube, this package
was premailed to registrants at major surgeons conven-
tions. Copies were also provided to sales representatives
for use in mailings within their territories and to be
placed in surgeons' mail boxes in hospitals.

Result:
No direct follow-up was done to determine a percentage
of return as those who received the package responded
by visiting Johnson & Johnson's booth at the conven-
tions. Sales managers for Johnson & Johnson attributed
several hundred thousand dollars in new business
to the effort.

Title: Discount Spectacular
Art Director: Dan Gregory
Copywriter: Robin Riggs
Design Agency: Epsilon
Client: Emery Worldwide

Air freight and express service has become almost
generic, with a huge number of companies competing
with essentially the same services at very similar prices.
This sticker-booklet promotion was aimed at getting
customers to ship with Emery more often. A calculator
was offered as a premium to those who made five or
eight shipments during the two-month promotional
period.

Result:
The response was 35% over the promotion goal. During
the two-month period, 39,419 shipments were generated
from the 259,150 Emery customers and prospects who
received a booklet. Of these, 5,053 made the full five or
eight shipments to qualify for the premium.

Title: AT&T Direct Marketing Centers
                   Introduction
Art Director: Noreen Young
Copywriter: Betty Bowes
Design Agency: Eastern Exclusives, Inc.
Client: AT&T Communications, Inc.

The photo on the cover of the piece represents power
and energy, attributes that AT&T wanted to express while
introducing a new direct marketing service. The variety of
services available was emphasized.

NOW DIRECT MARKETING SERVICES FROM THE COMPANY MOST QUALIFIED TO OFFER THEM...

WHO ELSE BUT AT&T!

FOR TELEMARKETING EXPERTISE AND EXPERIENCE—

Who else but the company that taught many of today's top telemarketing specialists and set the industry standards for training and performance... The company that maintains a permanent full-time staff of skilled telemarketing specialists? *Who else but AT&T!*

FOR NETWORK RELIABILITY—

Who else but the company that built the world's most powerful long-distance telephone system?... the company that created the AT&T 800 network and keeps it running virtually error-free, 24 hours a day, 7 days a week. *Who else but AT&T!*

FOR PROFESSIONAL SUPPORT—

Who else but the company that offers every customer local on-the-scene management support... the company whose Account Executives have an in-depth knowledge of each customer's business and its communication needs? *Who else but AT&T!*

FOR STATE-OF-THE-ART SYSTEMS—

Who else but the company that effectively integrates AT&T WATS, AT&T 800 Service, DIAL-IT 900 Service and AT&T Long-Distance Service to meet a wide variety of business needs?... The company world-renowned for innovative telecommunications technology? *Who else but AT&T!*

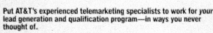

AT&T DIRECT MARKETING CENTERS

Put AT&T's experienced telemarketing specialists to work for *your* order processing and fulfillment program—in ways you never thought of.

CAPTURE CALLER DATA FULLY AND ACCURATELY.

As calls come in to your AT&T 800 number from a catalog, advertisement, radio or TV commercial, or direct mail promotion, trained AT&T telemarketing specialists will obtain and record the caller's name, address including zip code, phone number with area code, complete credit card data and media source.

RAPID RESPONSE FOR BETTER PERFORMANCE

Depending on your program, your dedicated AT&T Specialist initiates a product, magazine subscription or literature mailing. Fast response by your AT&T telemarketing team means sustained caller interest, fewer product returns, higher net sales.

INCLUDES COMPLETE PROGRAM ADMINISTRATION

Market planning, distribution of product or literature, plus program evaluation and analysis are all included in the Order Processing and Fulfillment function. Efficient, single source handling of your complete program.

Put AT&T's experienced telemarketing specialists to work for *your* lead generation and qualification program—in ways you never thought of.

GREATER SALES AT LOWER COSTS THROUGH SKILLFUL LEAD HANDLING.

AT&T pioneered the techniques of successful lead handling and qualification for its own products and services. Now these proven skills are available to you, including receipt and screening of calls, caller interaction to determine quality and interest, caller's purchase authority level, completion of lead report and assignment to its proper place in the lead management system.

INCLUDES COORDINATION WITH EXISTING SALES CHANNELS.

Successful sales lead handling requires detailed planning. Your AT&T Account Executive will work closely with you on marketing strategy and lead management for the most effective lead generation program.

AT&T IS IN ORDER PROCESSING

AT&T IS IN LEAD GENERATION

Title: AT&T Direct Marketing Centers
                    Introduction
Art Director: Noreen Young
Copywriter: Betty Bowes
Design Agency: Eastern Exclusives, Inc.
Client: AT&T Communications, Inc.

ANSWERING THE CALL FOR BUSINESS

Put AT&T's experienced telemarketing specialists to work for *your* market research program—in ways you never thought of.

PUT THE FIVE MAJOR ADVANTAGES OF TELEPHONE INTERVIEWING TO WORK FOR YOU.

Today approximately half of all research surveys are accomplished by telephone interviews. For five important reasons:
- More accurate sampling
- More efficient interviewer training and control
- Quicker, better validation
- Easier interview observation
- Lower cost per completed interview

Your AT&T telemarketing specialist will capture data accurately via telephone, identify the subject according to pre-selected demographic and psychographic criteria, and provide completed documentation on each interview.

ADD AT&T's "CUT-THROUGH" TECHNIQUE FOR SPECIAL IMPACT.

With AT&T's DIAL-IT™ 900 Service, phone market research can be accomplished by a "cut-through" feature. An individual can "cut-through" a recorded message for live interaction with the caller to determine firsthand the nature of the people responding to the program. Other marketing research services include market targeting; list development, the formatting and evaluation of results.

Put AT&T's experienced telemarketing specialists to work for *your* promotion program—in ways you never thought of.

HOW TO OBTAIN AN IMMEDIATE, HIGH RATE OF RESPONSE.

Conducting a traffic-building store contest … running a sweepstakes … getting the word out to employees … checking market response to a new product introduction … sending a message to shareholders. These are just some of the ways your customers can use AT&T 800 and DIAL-IT™ 900 numbers for promotion management. An AT&T telemarketing team can be deployed within 24 hours, fully scripted and trained, to handle any combination of incoming and outgoing communication, accurately, confidentially and with discipline.

INCLUDE YOUR AT&T ACCOUNT EXECUTIVE'S EXPERIENCE IN YOUR PROMOTION PLANNING.

Often, your trained, telemarketing-oriented AT&T Account Executive can suggest a telemarketing application to integrate and augment a planned product introduction, company policy communication, special promotion, and more. A good reason to keep your company's AT&T Account Executive informed of upcoming plans, programs and opportunities.

AT&T IS IN MARKET RESEARCH

AT&T IS IN PROMOTION MANAGEMENT

Title: Announcing The Greatest Expansion
Art Director: Joe Cupani
Copywriter: Steve Petoniak
Design Agency: Ogilvy & Mather Direct
Client: TWA

This accordion-fold piece was used to inform shippers of
new, expanded service available through TWA air cargo.

Title: Cystic Fibrosis
Art Director: Nancy Rice
Copywriter: Rod Kilpatrick
Design Agency: Fallon McElligott Rice
Client: Medtronic, Inc.

To introduce a new device for the early detection of
cystic fibrosis, Medtronic mailed this piece to pediatri-
cians and general practitioners, inviting them to attend a
seminar.

Result:
Those who received the piece, 30%, reserved a place at
the seminar.

WITH THE MEDTRONIC CF INDICATOR™ YOU CAN SCREEN FOR CYSTIC FIBROSIS WHILE THERE'S STILL TIME TO DO SOMETHING ABOUT IT.

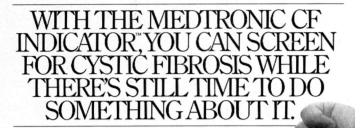

You already know the ugly statistics of cystic fibrosis.

In the United States, one out of 1,800 babies is born with it. And one out of 1,800 will die from it.

With early detection and treatment, CF victims can expect to live an average of 19.4 years before this genetic killer totally ravages their respiratory and gastrointestinal systems.

But one of the most shocking statistics of all is less well-known. According to many researchers, half of all CF victims die in early childhood. *Undiagnosed*.

The insidious symptoms of cystic fibrosis are often interpreted — even by the most skilled and informed physicians — as recurrent bronchitis, asthma, pneumonia, or allergy.

Thus, deprived of proper treatment, a child who was thought to be merely sick becomes another CF statistic.

THE SWEAT-TEST DILEMMA.

Clearly, there are many thousands of children with undiagnosed cystic fibrosis. Children who show few or anomalous symptoms, yet whose lives could be lengthened and improved dramatically if the right steps were taken soon enough.

For thirty years, the traditional laboratory sweat-test has provided a reliable diagnostic procedure. Through chemical analysis of dermal excretions, this test achieves a reasonable accuracy rate in the diagnosis of CF.

And yet, for a number of good reasons, many doctors are reluctant to use the laboratory sweat test for routine screening of possible CF cases — let alone as part of their well-baby care.

First, the test can be conducted only in specially equipped hospitals or Cystic Fibrosis Centers. Time and transportation can be a real burden for many patients and their families.

Second, the complicated testing procedures introduce an element of uncertainty into the results.

Third, the cost of the traditional sweat test may be prohibitive for screening purposes.

Because the test seems such a major undertaking, many physicians prefer not to alarm parents by recommending it — particularly since the chances of finding CF are relatively small.

THE MEDTRONIC® SOLUTION.

At Medtronic, Inc., we saw that something had to be done to bring cystic fibrosis screening to the children, parents and doctors who so desperately need it.

It was a logical extension of our quarter-century of pioneering work in the areas of cardiac pacemakers, heart valves, diagnostic instrumentation and neurological stimulation equipment.

Now, after years of research, we are more than pleased to announce the solution to the sweat-test dilemma:

The CF Indicator™
Using the basic laboratory sweat-test technology, the CF Indicator™ takes cystic fibrosis screening out of the "extreme measures" category — and brings it into your office.

The CF Indicator™ is fully ambulatory, and the test takes just 30-50 minutes from start to finish.

It is simple and practically foolproof. Extensive clinical trials have yielded an accuracy rate almost identical to that of the lab test.*

It is nonthreatening to administer — and also, therefore, to prescribe.

Warwick, W.J., Yeung, W., Huang, N., Du Hon, G., Waring, W., Cherian, A.G. *Evaluation of a New Sweat-Test Screening System: A Cooperative Study.* Copies available through Medtronic.

Perhaps most important, the CF Indicator™ costs only a fraction as much as the traditional sweat test. The compact testing unit is priced at just $250, and each test costs a mere $15 to administer.

Your patients will gratefully pay your small fee for the reassurance — or the hope of early treatment — the CF Indicator™ can offer. And the parents of CF infants will find this timely information invaluable for the purpose of family planning.

DISCOVER THIS IMPORTANT ADVANCE.

In order to introduce the CF Indicator™ to the medical community as rapidly as possible, Medtronic is sponsoring two free seminars at the Hyatt Regency Hotel in Minneapolis on Thursday, November 3 and Tuesday, November 8.

During the complimentary luncheon, the University of Minnesota's Dr. Warren Warwick will present a thorough review of the current state of cystic fibrosis knowledge.

In addition, the CF Indicator™ will be shown and discussed in far greater depth than this space allows – and the clinical data concerning this revolutionary new screening technique will be examined. We will call you during the next several days to secure your reservation for the seminar of your choice. Or you may mail the attached postage-paid card. In either case, your nurse or lab technician is invited to join you; and reservations for both of you are required.

Should you have any questions in the meantime you are welcome to call Medtronic at 574-6045 during regular business hours.

(Outside the Twin Cities metro area, call collect.)

We strongly urge your participation in this extremely important seminar.

It could brighten the prognosis for CF victims of today — and for CF victims yet unborn.

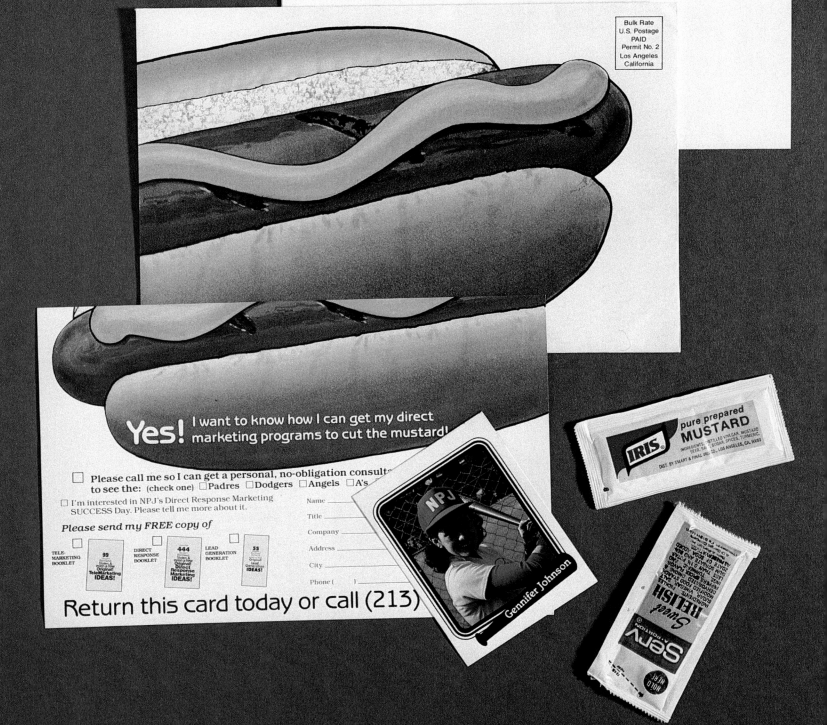

NPJ Nelson • Panullo • Jutkins
Direct Marketing, Inc.

April 23, 1900 . . .

In Hole-in-the-Wall, Colorado, Butch
Cassidy and the Sundance Kid were
planning their first heist.

Bulk Rate
U.S. Postage
PAID
Permit No. 2
Los Angeles
California

Yes! I want to know how I can get my direct
marketing programs to cut the mustard!

☐ **Please call me** so I can get a personal, no-obligation consult
to see the: (check one) ☐Padres ☐Dodgers ☐Angels ☐A's

☐ I'm interested in NPJ's Direct Response Marketing
SUCCESS Day. Please tell me more about it.

Please send my FREE copy of

☐ TELE-
MARKETING
BOOKLET

☐ 99
Stories & more
Original
TeleMarketing
IDEAS!

☐ DIRECT
RESPONSE
BOOKLET

☐ 444
Stories &
more a free
Original
Direct
Response
Marketing
IDEAS!

☐ LEAD
GENERATION
BOOKLET

☐ 55
Stories &
more a free
Lead
Generation
IDEAS!

Name
Title
Company
Address
City
Phone (   )

Return this card today or call (213)

pure prepared
MUSTARD
IRIS

Sweet
RELISH
Serv

Gennifer Johnson

Title: Get Yer Red Hots!
Art Directors: Donna Panullo and David Panullo
Copywriters: Steve Murphy and Paul Nelson
Design Agency: Nelson, Panullo, Jutlins Direct
                    Marketing
Client: Nelson, Panullo, Jutlins Direct
                    Marketing

This self promotion for a small direct marketing agency
used a timely baseball theme and an offer of free game
tickets to generate new business leads. Graphics
featuring hot dogs, baseball cards, packets of mustard
and relish, and entertaining copy were used displaying
the creativity of the agency staff.

Result:
Within one week of mailing 6,000 pieces, the effort had
pulled a response just over 1%, generating 60 new
business leads.

Title: Low Cost Long Distance
Art Director: Richard M. Ference
Copywriter: Spencer Lambert
Design Agency: Benton & Bowles Direct
Client: MCI Communications

The quality, convenience and reliability of MCI's low-cost
long distance telephone service were stressed in this
mailing to commercial prospects. The piece directly
confronts the fears of business customers, assuring them
that MCI's services are as good as those of competitor
AT&T.

Whales are New England's wandering giants, and the best way to observe these majestic creatures is on a New England Aquarium Whale Watch.

Many whales spend their winters in the Caribbean, mating and rearing their young. But from April to October, they roam the rich feeding grounds between Labrador and Cape Cod. Here, your expedition begins.

A scenic cruise takes you to one of the most fertile whale habitats – Stellwagen Bank, 27 miles east of Boston. Typical sightings include Humpback, Finback or Minke Whales, yet as many as 20 varieties can be found in these waters.

The most playful whale is the Humpback. They roll, wave their flippers, flap their flukes, or even breach the surface by heaving their 50-ton bodies high into the air. These acrobatics have baffled men for centuries, and thrilled whale watchers for years.

The expeditions last four or five hours, depending on the wind, the waves and the whales. During the voyage, you'll be able to handle whale artifacts, and learn all about the habits of these fascinating marine mammals from our trained biologists.

Whale Watch schedule:
May 1-October 14
Monday-Thursday, 11 AM
Friday-Sunday, 8:30 AM, 2:30 PM
Actual departure schedule subject to change.

Whale Watch rates:

	General	Member*	Schools
Adults	$20.00	$17.00	$10.00
Children (5-15 yrs.)	16.00	14.50	10.00
Seniors	17.00	15.50	10.00
Military	17.00	15.50	10.00
College	17.00	15.50	10.00

*These are also the group rates for 20 or more people.

Charter groups are welcome, and special rates are available. School groups of 20 or more are discounted Monday through Thursday in the months of May, June, September and October.

Reservations are required. If the Captain is forced to cancel an expedition for safety reasons, you may choose between an alternate date or a full refund. Due to demand, however, there are no refunds for customer cancellations or no shows.

Aquarium Whale Watches boast an incredible 99.99% sight ratio. However, in the rare event that your excursion does not see a whale, we'll be happy to reschedule you for another opportunity at no charge.

Your Whale Watch will be aboard the Aquarium's own vessel. She's a comfortable, 96-foot, 149-passenger ship that's fully heated and air-conditioned. And if you get hungry, there's a full galley serving filling chowders, sandwiches, snacks and beverages.

So this year, why not try something really exhilarating. Come face to face with a wandering giant, on a New England Aquarium Whale Watch.

It's a mammoth experience you'll never forget.

For more information call (617) 723-2206.

New England Aquarium

And this could be one of them.

Title:	Whale Watch Pop-Up
Art Director:	Steve Snider
Copywriter:	Jonathan Plazonja
Design Agency:	Arnold & Company, Inc.
Client:	New England Aquarium

In the New England area, there is great competition among companies offering boat tours to view whales. To increase tour bookings for the New England Aquarium from corporate and university groups, an oversized "pop-up" mailer was designed which would impress recipients with the size of the animals, generating interest in whale watching tours. The novel approach also set the New England Aquarium apart from other tour operators.

Result:
In the four months following the mailing, charter and group tour business exceeded projections by 80%.

Title:	How We Gave Its Bark Some Bite
Art Director:	Dennis Soohoo
Copywriters:	Mark Levit, Rick DeDonato
Design Agency:	Levit & Sherman Advertising
Client:	Levit & Sherman Advertising

To generate new business leads, Levit & Sherman Advertising developed this self promotional mailing.

Result:
The agency increased its billings 13% during the period the pieces were mailed.

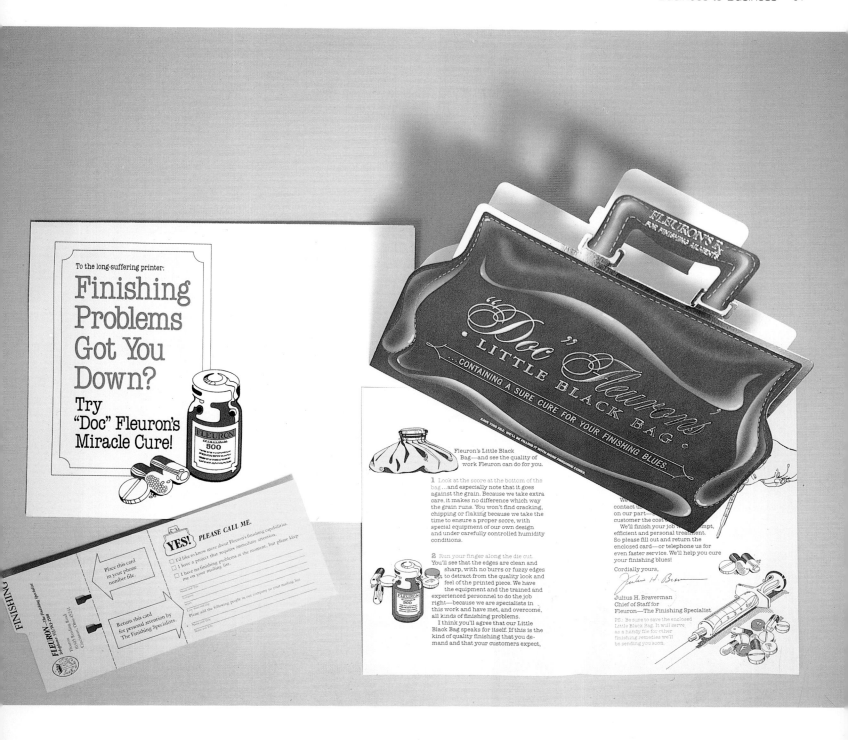

Title: Finishing Problems
Art Director: John G. Feldman
Copywriter: Daryl Knauer
Design Agency: Brewer, Jones & Feldman Inc.
Client: Fleuron

A Cincinnati printer, Fleuron specializes in finishing
services such as scoring, folding, and die-cutting for other
printers. This package was developed to make other
printers aware of Fleuron's services.

ONE CALL.
WESTERN UNION TRAVEL INDUSTRY SERVICES, INC.
5519 ARAPAHO, SUITE 211, DALLAS, TEXAS 75248

John F. Richard
President

Dear Meeting Planner:

Thank you for your request for more information about One Call.

Like all good ideas, the idea behind One Call is simple:

...ork with.

...ry skillful at
...a service that

...way...to get

...personally
...you like doing
...the same set

☐ One Call sounds like a sensible way to plan meeting...
I'd like to subscribe. I und...
subscription fee of $75 l...

SUBSCRIPTION FORM

To subscribe to One Call, complete and
return this form. Or to subscribe faster,
call toll-free: 800-847-2255.

ONE CALL.

ONE CALL.
800-847-2255
WESTERN UNION TRAVEL INDUSTRY SERVICES, INC.
5519 ARAPAHO, SUITE 211, DALLAS, TEXAS 75248

**SAVE THIS CARD AND USE IT TO
PLAN YOUR NEXT MEETING
WITH ONE CALL.**

When you're planning a meeting for 25 or more people,
there's no easier way to do it than with One Call.
With just one call, you get competitive bids from hotels,
airlines, conference centers, and ground transportation
companies. Then you can quickly negotiate all the
arrangements necessary for a highly successful and
enjoyable meeting.

BUSINESS REPLY MAIL
FIRST CLASS   PERMIT NO. 4494   DALLAS, TEXAS
POSTAGE WILL BE PAID BY ADDRESSEE

ONE CALL.
WESTERN UNION TRAVEL INDUSTRY SERVICES, INC.
5519 ARAPAHO, SUITE 211
DALLAS, TEXAS 75248

ONE CALL.
WESTERN UNION TRAVEL INDUSTRY SERVICES, INC.
5519 ARAPAHO, SUITE 211, DALLAS, TEXAS 75248

HERE'S THE INFORMATION...
IT CUTS MEETING PLANNIN...

**ONE CALL.
IF YOU'RE PLANNING A MEETING,
IT CAN HELP YOU CONQUER
A MOUNTAIN.**

**ONE CALL
WORLDWIDE
DIRECTORY**

AIRLINES
HOTELS
CAR RENTAL COMPANIES
MOTORCOACH COMPANIES
CRUISE LINES
TOUR OPERATORS

ONE CALL
800-847-2255

Title:	One Call Fulfillment Mailing
Art Director:	Michael Campbell
Copywriter:	James Overall
Design Agency:	Scali, McCabe, Sloves Direct Response
Client:	Western Union

This fulfillment kit was sent to prospects who responded
to advertising for Western Union's One Call travel
planning service. The kit provides details on the service
in an entertaining and easy-to-comprehend style in order
to prompt recipients to use One Call.

A SQUARE FOOT OF THE MOST BEAUTIFUL, THE MOST PROFITABLE BRUCE HARDWOOD FLOORING EVER... INTRODUCING

THE NEW BRUCE DIY SOLID OAK FLOORING PROGRAM

We invite you to preview the new Bruce DIY Program at the National Hardware Show August 12 through August 15.

At McCormick Place West   First Level Booth #8328

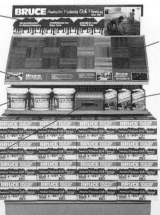

A colorful, attention grabbing header with an actual installation photo. Shows how easy it is to install Bruce parquet.

Product identification tags show actual 4-color room scenes of Bruce parquet and emphasize the features and benefits.

Bruce Everbond LP® Adhesive specifically designed for easy installation of Bruce solid oak parquet.

Bruce trowels for easy application of the adhesive.

24" × 48" sample board actual product in 3 color s show the warmth and b of Bruce parquet.

Additional profit generating floor care products. Products that are designed to keep Bruce floors beautiful for years and years after the sa and to keep your customers comin back for repeat business.

Colorful product cartons designed just for the DIY market.

- 4 easy steps to install Bruce solid oak flooring. Plus complete installation instructions packed in every carton.
- Floor care information on the exterior of each carton shows how easy Bruce parquet is to care for.
- Quick reference chart converts room dimensions to actual number of cartons required. Plus a recommended tool list.
- Suggestions for different applications of Bruce solid oak parquet.

We Just Wanted To Get A Foot In The Door...

SPECIAL DELIVERY

SPECIAL DELIVERY

Title: Bruce DIY Oak Flooring
Art Directors: Jim Haigler, Judah Denny
Copywriters: John Bolton, Linda Shea
Design Agency: Foote, Cone & Belding/Impact
Client: Bruce Hardwood Floors

Bruce was introducing a new line of do-it-yourself oak flooring and a new retail display at a major hardware retail convention. Samples of the new flooring were sent special delivery to buyers for the 100 leading home improvment retailers, encouraging them to visit Bruce's booth at the show.

Result:
Over 20% of those who received the mailing visited the Bruce booth during the show.

Title: Great Line
Art Director: John Morrison
Copywriter: Rod Kilpatrick
Design Agency: Fallon McElligott Rice
Client: American Sharcom

American Sharcom sent this promo piece to businesses to emphasize the quality of their long distance phone service. The message was that your savings don't end when you hang up the phone the way they do with other long distance services.

Title: Giants of the Gridiron
Art Director: Kelly Gothier
Copywriter: Bob Larranaga
Design Agency: Associates & Larranaga Advertising
Client: Pillsbury, Inc.

To generate interesting upcoming sales promotions for Green Giant frozen vegetables, a locker containing football paraphenalia and a challenge to "play ball" was sent to food brokers. Each entrant had to correctly answer questions about upcoming promotions to gain yardage. Entrants were ranked by the number of yards gained and prizes were awarded accordingly.

Result:
Over 90% of the recipients responded to the series of four mailers.

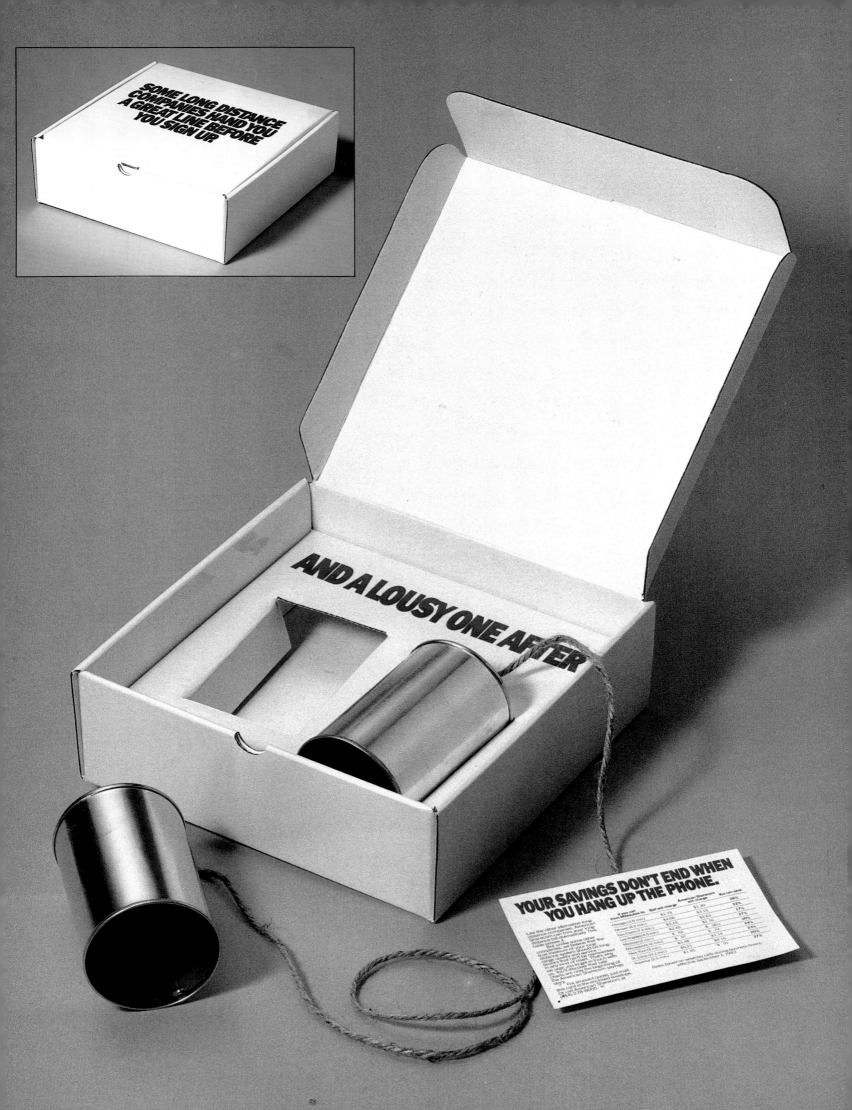

SOME LONG DISTANCE
COMPANIES HAND YOU
A GREAT LINE BEFORE
YOU SIGN UP.

AND A LOUSY ONE AFTER.

YOUR SAVINGS DON'T END WHEN
YOU HANG UP THE PHONE.

PUZZLED?
Keep going.
The pieces will
all fall together.

Title: Puzzled?
Art Director: Ray Eisenmenger
Copywriters: Robert J. Comein, Michael Eleder
Design Agency: Circle Advertising
Client: Andrew Corporation

Improved performance standards for this new microwave
antenna prompted a mailing to alert potential customers.
Magazine ads, which had introduced the product three
months earlier, were generating a good response. To
build on the ad campaign's recognition and lower
production costs, four-color graphics from the ad were re-
used and the new information highlighted through
expanded copy.

Result:
A mailing of 6,000 pieces covered the target industry and
prospects began responding within two days.

Now you have the whole picture. You've probably seen this ad but we want to re-emphasize some important points about our <u>NEW</u> SHX™ Super High Performance Antenna.

Andrew SHX antennas have always provided excellent pattern discrimination and near symmetrical E- and H-plane performance. Now a new version, Type SHX10B, has improved patterns and symmetry with 40 dB cross polarization discrimination.

PATTERN ENVELOPES FOR SHX10B

— E plane   — H plane

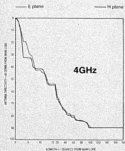

4GHz

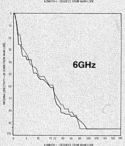

6GHz

Frequency coordination is simplified with Andrew's superior pattern technology. The patented feed cone design produces symmetrical E- and H-plane pattern performance. The separate, precision formed, non-structural aluminum reflector is factory aligned, and protected from damage from external forces. The SHX antenna is capable of operation in several single and multi-band combinations.

Patented

Now there's new evidence of the Andrew SHX™ super high performance antenna's unique performance. Our symmetrical E- and H-plane pattern technology has been granted U.S. Patent No. 4,410,892. That news won't surprise the many users who have already solved difficult frequency coordination problems with this antenna.

The SHX is all metal for strength and dependability. It is shipped, fully assembled, from Andrew's midwest location, on an exclusive steel skid for maximum protection enroute. To suit your specific needs a wide range of options is available, including: various mounts, access kits, combiners, and waveguides.

We'll be glad to send you complete details. Ask for Bulletin 1281. Andrew Corporation; 10500 West 153rd Street; Orland Park, IL; 60462. (312) 349-3300. TLX: 25-3897.

ANDREW
Our concern *is* communications.

All metal construction provides exceptional durability and reliability. Welded construction combined with external bracing means rigidity and improved transfer of loads to the mount. Protective primer ensures antenna durability. The TEGLAR™ long-life radome sheds rain, snow, ice and dirt to assure optimum performance.

A complete list of accessories is available for your SHX antenna installation, beginning with a choice of three rugged, galvanized steel mounts. Antenna adjustment kits can be added to simplify alignment. A circular waveguide support system, upper, lower, top and front access kits, a side ladder, antenna and radome repair kit, and ice shield can be added to your antenna.

Top quality circular or **HELIAX**® elliptical waveguide, associated hangers and transitions are available as part of the Andrew horn antenna system. Several combining networks including a 4- port combiner for simultaneous dual frequency band, dual polarized operation, and Lectrodryer pressurization equipment can be added to the system.

To complete your antenna system, choose one of our GRASIS® guyed or self-supporting towers, and a concrete or PLASTIDOME® shelter, optionally equipped at the factory with any desired equipment. Choose Andrew field service for complete systems capability, including pre-planning, program management, site civil work, installation supervision, delivery, tower erection, assembly, alignment and system testing for total turnkey operation.

To find out more about this antenna and our Complete Systems Capability, contact your Andrew Sales Engineer.

ANDREW
Our concern *is* communications.

If you've been using
Enide, take note...

Dear Tobacco Farmer:

How would you like to cut your herbicide costs in half (or close to it)? By
switching to Devrinol® 50-WP selective herbicide, you can.

Because Devrinol 50-WP is the tobacco herbicide that performs just as well
as Enide 90-WP* (in fact, it performs so well, it's guaranteed); only it costs up to
50% less at transplant or lay-by.

Pound for pound, Devrinol and Enide cost about the same, but there's one
important difference:

You need to buy up to twice as much Enide to equal the control
you get with Devrinol. (See the enclosed brochure for exact rate
information.)

As you would expect, there's no stunting with Devrinol...you get control of
both grasses and weeds, including Ragweed suppression...and you get the Stauffer
guarantee.

So, give yourself a break this season. Get Devrinol 50-WP, the herbicide that's
guaranteed to work...at just about half the cost.

Sincerely,

Ken Stroud

W. Ken Stroud
District Sales Manager,
North and South Carolina

P.S. Now you can take a break, too. Be sure to enter the Devrinol GREAT DOUBLE

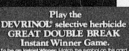

Play the
DEVRINOL® selective herbicide
GREAT DOUBLE BREAK
Instant Winner Game.

GET A BREAK
Save up to 50%

TAKE A BREAK
Win a free trip

Devrinol® offers you a double break.
Selective Herbicide

Title: Mobile Phone
Art Director: Len Sherman
Copywriter: Bruce Lee
Design Agency: Scali, McCabe, Sloves Direct Response
Client: Western Union

A free test drive was offered to attract potential buyers of a new cellular mobile phone. The phone, which cost $2,500, was shown as a breakthrough in terms of its sound quality, dependability, and service, and as a way to enhance the user's job performance.

Result:
In the first eight weeks of the campaign, more than 20,000 qualified sales leads were generated.

Title: Get a Break/Take a Break
Art Director: Deborah Lyons
Copywriter: Valerie Gelb
Design Agency: Stone & Adler, Inc.
Client: Stauffer Chemical Company

Although this herbicide was quickly losing market share, it offered significant cost savings over competing products, a fact that was almost unknown among its users. The client requested a sweepstakes, with the prize being a free trip, to revive interest in the product, and this was integrated to highlight the cost savings.

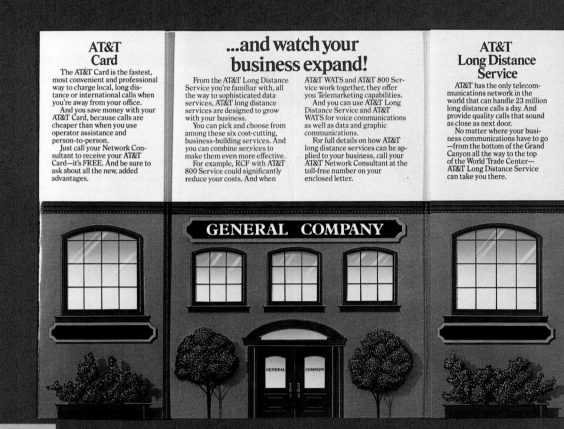

Title: Open Your Business
Art Director: Lynn Herring
Copywriter: Wendy Wishnie
Design Agency: Stone & Adler, Inc.
Client: AT&T

To stimulate interest in AT&T's long distance services among low-frequency business users, normally an unprofitable segment, the services were characterized as "business builders" through strong graphics. The piece folds out to illustrate an expanding business.

Result:
The promotion resulted in a 20-to-1 revenue to expense ratio, three times higher than needed for acceptable profitability.

AT&T WATS

AT&T WATS is a special service for outgoing calling that can cost you much less than regular long distance.

AT&T WATS offers you cost-saving ways to keep in touch with customers, suppliers and sales reps, to help your business save money and increase profits.

AT&T WATS is available 24 hours a day, seven days a week. And it reaches everywhere, even remote geographical areas, and gives you long distance calls that sound as close as next door.

RCF-AT&T 800 Service

Remote Call Forwarding (RCF) combined with AT&T Long Distance Service makes it possible to offer a local phone number in almost any city ... calls are automatically forwarded to your office.

When you combine AT&T 800 Service with RCF, calls are forwarded over AT&T 800 Service, so your costs could be significantly reduced.

Your local identity is reinforced with listings in the local White and Yellow Pages for those cities.

...and watch your business expand!

From the AT&T Long Distance Service you're familiar with, all the way to sophisticated data services, AT&T long distance services are designed to grow with your business.

You can pick and choose from among these six cost-cutting, business-building services. And you can combine services to make them even more effective.

For example, RCF with AT&T 800 Service could significantly reduce your costs. And when

AT&T WATS and AT&T 800 Service work together, they offer you Telemarketing capabilities.

And you can use AT&T Long Distance Service and AT&T WATS for voice communications as well as data and graphic communications.

For full details on how AT&T long distance services can be applied to your business, call your AT&T Network Consultant at the toll-free number on your enclosed letter.

AT&T 800 Service

More prospects and customers are likely to call your business to order, reorder or inquire about your products and services when you offer a toll-free AT&T 800 Service number for incoming calls.

AT&T also offers a number of options you can add to your AT&T 800 Service to make it even more convenient and effective.

And AT&T 800 Service-Canada makes it possible to offer Canadian prospects and customers instant, toll-free access to your business.

DATAPHONE® Digital Service

As you well know, downtime on a data communications system can mean backlogs, overtime, expensive repairs, delayed orders, poor customer service ... all adding up to higher costs and reduced revenue.

Well, AT&T has developed a virtually flawless way for machines to "talk."

DATAPHONE Digital Service is part of the ACCUNET™ family of services. It's "up" over 99% of the time. And it's guaranteed 99.5% error free.

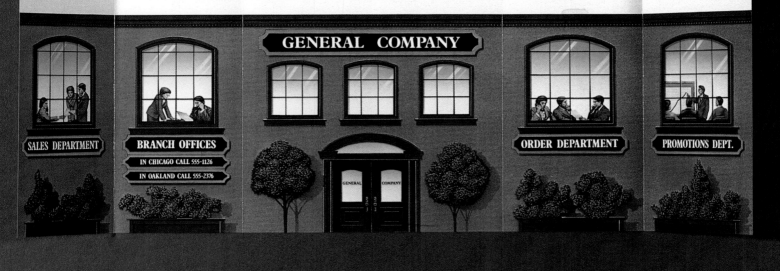

GENERAL COMPANY

SALES DEPARTMENT

BRANCH OFFICES
IN CHICAGO CALL 555-1126
IN OAKLAND CALL 555-2376

ORDER DEPARTMENT

PROMOTIONS DEPT.

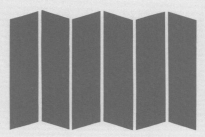

Title: Your Free Mailbox Is Enclosed
Art Director: Tom DeBow
Copywriters: Ann Goodstein, George Rockmore
Design Agency: T.J. DeBow and Company, Ltd.
Client: ITT Communications Services Group

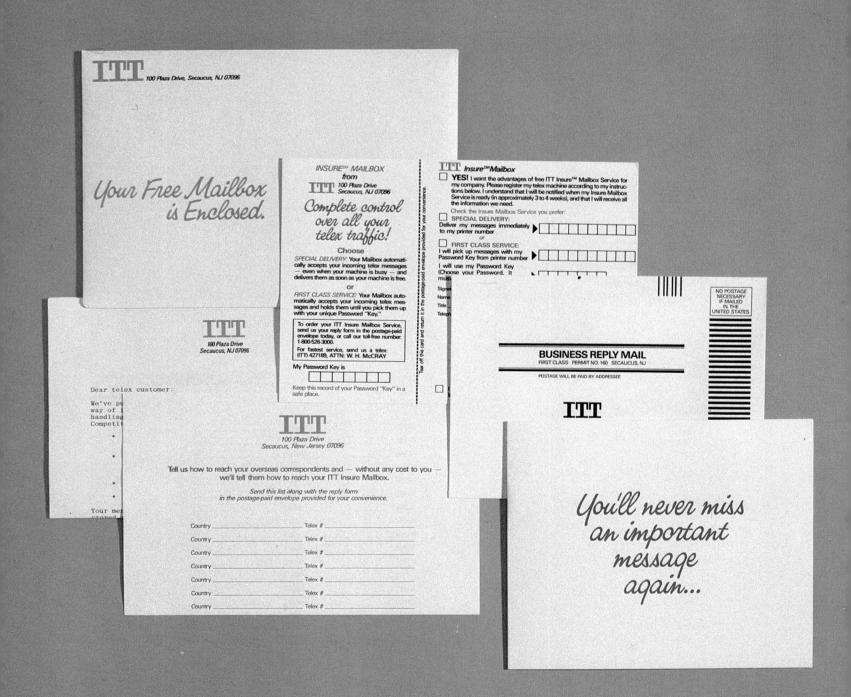

The mailbox was devised as a symbol to represent ITT's Insure Service. The telecommunications service accepts and holds telex messages for its clients until they are ready to retrieve them. The message was that Insure Service worked like a mailbox for incoming telexes and that, like a mailbox, was simple to understand and easy to use.

Result:
Responses exceeded those of previous efforts by 30% to 50%.

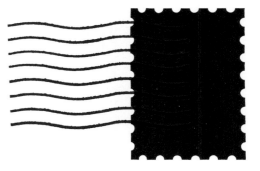

Inter·Continental Hotels
Americas Division
cordially invites you and your agents
to be our guests for complimentary V.I.P. Weekends
at any of our world-class hotels
in
North and South America.
Any time before June 30, 1985.

R.S.V.P. by September 15, 1984.

Luxur
for yo

Comp

R.S.V.P.

Inter-Continental Hot
11501 Georgia Avenue
Suite 405
Wheaton, MD 20902

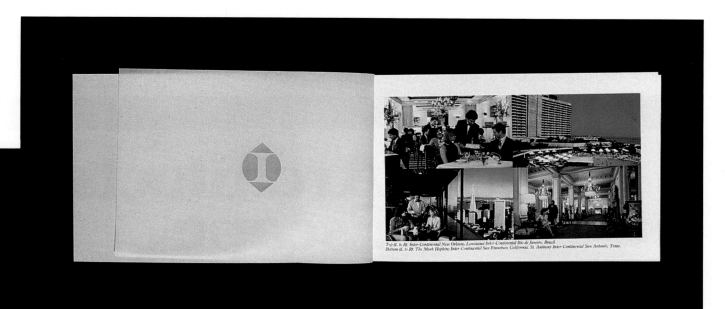

Top (L. to R): Inter-Continental New Orleans, Louisiana; Inter-Continental Rio de Janeiro, Brazil.
Bottom (L. to R): The Mark Hopkins Inter-Continental San Francisco, California; St. Anthony Inter-Continental San Antonio, Texas.

INTER•CONTINENTAL HOTELS
Americas Division

World-class hotels in North and South America's most exciting cities.

Title:	Luxurious Weekend Escapes
Art Directors:	Cindy Cole, Pat Cunningham
Copywriters:	Cindy Cole, Chris Spillman
Design Agency:	Earle Palmer Brown/Brown Direct
Client:	InterContinental Hotels

To increase the awareness of InterContinental Hotels in North and South America among travel agencies with $1 million or more in annual billings, agency managers were sent an invitation to stay at an InterContinental for a weekend.

Result:
More than half of the agency managers requested certificates for accommodations.

Great Architects of Escape

Kevin Callahan

Title: Great Architects of Escape
Art Directors: Robert Patrick, Ed Galog
Copywriters: John Bodnar, Ed Galog
Design Agency: STG Marketing Communications. Inc.
Client: Philips Electronic Instruments, Inc.

This piece was developed to introduce Philips' line of security screening systems to security officers at correctional institutions and to architects who design correctional facilities. The illustrations of safecrackers and other thugs humorously express the point.

Result:

The piece generated a 27% response, uncovering a number of new construction and renovation projects for the sales force to follow up on.

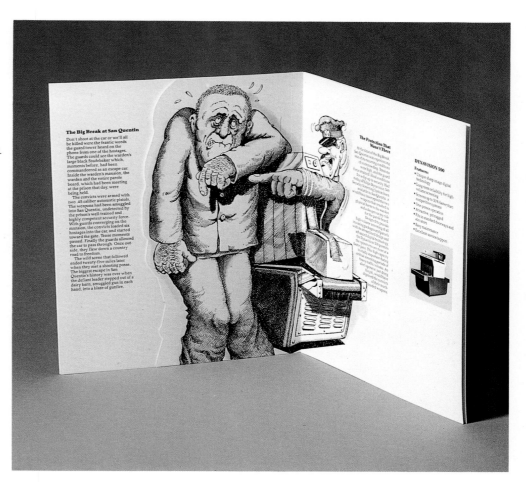

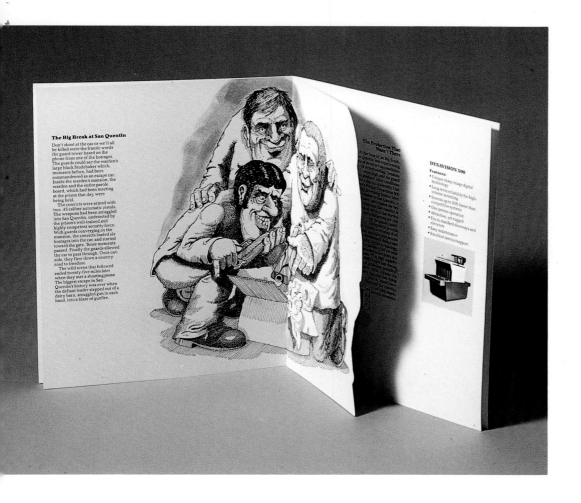

Title: On People's 10th Birthday
Art Directors: Arthur Beckenstein, Dick Martell
Copywriter: Harry Welsh
Design Agency: People Promotion
Client: People Magazine

As People Magazine neared its tenth anniversary, a sales promotion piece was created to increase advertising sales for the special anniversary issue.

Result:
More ad pages were sold for the anniversary issue than for any other single issue in the magazine's history.

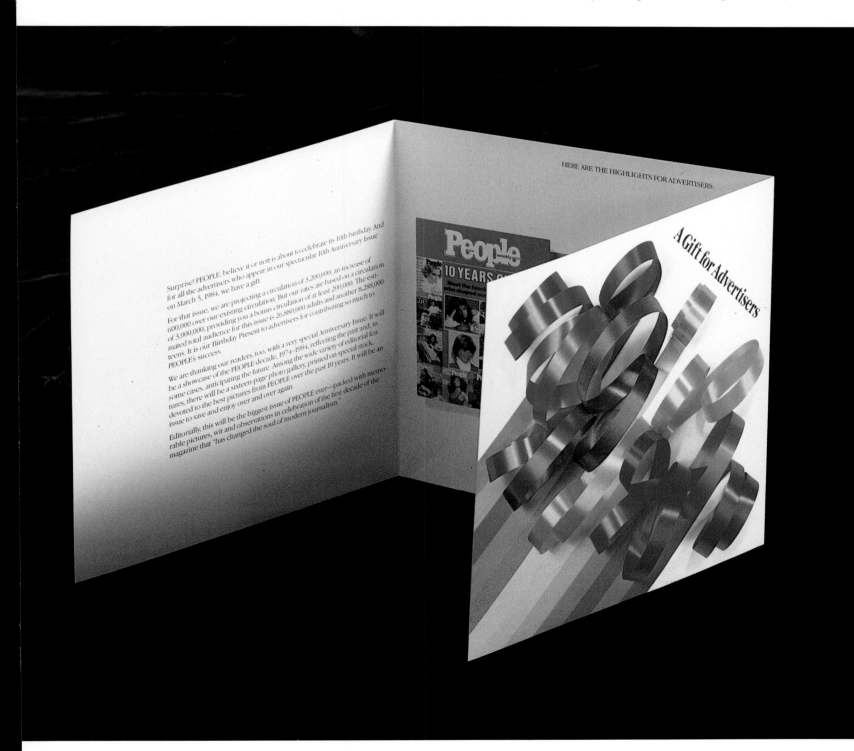

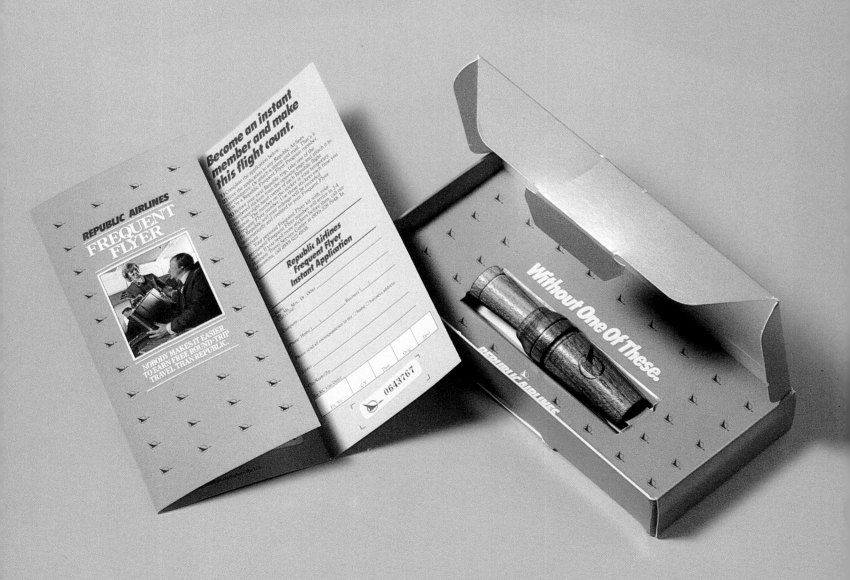

Title: Memphis Duck Caller
Art Director: Terrell Daniels
Copywriter: Patrick Hanlon
Design Agency: Campbell-Mithun, Inc.
Client: Republic Airlines

An attention-getting promotion was needed to spur
interest in Republic Airlines' Frequent Flyer program for
business travelers. Clever copy and a duck call (alluding
to the airline's logo, which features a duck) were
combined in an eye-catching package to sell the
program's benefits.

Result:
A return of 14% on the mailing resulted in 2,108 new
clients enrolled in the Frequent Flyer program.

Title: MCI WATTS
Art Director: Richard M. Ference
Copywriter: Spencer Lambert
Design Agency: Benton & Bowles Direct
Client: MCI Communications

When MCI introduced its new WATS service, this piece
was developed to inform time-pressured corporate
decision makers of the service and convenience available
to them and that it was a low-cost alternative to
AT&T's WATS lines.

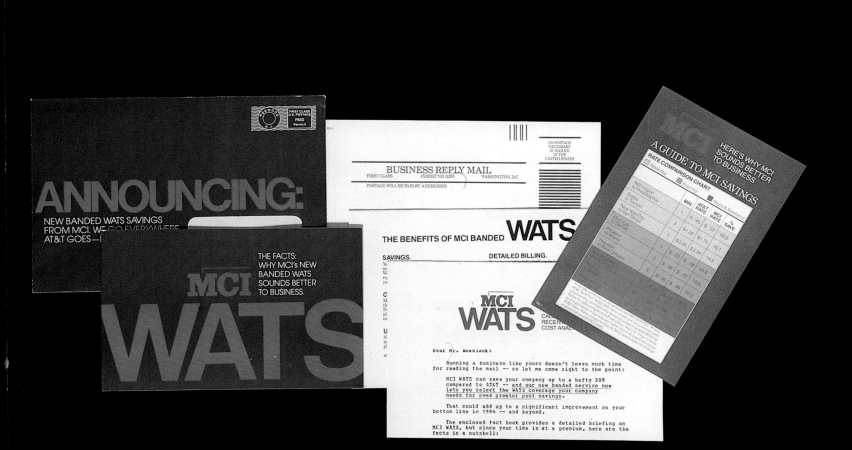

Title: VisiCorp VisiWord Mailer
Art Director: Wayne Kosaka
Copywriter: Carleton Prince
Design Agency: Foote, Cone & Belding/Impact
Client: VisiCorp

The intent of this effort was to sell packages including word processing software, tutorial software, and a self-study book to customers who had registered warranties with VisiCorp.

Title: Pop-Up House
Art Directors: Tom Tarvin, Bruce Shafer
Copywriter: Don Kortekamp
Design Agency: Sive Associates
Client: Senco Fastening Systems

An increase in the rate of new construction generated a
need by builders for ways to speed up production. The
benefits of the Carlson/Senco fastening system—superior
quality construction, faster production, and lower labor
costs—were sold through this mailing.

Result:
Inquiries increased by 400%.

Title: You're Invited to the Launch
Art Director: Timothy Savage
Copywriter: Joel J. Blattstein
Design Agency: Schein/Blattstein Advertising, Inc.
Client: Sailor Publications, Inc.

This piece was mailed to solicit subscriptions to a new publication. One of the publication's prime selling points was that it's issued 22 times per year, rather than the more ordinary 12 times.

Title: Freedom
Art Director: Jolene Rickard
Copywriter: Mike Edelstein
Design Agency: Grey Direct
Client: Lanier, Inc.

To reposition Lanier as a supplier of state-of-the-art office automation equipment, rather than of dictation equipment, an attention-getting piece was developed which promised executives "more freedom on the job."

Result:
The package pulled a 339% better response than the previous control package, lowered cost per inquiry by 56%, and increased the sales per lead by 100%.

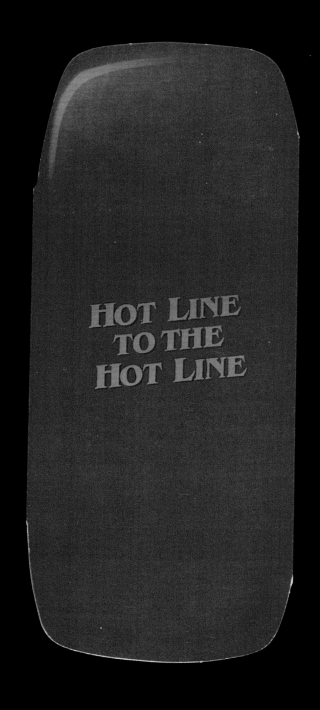

Title:	Hot Line
Art Director:	Teri Habig
Copywriter:	David Wesolowski
Design Agency:	Keller Crescent Advertising
Client:	Magic Chef, Inc.

Magic Chef wanted to recruit new dealers for its appliances and convert dealers selling only one Magic Chef product to full-line dealers. A series of local showings of Magic Chef's 1984 product line were arranged, and this package was pre-mailed to attract attendance. The specific objects were to garner a 13% response from new dealers; a 25% response from existing, single product dealers; convert 20% of those responding to full-time dealers; generate $500,000 in sales to new dealers and $500,000 in sales of new products to existing dealers.

Result:
The piece attracted 45% of those who weren't Magic Chef dealers and 75% of those who were existing, single-product dealers to the showings. Of those, 18% were converted to full-line dealers, generating $800,000 in sales to new dealers and $1.2 million in sales of new products to existing dealers.

paper specifiers, and printers. This piece showed the versatility of Lewmar paper for die cutting, hot foil stamping, scoring, printing, and packaging. Also, a contest provided free gifts to customers ordering specific papers.

Result:
Industry reaction to the piece was overwhelming.

Lewmar Suits Your Paper Needs!

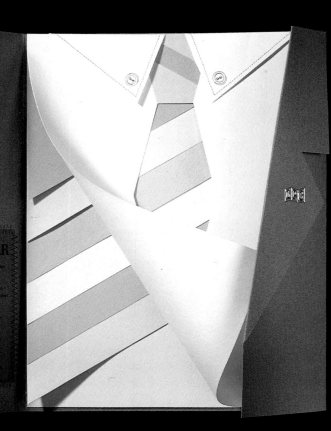

Finally! A Paper Promotion That Suits Your Needs!

Choose a free gift when you order 4 or more cartons (folio size) or 10 or more cartons (cut size) of GILBERT® oxford or Curtis Flannel. Specify to your printer to purchase either GILBERT® oxford or Curtis Flannel from Lewmar Paper Company and your printer can also receive a free gift. This promotion ends December 31, 1984 and supplies are limited, so enter early. They'll warm up your print! **You may enter as often as you like!**

Gifts are only redeemable at

bloomingdale's
SHORT HILLS

Please cut here ✂

Order Form
(You and your printer may each order (1) of the following fine gifts.)

Send Mr. Gary Pedinoff
certificate(s) Lewmar Paper Company
to: 370 Adams Street
Newark, NJ 07114
(201) 589-2800

_____ 4 oz. Grey Flannel spray cologne in Grey Flannel pouch

_____ Bloomingdale's Traditionalist button-down oxford shirts

_____ Flannel Pajamas   neck sizes _____   sleeve sizes _____

_____ Flannel Night Shirt

full _____   fitted _____

(No substitutions. Colors depend on   Colors: _____ white   _____ blue   _____ pink
availability.)   _____ ecru   _____ yellow

Printer

YES, I am interested in Curtis Flannel and GILBERT® Oxford. Lewmar, show me how you can suit my paper needs. Please send me the following:

☐ Curtis Flannel Printed Samples

☐ GILBERT® Oxford Printed Samples

☐ GILBERT® Oxford Fashion Box (plain sheets and envelopes)

LPC Lewmar Paper Company

Please print

Name _____

Title _____

Company _____

Address _____

City _____ State _____ Zip _____

Telephone Number (_____)
AREA CODE

State _____ Zip _____

Number (_____)
AREA CODE

_____ations

Quantity _____ Size _____ Basis Wt. _____ Color _____

Grade of Paper _____ Purchase Order # _____

For Lewmar Use Only

Confirming Purchase Order # _____   Authorized Signature _____   Date _____

RCA Cylix keeps your network running smoothly

When you run with RCA Cylix, you're running with the stars. Because we're a satellite based, value-added network. Providing end-to-end management and a permanent virtual circuit that's perfect for transaction oriented applications anywhere in the continental United States or Alaska.

We'll get you off to a winning start, too. One phone call puts our experienced people to work for you. Installing your network. Handling all those dealings with all those phone companies. And then keeping your network running smoothly thanks to our unique service concept. Plus, when

you're ready to grow, our design flexibility makes that growth both easy and cost effective.

Whether it's state-of-the-art technology, technical expertise or on-going guidance you want, you'll find we can provide it.

That kind of convenience, efficiency and service is what single vendor simplicity is all about. But it's only part of the value our value-added network can offer.

Title: Runner's Guide
Art Director: Eddie Tucker
Copywriters: Bob Gilbert, Brett Robbs
Design Agency: Ward, Archer & Associates
Client: RCA CYLIX Communications Network

Since the breakup of AT&T, corporate data processing managers have been forced to deal with a number of telecommunications companies, rather than just one. A lighthearted approach was used to break through the clutter of direct mail these professionals receive and tell them that RCA's CYLIX Network could save them time and energy.

Result:
The effort exceeded the return of previous mailings for CYLIX by drawing a response rate greater than 8%.

RCA Cylix Communications Network
800 Ridge Lake Boulevard | Memphis, TN 38119-9404

We've got a free runner's shirt just for you
and tips for a smooth running data network.

Title: Need a Hand?
Art Director: Eddie Tucker
Copywriters: Joy Blair, Brett Robbs
Design Agency: Ward Archer & Associates
Client: RCA CYLIX Communications
                    Network

The brochure was mailed concurrently with the appearance of a similar ad in trade publications reaching data processing managers. A real string was used to close the brochure, involving the recipient by having them cut the string.

Need a hand with your data networking?

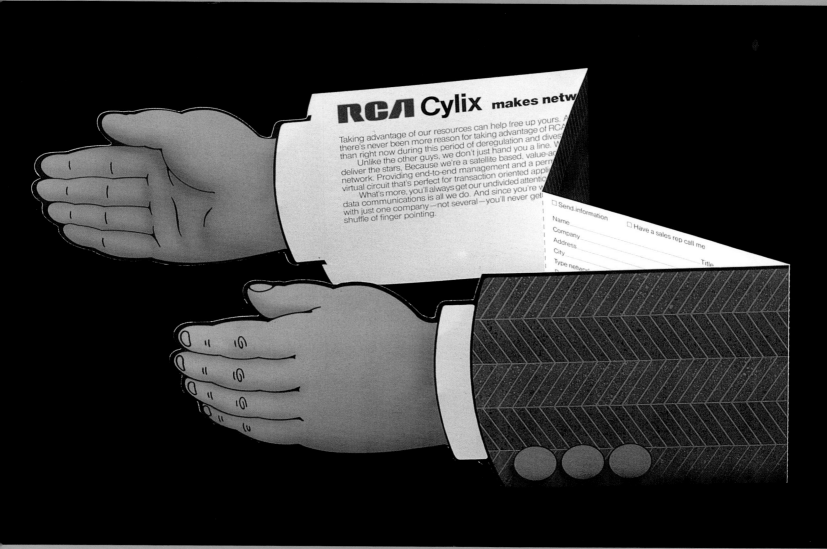

RCA Cylix makes netw

Taking advantage of our resources can help free up yours. A
there's never been more reason for taking advantage of RCA
than right now during this period of deregulation and dives
Unlike the other guys, we don't just hand you a line. W
deliver the stars, Because we're a satellite based, value-ac
network. Providing end-to-end management and a perm
virtual circuit that's perfect for transaction oriented appli
What's more, you'll always get our undivided attentic
data communications is all we do. And since you're
with just one company—not several—you'll never get
shuffle of finger pointing.

☐ Send information

Name_____   ☐ Have a sales rep call me
Company_____
Address_____
City_____   Title
Type netwo

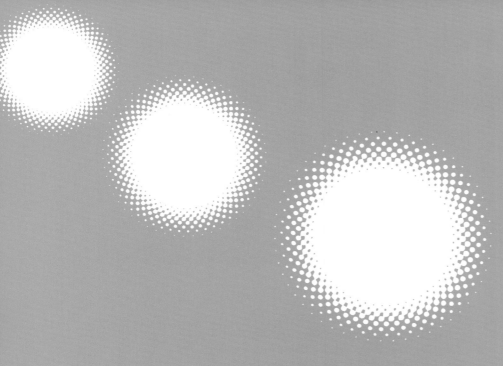

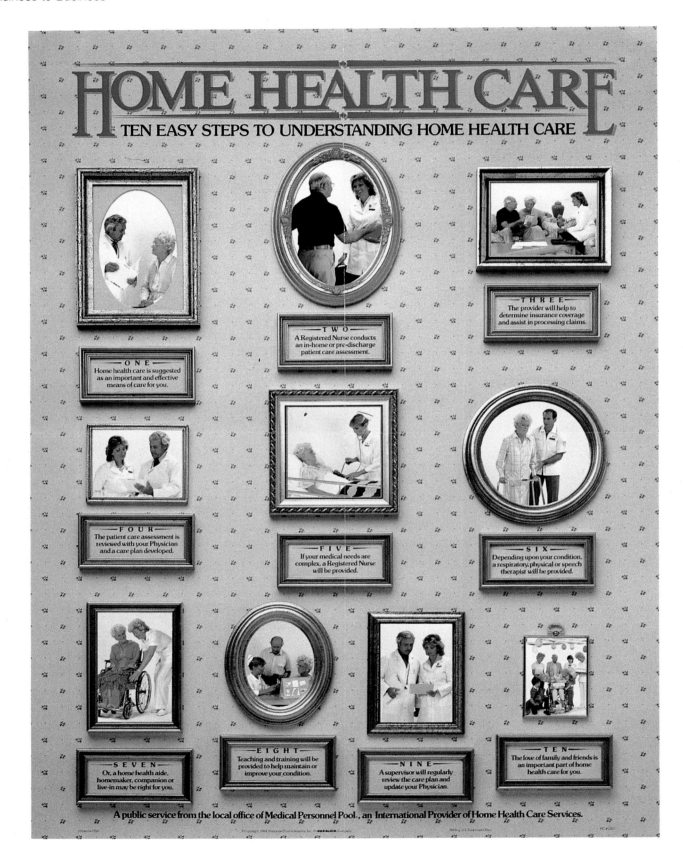

Title: Physician's Home Health Care Teaching Kit
Art Director: Gary Lucas
Copywriter: Jan Sabin
Design Agency: Rich Field Agency

Reaching physicians through direct mail is difficult because their mail is often opened and pre-screened by others. Through research and observation, the agency found that mailing tubes and boxes had a higher chance of getting to the doctors unopened. Accordingly, a boxed mailing was prepared to introduce literature designed to educate patients going into home care.

Take one

The first step to understanding Home Health Care.

TEN EASY STEPS TO UNDERSTANDING HOME HEALTH CARE

Title: A Rose of a Different Color
Art Director: Dennis Tabor
Copywriter: Brian Ross
Design Agency: Pihas, Schmidt, Westerdahl
Client: Portland Chamber of Commerce

The black cloth rose was the first in a series of mailings designed to convince corporate decision makers that the city of Portland, Oregon wasn't anti-business and desired new businesses for the area.

Title: Some Hot Air About Portland
Art Director: Dennis Tabor
Copywriter: Brian Ross
Design Agency: Pihas, Schmidt, Westerdahl
Client: Portland Chamber of Commerce

This was the second in a series of mailings designed to attract new commercial and industrial businesses to Portland, Oregon.

These packages were mailed on May 9, June 7, and July 31

May 9

Now you can attract some of the world's
highest-spending customers to your store...
Find out how-inside.

RELATED SERVICES COMPANY, INC.

ano, New York, NY 10017

May 9, 1984

It helps customers to find you, and -- over
of service you provide.

Card® sign -- the most important sign you can
instantly recognized by some of the highest
can Express Cardmembers.

akes good business sense.

pending limit. Their purchases are
and payment patterns and personal
flexibility to spend as they choose.

ardholders -- the average Cardmember
nk card charge.

the card in hand, they're more

ong
r
als.

d on
nce
antity.

sales.

Call this toll-free number
and ask for your American Express
traffic builders today

800-327-1005

They'll be on their way to you
within three weeks

6316721117

0113

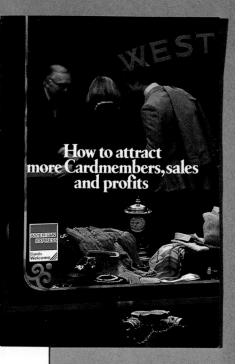

WEST

How to attract
more Cardmembers, sales
and profits

AMERICAN
EXPRESS
Cards
Welcome

June 7

AMERICAN
EXPRESS
®

AMERICAN EXPRESS TRAVEL RELATED SERVICES COMPANY, INC.

e, New York, NY 10017

June 7, 1984

☐ Yes, I want all my staff to
"spot the imposter."

Please send me:
_____ Posters
  Qty.
_____ Stickers
  Qty.
_____ Fraud Education Materials
  Qty.

Store Name _____

Owner/Manager _____

Address _____

City & State _____ Zip _____

ise -- increasing sales and boosting profits for
is credit card fraud.

riority on safe-guarding your profits. Because
rs is prevention, we've designed a wide range
T detect fraud.

to accept the Card -- as well as when not to

the American Express® Card of the vital proce-
a special sticker to place on your cash registers.
ps to follow in processing Card transactions.
customer sales and at the same time helps stop

ud, I've also enclosed a four-color poster
g signs to look for. I suggest you post it in
s -- a staff lounge, for example.

astic" of all kinds is an ever-growing part of business life. I know this informa-
be valuable in helping your staff handle not just the American Express Card, but
and charge cards -- including your own -- smoothly and securely.

ou need more stickers, posters or other fraud education materials, please use the
ostage paid order card to let us know.

Cordially,

Mark David
Mark David
Territory Manager

r your convenience, please enter your American Express merchant number and floor
ut on the enclosed sticker.

MR ARMANDO BARRA
PRESIDENT
BARRA OF ITALY
417 PARK AVE
NEW YORK NY   10022

SPOTLIGHT
ON BUSINESS

Can you spot a card carrying imposter in your store?

Title: Spotlight on Business, American Express Marketing Partnership
Art Directors: Robert Cesiro, Stefanie Palermo
Copywriters: Larilee Frazier, Sue Enterline, and Sheldon Gewirtz
Design Agency: Ogilvy & Mather Direct
Client: American Express Service Establishment (retail)

This campaign was designed to build goodwill between the client, American Express, and small retail establishments by providing owner/managers with helpful business information. A visual style and "Spotlight" logo were designed to create continuity for the series. Each package included a response device, although response was not the campaign's purpose.

Two of these "customers" are imposters. Can you spot them?

1. Is there a close match between the signature on the Card and the signature on the charge slip?
2. Has the Card been altered?
3. Does the "member since" date match the approximate age of the customer?
4. Are the valid dates correct?
5. Does the name fit the face?
6. Has the customer selected a strange assortment of unrelated items to purchase? Is he buying heavily with a new Card?
7. Is the customer deliberately causing confusion? Especially at closing time?

"Plastic" card criminals come in all shapes and sizes. Some look the part more than others. That's why, after sizing up a customer with these seven steps, it's important to rely on one other criterion: judgement. Without it, you may have guessed the real Terry James as the woman on the left. Or the man on the right—when in fact, our genuine Cardmember is the man in the middle.

To tell the truth, there's no one in a better position to stop fraud than you. You're the last obstacle between an imposter and the front door. And that makes you a very important person. Will you help?

Want to boost sales quickly?
Your best prospects are waiting to hear fr

July 31

Find out how using the American Express®
Cardmember List can help increase
your business. Return this card today.

☐ I'd like to find out how to use the American Express
Cardmember List in my own Direct Mail campaign.
Please send me the American Express List Services
Guide, including an order form for the American Express
Cardmember List.

Name
Title
Store Name
Address
City & State   Zip

AMERICAN EXPRESS TRAVEL RELATED SERVICES COMPANY, INC.
708 Third Avenue, New York, NY 10017

Mr Dennis Chandler   July 31, 1984
Store Manager
East Flower Ltd
Southflower Market
1045 Second Ave
New York NY 10022

Dear Mr Chandler:

It's no secret that in business, we've all got our hands full trying to find new ways of
attracting customers.

Mark David
Territory Manager

Direct Mail:
Simple Way
To Succeed

MAIL

Title: Mailbox
Art Director: Robert Cesiro
Copywriters: Sheldon Gewirtz, Sue Enterline
Design Agency: Ogilvy & Mather Direct
Client: American Express Company

To win goodwill for American Express, this package was
designed to provide owners and managers of small retail
establishments with an introduction to the possibilities of
direct mail advertising.

Result:
Though response was not the goal of the package, 2.6%
of the recipients returned an enclosed reply card.

Title: Fireman's Hat
Art Director: Dean Hanson
Copywriter: Rod Kilpatrick
Design Agency: Fallon McElligot Rice
Client: Interline

The breakup of AT&T deprived corporate communications
managers of their major source of information and
support. Interline wished to emphasize the consequences
of this change to the managers and to offer itself as a
single-source telecommunications support service. The
mailings were sent to telecommunications managers of
the Fortune 500 companies.

Title: It's High Time
Art Director: Steve Erenberg
Copywriter: Robert DeBear
Design Agency: Pace Advertising
Client: Copeland Distributors

As part of a start-up business venture, this mailing went to retailers of crafts supplies.

Result:
Over 17% recipients sent back the reply card requesting a copy of Copeland's catalog.

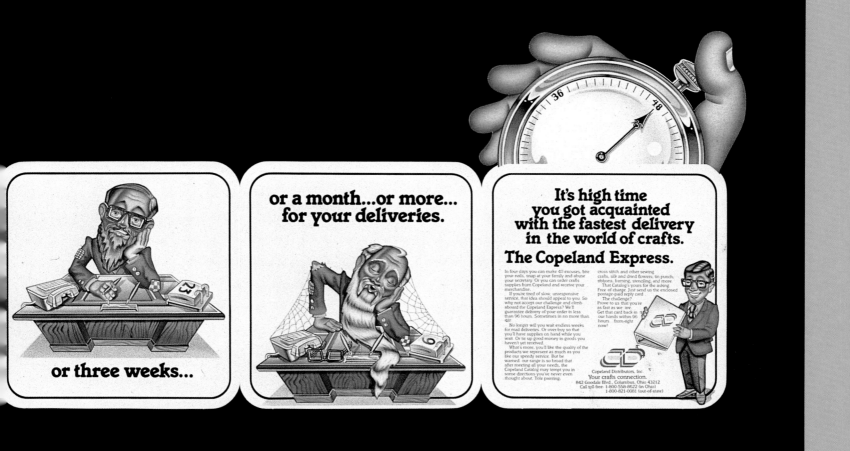

- Vehicle propulsion
- Gear boxes with planetary hubs for transmissions
- Chain and sprocket drives
- Swing drives
- Sweepers
- Auger/screw drives
- Agricultural implement rotation
- Mixers
- Forage harvesters
- Hoists and winches
- Conveyor drives
- Grapples
- Trenchers
- Drilling equipment drives
- Positioning, clamping

The power to move:

No other form of motive power matches the versatility and sheer power capacity of a high torque, low speed hydraulic drive system.

Its extremely high power-to-weight ratio, its ability to reverse motor direction instantly without sacrificing efficiency, its compactness... nothing comes close to the HTLS hydraulic drive.

- **Double the sideload capacity, plus half again the thrust load capacity of most other HTLS motors**
  ...eliminates the need for outboard bearings in many drive systems, lets you use a smaller, simpler, less costly installation.

- **Flexible speed control**
  ...provides considerable power over a wide speed range without danger of stall or burnout as compared to mechanical and electrical drives.

- **Totally field serviceable**
  ...all parts, including flanges and valving, can easily be replaced in the field — which means reduced downtime and increased productivity.

- **The advantage of a Vickers total system and total support**
  ...Vickers HTLS motors combine with Vickers pumps and valves to deliver a total, integrated hydraulic drive system functioning at optimum efficiency, plus the backup support of the worldwide Vickers network of distributors, service centers, and field service engineers.

The dynamic

advantage of
superior performance

Ideal for applications such as:

- Vehicle propulsion ☐ Gear boxes with planetary hubs for transmissions ☐ Chain and sprocket drives ☐ Swing drives ☐ Sweepers ☐ Auger/screw drives ☐ Agricultural implement rotation ☐ Mixers ☐ Forage harvesters ☐ Hoists and winches ☐ Conveyor drives ☐ Grapples ☐ Trenchers ☐ Drilling equipment drives ☐ Positioning, clamping

performance edge of the Vickers HMA...

The power to move:

No other form of motive power matches the versatility and sheer power capacity of a high torque, low speed hydraulic drive system.

Its extremely high power-to-weight ratio, its ability to reverse motor direction instantly without sacrificing efficiency, its compactness... nothing comes close to the HTLS hydraulic drive.

- Double the sideload capacity, plus half again the thrust load capacity of most other HTLS motors ...eliminates the need for outboard bearings in many drive systems, lets you use a smaller, simpler, less costly installation.

- Flexible speed control ...provides considerable power over a wide speed range without danger of stall or burnout as compared to mechanical and electrical drives.

- Totally field serviceable ...all parts, including flanges and valving, can easily be replaced in the field — which means reduced downtime and increased productivity.

- The advantage of a Vickers total system and total support ...Vickers HTLS motors combine with Vickers pumps and valves to deliver a total, integrated hydraulic drive system functioning at optimum efficiency, plus the backup support of the worldwide Vickers network of distributors, service centers, and field service engineers.

Title:	The Dynamic Power
Art Director:	Bill Smith
Copywriter:	Don Newell
Design Agency:	Gray & Kilgore
Client:	Vickers, Inc.

For clients who receive numerous direct mail messages every day, the challenge was to quickly show the power capacity of the Vickers HMA, high-torque, low-speed motor.

Result:
Estimated sales of $418,000 gave the effort a revenue to expense ratio of 64:1.

2

Consumer

Pieces Mailed Directly to Consumers

Despite the explosion of direct mail to businesses caused by the seemingly endless increases in the cost of making sales calls, the number of direct mail pieces sent to consumers is still far greater than those sent to businesses.

Naturally, therefore, the largest single category of entries to the Caples Awards Program was those directed to consumers.

The appeals ranged from items traditionally promoted through direct mail—such as magazine subscriptions and insurance—to less common ones, including disposable diapers and children's television programming.

As always, the lynchpin of promotions for magazine subscriptions and for book clubs was the free offer. The popularity of sweepstakes is undiminished. Perhaps the most alluring of these was created for the Doubleday Book Club (page 125). The package included a replica of an airline boarding card. The recipient's name was typed in, along with the destination— Greece—and a number to be used in a lottery drawing. The winner also received $5,000. This sweepstakes was coupled to a giveaway: each new subscriber was guaranteed a tote bag and a best-selling hardcover book.

Designers for Time, Inc.'s *Discover* magazine sought to exploit their audience's natural interest in technology by offering a calculator/watch as a premium (page 76). The technology theme was continued inside the package with photos of scientists working in labs, an astronomer calibrating a mammoth telescope, a rocket lifting off. The whole affair was delivered in a silver mylar envelope with red and black banners trumpeting the free calculator/watch offer.

Premiums were devised for clients offering other kinds of goods and services, as well. Ogilvy & Mather Direct, promoting the Huggies brand of disposable diapers for Kimberly-Clark, developed two booklets for expectant mothers (page 96). The booklets gave mothers basic information on child care and served as a delivery vehicle for cents-off coupons on Huggies diapers. As their research had shown that couples having children rely on other parents for advice, O&M encouraged new mothers and fathers to pass the word about Huggies' educational materials to others through a "Friend, Get A Friend" program.

A unique mailing, similar in concept to listener promotions done by radio stations, encouraged pre-teenagers to view Nickelodeon, a pay-TV service that was perceived as a children's channel (page 78). To stimulate viewing by pre-teenagers, the mailing included a Nickelodeon Quiz Card. The recipients could find the answers to the questions by watching Nickelodeon programs, and then use the completed game card to qualify for prizes. A special insert card explained Nickelodeon programming and the intent of the contest.

A more traditional kind of direct mail promotion is typified by the Playtex Pantyhose Fit Kit (page 84) designed by Wunderman, Ricotta & Kline. The mailing tells customers how to measure themselves for made-to-order, computer-fitted pantyhose. These pantyhose are only available by mail, harking back to the earliest days of direct mail, when the medium was used primarily to sell products not available through retailers, rather than as a support for retail goods and services.

The level of visual sophistication of these consumer pieces demonstrates the skill of direct mail practitioners. Packages such as the one designed for Carson, Pirie, Scott's Corporate Level Club rival the best print advertising and catalogs in presentation (page 94). The classic black background and rich, "portfolio" packaging reflect perfectly the high-style sensibility of the women who are its prime targets.

As noted in the Foreword, the original watchwords of direct mail advertising may have been *free* and *ugly*. As these consumer pieces show, the lure of a free gift is still a prime method for moving customers to action, but no one would suggest that the mail packages themselves are ugly.

Title: Curious?
Art Directors: Deanna Lorenze
Copywriters: Dawne Steward
Design Agency: Time, Inc.
Client: Discover Magazine

To encourage readership for *Discover* magazine, the publisher announced a free gift certificate for a calculator/watch.

HOP ABOARD DISCOVER'S FANTASTIC VOYAGE INTO TO

YOU'LL DISCOVER breathtaking vistas in outer space...amazing new satellites in orbit...unexplored planets...ancient stars...and mysterious pulsing quasars like fiery sentinels guarding the boundaries of the cosmos. You'll blast off with NASA's top astronauts...witness the dramatic impact of the Space Shuttle, and man's courageous quest to conquer the heavens.

YOU'LL DISCOVER wondrous

new breakthroughs in medicine that will really open your eyes...ultra-modern lasers that do the work of scalpels...computers that can diagnose illness...an intriguing new germ called a prion, which may provide clues to battling several deadly diseases...computers that galvanize impaired muscles into action again.

YOU'LL DISCOVER new insights about the way we play, think, and live...how exer-

cise affects our bodies and minds...how pets can ease depression and lower blood pressure...why Japanese children outperform their American counterparts on intelligence tests...or how scientists are de-mystifying the process of memory.

YOU'LL DISCOVER the sheer exhilaration of traveling into the future. Experience how the earth will look in 250 million years... see a futuristic fighter plane controlled by human

voice...visi
scanner the

DISC
tainment, N
will bring t
written with
jump at the
and stimul
more abou
every mon

THE WAYWARD SATELLITE

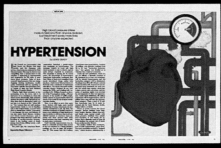
HYPERTENSION

MEMORY

A Voice

THE SILENT BATTLE

DIAGNOSIS BY COMPUTER

I.Q.

The Sha of Tom

EXPLORING THE EDGE OF THE UNIVERSE

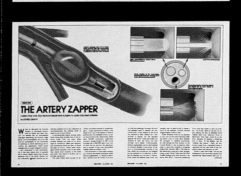
THE ARTERY ZAPPER

EXERCISE

DISCOVER
AMERICA'S LEADING SCIENCE MAGAZINE

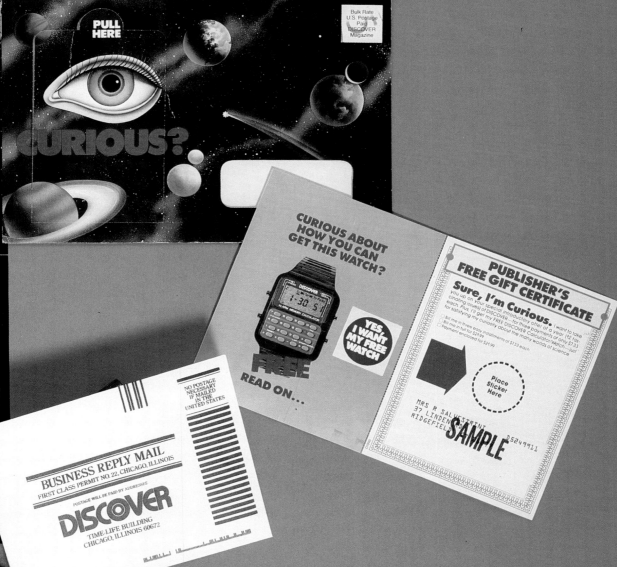

Title:	Nickelodeon Challenge Quiz
Art Director:	Len Sherman
Copywriters:	Bruce Lee, Robert Culver
Design Agency:	Scali, McCabe & Sloves Direct
Client:	Warner/Amex Satellite Entertainment Company

Nickelodeon is a cable TV channel devoted to quality television programming for children ages four to 16. This mailing was devised to increase Nickelodeon viewership among pre-teenagers, most of whom regarded it as a service for young children.

Result:
The number of pre-teen viewers jumped 60% within a few weeks of the mailing. In addition, over 2,000 of these viewers returned the Nickelodeon Challenge Quiz Answer Card.

The making of an American Express® Cardmember

(By way of the Special Graduating Student Program)*

Before

Well known to mother, father, three roommates, two political science professors and one local tennis shoe outlet.

After

Recognized by the world of restaurants, hotels, great stores, theatres, airline, train and car-rental counters, ski lifts and bookstores.

Bad mood. Bank closed at 3:00. Couldn't have happened on worse day.

Tape of favorite group. Missed last concert. Heard it was great.

Bitten fingernails. Might not be able to book hotel reservations for parents' visit to campus. Forgot to send deposit.

Sunday paper. Classifieds circled in red, latest draft of resume, appointment calendar.

Roommate's umbrella, invaluable in rain.

High tops. Essential part of going home for the holidays. Ankle support needed for long wait at airline counter.

Voilà! Energized aura. Life is a great deal more convenient with the American Express Card. Especially when you're in a hurry.

Tape of favorite group. Haven't missed a concert since the Card.

Same pearls. New suit. Some things never change. But some things will never be the same. More reason to have the Card.

Trade journal. Always carried. Often read. Sign of sound business instincts. Like the Card.

De rigueur attaché; contains vacation tickets charged to the Card, address of lunch meeting, recommended office reading and roommate's new umbrella.

Going places much easier with the American Express Card. To say the least.

*You may qualify for the Card if you have accepted a career-oriented job with a salary of $10,000 or more.

Title:	The Making of an American Express Cardmember
Art Director:	Maria Lucca
Copywriter:	Sheila Zubrod
Design Agency:	Ogilvy & Mather Direct
Client:	American Express Company

The American Express card has traditionally been known as a credit card for business people and others with an upper middle class income. To encourage college students to apply, this mailing solicited college seniors who had accepted a career-oriented job paying $10,000 or more as new card members.

Title: Apple II Power
Art Director: Doug Hamer
Copywriter: George Duncan
Design Agency: George Duncan Associates
Client: inCider Magazine

The magazine for Apple computer users, inCider, was transformed from a publication for hobbyists with a high level of technical knowlege to a family-oriented journal emphasizing off-the-shelf solutions to family computing needs.

Result:
The early returns indicated a response rate of 2%, which met goals for the repositioning effort.

Title: Passport
Art Director: Frank Golia
Copywriter: Geoffrey Alan Moore
Design Agency: Benton & Bowles Direct
Client: Signature Magazine

Signature Magazine was originally sent only to readers
who had a Diner's Club credit card. In order to widen its
readership, this mailing was sent to higher income
households outside the Diner's Club membership.

SIGNATURE. The good life just got better.

Title: Playtex Fit Kit
Art Director: Laura Astuto
Copywriter: Beth Griffen
Design Agency: Wunderman, Ricotta & Kline
Client: Playtex

Playtex introduced its made-to-measure pantyhose by
mailing this Fit Kit. The pantyhose are computer-tailored
to the individual measurements supplied by the customers and are only sold through mail order.

Here's how to get pantyhose that fit like they're made for your legs only.

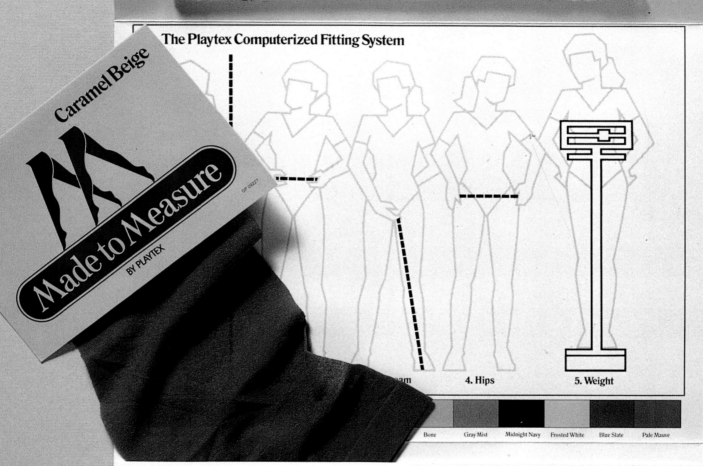

The Playtex Computerized Fitting System

Caramel Beige

Made to Measure
BY PLAYTEX

GP 09227

4. Hips 5. Weight

Bone   Gray Mist   Midnight Navy   Frosted White   Blue Slate   Pale Mauve

Here's a foolproof way to find perfect fitting pantyhose.

Introducing the computerized fitting system of Made to Measure® Pantyhose by Playtex.®

Now by following a few simple steps, you can own pantyhose perfectly proportioned to your body.

Say so-long to pantyhose that bag at the knees, sag at the crotch, bind at the waist.

And get acquainted with pantyhose that fit like they were made just for you.

Using the Fit Kit tape measure, take your height, hip, waist and inseam measurements and jot them down on the order form we've provided. Add your weight to the list, and Playtex will take it from there.

Not only will our computer provide you with pantyhose made for your mea-

surements, it'll even store your measurements for easy reorders.

Made to Measure Pantyhose offer you more than a terrific fit. They give you 12 great colors, too. Choose your favorites from the color bar above and mark them off on the order form.

Next, check your style. Made to Measure Pantyhose has them all: Regular, Light Support and Control Top.

At Playtex, we offer a No-Quibble Money-Back Guarantee. If you're not absolutely delighted with the way our pantyhose fit, you can return them for a full refund or replacement.

So send in your order form and give Made to Measure Pantyhose a try. One wearing will prove that when it comes to fit, other pantyhose just don't measure up.

Made to Measure
BY PLAYTEX

GP 09227

Title: The Union Dissolved
Art Director: Ron Wilcox
Copywriter: Paul Dexter
Design Agency: Time-Life Books
Client: Time-Life Books

This effort was created for an existing series of books.
Using the major battles of the U.S. Civil War, the package
pitched the series to military history enthusiasts.

Result:
Produced higher results than previous series mailings and
became the control package.

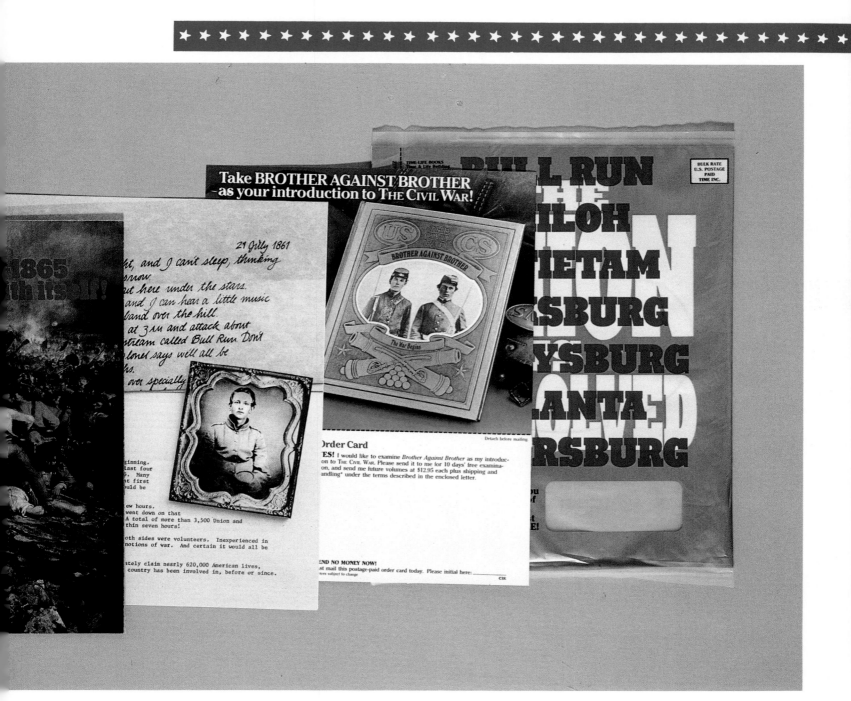

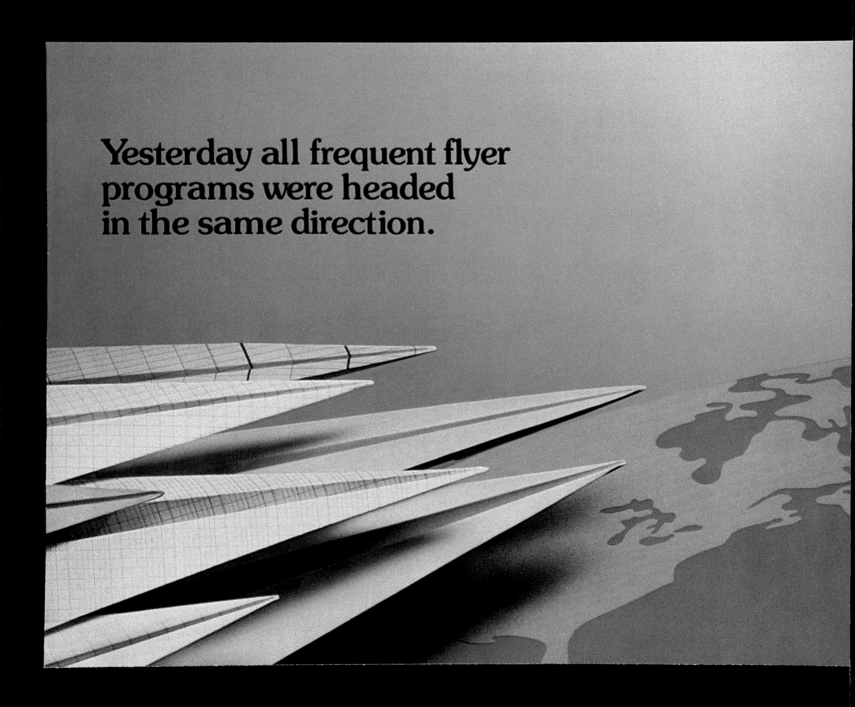

Title: Paper Planes
Art Directors: Hank Stromberg, Jack Newman
Copywriters: Ellen Kahn-Piderit, Elizabeth Schworm
Design Agency: Ogilvy & Mather Direct
Client: Trans World Airlines

Responding to waning interest in TWA's Frequent Flight Bonus program, this piece had to not only generate new excitement among frequent flyers, but also had to be produced, from concept to printed pieces, in three weeks.

We've made special arrangements with the luxurious Orient Express... so now you can enjoy a free trip for two from Venice to London! Just picture yourself on this opulent railway. Your 25-hour trip will be filled with sumptuous meals, elegant surroundings—all the art and ambience of the original Orient Express. You'll discover why it is called the train of kings—and the king of trains.

Best of all, you can start earning every one of these awards right now. And there's one more item of special interest...

A limited-time bonus mileage offer.

To help you celebrate the all-new FFB with us, we're even making your shorter TWA flights count for more. From now until December 31, 1983, any nonstop TWA flight you take over 200 actual miles will earn you at least 1,000 miles credit. We'll take your actual mileage flown, and then award you enough additional mileage to bring your total to 1,000 miles. And that's in addition to any class-of-service bonuses you may be entitled to!

Start earning your new awards today.

Our FFB program just keeps getting better! And we wanted you to know about it right away. Remember, just use your Personal I.D. Stickers every time you fly TWA. Starting October 15, be sure to use them on your Eastern and Qantas flights. You'll receive more details soon, in your next mileage update mailing. In November, you'll be able to claim your new travel awards. But even before you do, we're confident you'll agree that only one frequent flyer program can take you in all these fabulous directions...TWA's all-new FFB!

...the spectacular ruins at Machu Picchu, Peru.

Experience the world-famous Sydney Opera House.

American Motors needed a package to convince owners of imported cars that the American-built Renault Alliance and Encore compared favorably to imports. A financing offer was added to build traffic in AMC/Renault auto dealerships.

Encore S
3-door Hatchback

European technology means. . .

Performance on the road

Now is your opportunity to experience the rid
that has been acclaimed throughout North
America. Take an Alliance Sedan or an Encor
Hatchback for a test drive and you'll undoubt-
edly be impressed by its superior handling.
And you'll feel the ride and comfort created by
Renault's patented suspension system.

Renault's suspension is a result of our many
years of racing experience. The front suspension was designed to provide excellent road
holding qualities, superior riding comfort and
quick steering response. The system features
independent coil springs on MacPherson-typ
struts with negative scrub radius design and
stabilizer bar. The rear suspension is fully inde

New from
TIME LIFE BOOKS

Now you can indulge in delicious desserts!
If you love to make a special treat for your family, wait until you try these recipes!

Mocha Sherbet

Fresh Strawberry Sorbet

Papaye-Mango Ice

Chicken Diable

Chicken à la Grecque

Chicken Valencia

Fresh Ways with Poultry

Beginning the day with good nutritional sense

Recommended Daily Allowances for a Healthy Diet

Up-to-date information on diet and nutrition.
Find out your recommended daily individual calorie, cholesterol, protein, fats and sodium allowances—depending on your age and sex. Then feast on delicious, nutritious HEALTHY HOME COOKING dishes that help you look good and feel good.

Sole en Papillote

Baked Fish Plaki

Step-by-step full-color photographs show you how to do it!
Easy-to-follow photographs with special tips and tricks show you how to prepare the critical steps of some special dishes, taking the guesswork out of trying recipes for the first time.

Raspberry Chicken

Vegetable Lasagne Roll-ups

Try one of these delicious recipes tonight!

Punch out token and place on card at right

Place 10-day FREE examination token here.
Just moisten back of token No glue needed.

Prepublication Reservation Card

▲ Detach here before mailing

YES! I'd like to kitchen-test *Fresh Ways with Poultry*, as soon as it's published, as my introduction to HEALTHY HOME COOKING. Please send it to me for a 10-day FREE examination along with future volumes, each at $12.95 plus shipping and handling, under the terms described in the enclosed letter.

Fresh Ways with Poultry
Yours to examine for 10 days FREE as your introduction to

New from
TIME LIFE BOOKS

Healthy Home Cooking

SEND NO MONEY NOW! Just detach and mail this postage-paid card today. Please initial here _____

Time-Life Books
Time & Life Building
Chicago, Illinois 60611

**Delectable.
Mouth-watering.
And nutritious, too.**

Healthy Home Cooking

Advance Notice

TIME LIFE BOOKS

FREE recipe inside!
Raspberry Chicken

Title: Healthy Home Cooking
Art Director: Kathleen Tresnak
Copywriter: Diana Finegold
Design Agency: Time-Life Books
Client: Time-Life Books

This series of cookbooks was aimed at a narrow segment of the crowded cookbook market. While not dietetic, the recipes were lower in calories, sodium, fats, and cholesterol than those found in other cookbooks. The mailing had to communicate these benefits to its audience of 25 to 45 year old females with $30,000 or more in household income.

Title: Always Changing
Art Director: Randal Fleck
Copywriters: Susan Webber, Don Pinto
Design Agency: Grey Direct
Client: Meredith Publishing Company

The market for cookbooks issued in series is normally crowded. This effort had to distinguish the Cookbook Collection from its competitors and appeal to a more affluent reading audience.

Result:
The response rate was 32% over pre-mailing projections.

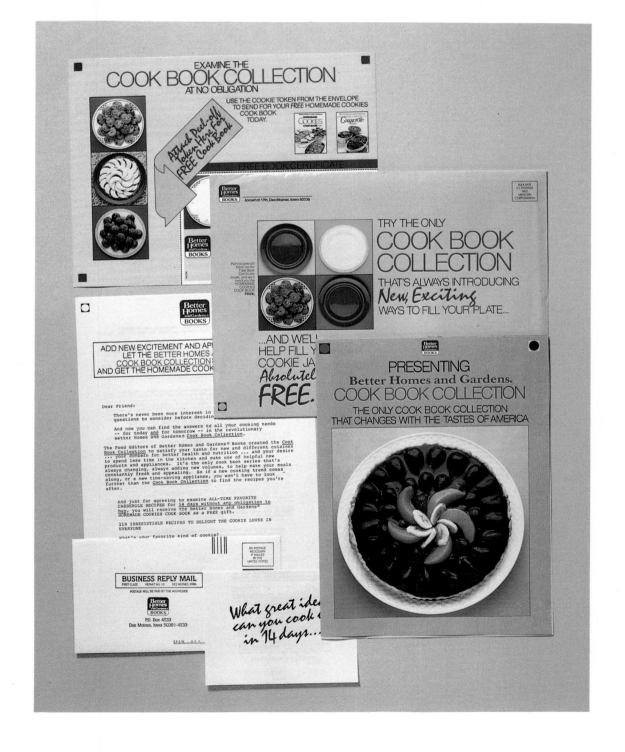

Title: Corporate Level
Client: Carson, Pirie, Scott & Company

To introduce a new retailing concept and to solicit credit card members for a corporate level account this ad was sent to upscale busy working women who don't always have time to shop.

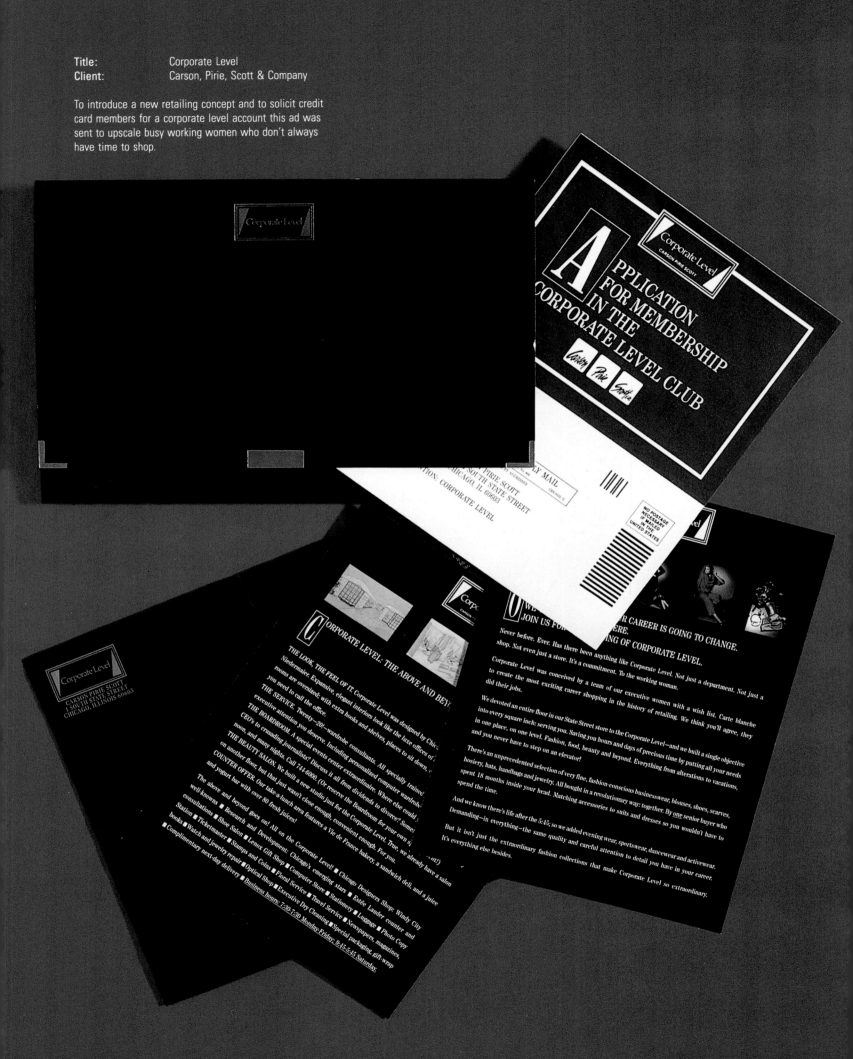

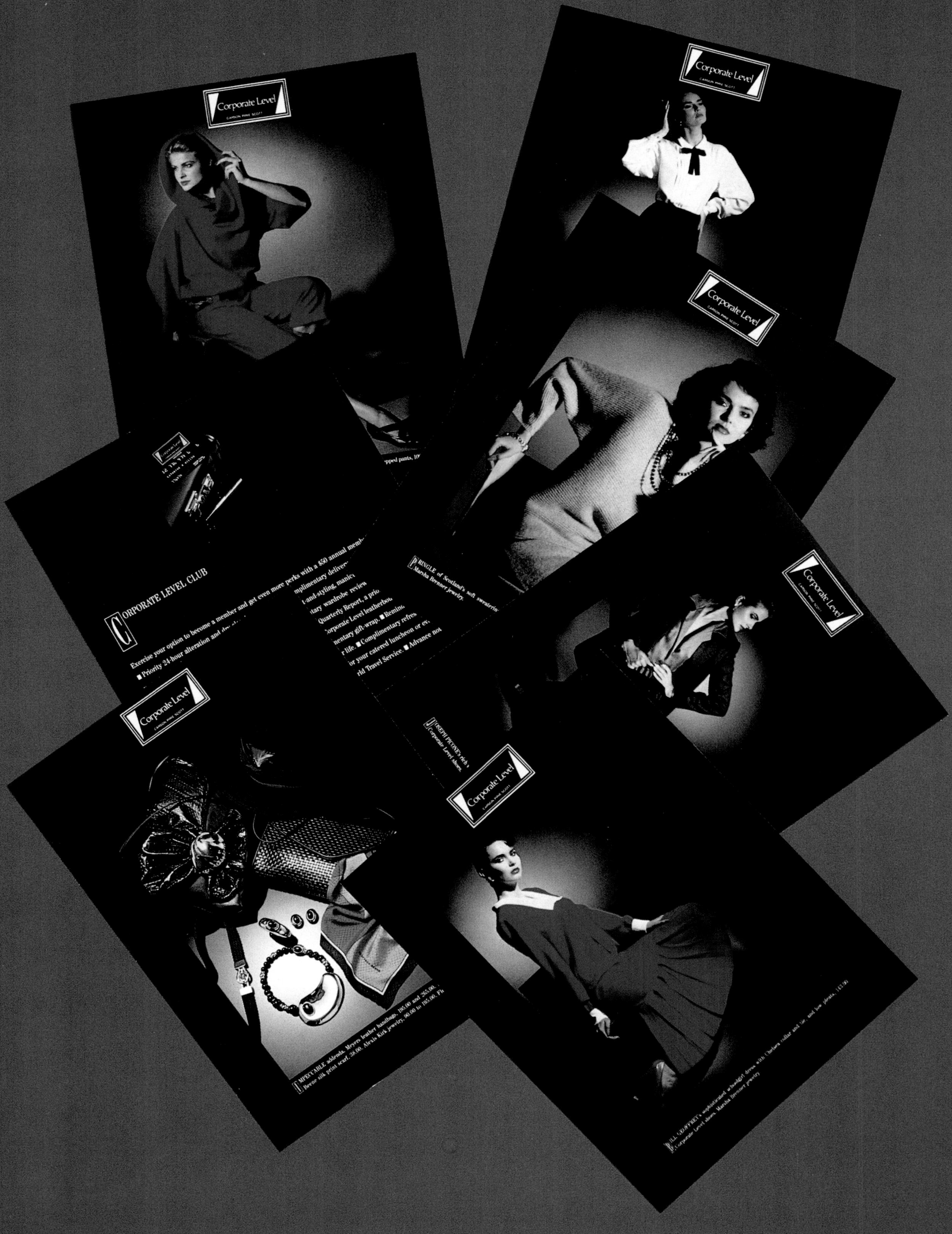
Corporate Level
CARSON PIRIE SCOTT
CORPORATE LEVEL CLUB

Title: Beginnings
Art Directors: Joe Cupani, Herb Ackerman
Copywriters: Robert Chambers, Gretchen McKee
                  and Virginia Lemmon
Design Agency: Ogilvy & Mather Direct
Client: Kimberly-Clark Corporation

With 10,000 new babies being born every day, and a highly competitive market for disposable diapers, Kimberly-Clark wanted a mailer that would help establish brand loyalty. Two booklets for new mothers were designed to enhance the image of the Huggies brand and serve as a delivery vehicle for cents-off coupons.

Result:
Coupon redemptions and use of the reply card exceeded projections. Response to the "Friend Get A Friend" program was over 15%.

Title:	Berenstain Bears Books
Art Director:	John Pittari
Copywriter:	Nancy B. Ryan
Design Agency:	Grolier Enterprise Corporation
Client:	Grolier Enterprise Corporation

This mailing introduced a new series of hardcover Berenstain Bears books for children. The books deal with the concerns and fears of pre-schoolers—from the first visit to a doctor to the arrival of a new baby—in a humorous way.

Title: Asking the Right Questions
Art Director: R. Ross
Copywriter: R. Green
Design Agency: Computer Marketing Services
Client: CNA Insurance

CNA Insurance uses a network of independent insurance agents to sell its products. This effort was geared to lowering the cost of sale to those agents and CNA by generating a large number of leads.

Result:
Response to the piece averaged 5%, with some mailing lists performing at up to 13%. The sales conversion rate averaged nearly 20%, assuring CNA of a lower cost per sale.

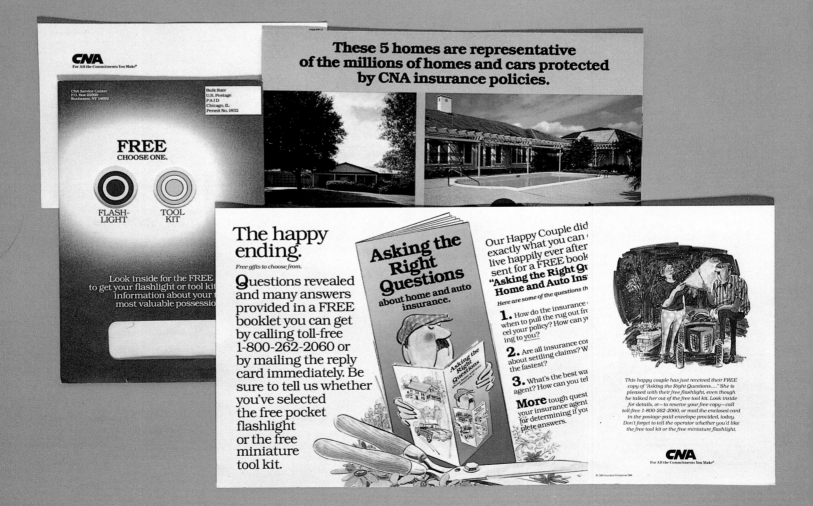

Title: Preserving Your Affluence
Art Director: R. Ross
Copywriter: R. Green
Design Agency: Computer Marketing Services
Client: CNA Insurance

CNA's Universal Security Plan was aimed at affluent consumers with sufficient income and possessions to need a comprehensive package of insurance products. The package was designed to generate enough sales leads to lower the cost of sale for CNA's independent agents, and to position CNA and its agents as professional, innovative sellers of insurance protection.

Result:
Between 3% and 4% of the recipients responded to the mailing.

Title: American Symphony Orchestra
Art Directors: Gloria Moyer, Donald Van Hook
Copywriter: Ronald S. Moyer
Design Agency: RSM Marketing
Client: American Symphony Orchestra

To improve season ticket sales for the American
Symphony Orchestra's 1984–1985 season, the agency
created this mailing package and targeted it to affluent
households in the region.

Result:
Season ticket sales increased 35.5% over the previous
year.

Title: Relive the Memories
Art Director: Shahen Zarookian
Copywriters: Barry Silverstein, Beth Lipsey
Design Agency: Directech, Inc.
Client: Polaroid Corporation

Sales of Polaroid films are typically slow during the fall
season. This effort was created to encourage film use
and to test a mail-in offer for enlarged photos from
consumers' Polaroid prints.

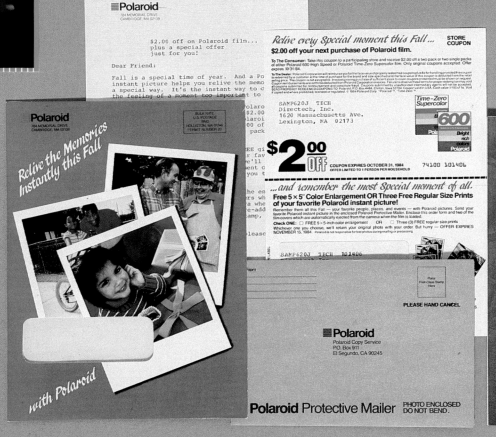
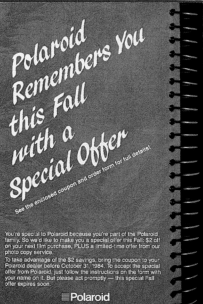

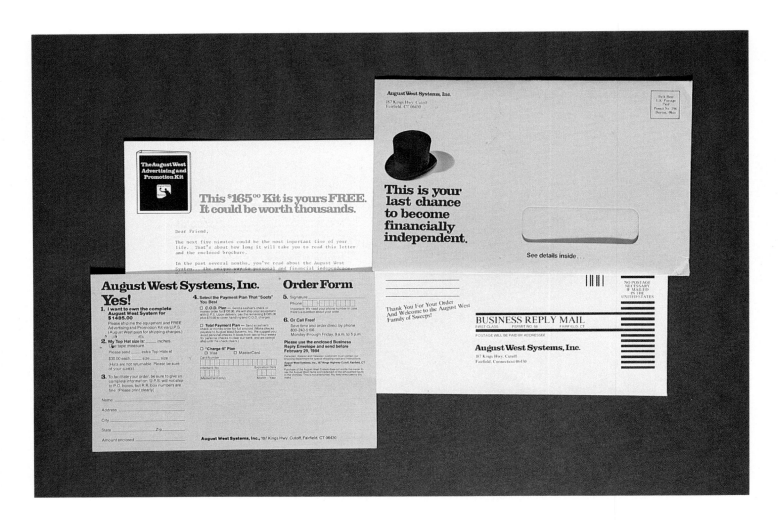

Title:	August West Last Chance
Art Director:	Tony Vernon
Copywriters:	Laura Yaro, Jan S. Moore
Design Agency:	Parhelion Direct
Client:	August West Systems, Inc.

August West needed to remove unqualified prospects from its sales lead list, which contained names of inquirers who had responded up to 36 months before this mailing. The piece gave them a "last chance" and included a special low-price offer to create sales during the company's slow sales season.

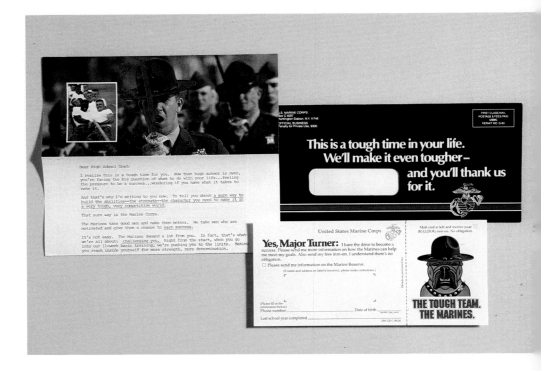

Title:	This Is A Tough Time
Art Director:	Louis Deliz
Copywriters:	Shelley Mazor, David Willis
Design Agency:	Soskin/Thompson Associates
Client:	U.S. Marine Corps

In an effort to build enlistments into the Marine Corps by high school graduates 17 to 21 years old, this mailing was developed to run against the control package.

Title:	The Homestead
Art Director:	Neil Wagner
Copywriters:	John Tobias, Jenny Raybould
Design Agency:	Ogilvy & Mather Direct
Client:	American Express Company

To help one of its service establishments sell a series of theme weekends, American Express had this package created and mailed it with brochures supplied by The Homestead, a distinguished resort hotel.

Result:
The Homestead booked $35,000 worth of theme weekends through the effort, and received 150 additional inquiries about the resort.

Title: Weekends At The Registry
Art Directors: Celesta Segerstrom, Nan Yawitz
Copywriters: Marty M. Morgan, Chuck Bua
Design Agency: Keller Crescent Company
Southwest
Client: Registry Hotels

To accommodate the need for the individual units of this chain to promote varied weekend accommodation packages, yet share production expenses to lower costs, this folder was created. Four-color inserts promote individual locations, and details on the packages were surprinted on the inserts as they became available.

WEEKENDS AT THE REGISTRY CHARLOTTE ARE A CUT ABOVE THE REST.

RELAX. FIND A COMFORTABLE CHAIR. THEN OPEN THIS PACKAGE AND BROWSE THROUGH OUR LARGEST SELECTION OF TODAY'S BEST BOOKS.

BULK RATE
U.S. POSTAGE
PAID
Book-of-the-Month Club, Inc.

LIST YOUR 4 FAVORITES. THEY'RE YOURS FOR ONLY $2.

3-04
663/7

AND DON'T FORGET YOUR EXTRA BOOK.

Please enroll me as a member of Book-of-the-Month Club and send me the books I have listed by number above. Bill me only $2, plus a charge for shipping and handling. I agree to buy just 4 more books during the next two years. A shipping and handling charge is added to each shipment.

B□MC

Book-of-the-Month Club, Inc.
Camp Hill, Pennsylvania 17012

Look through our largest selection of today's books and select any 4 for only $2. Save up to $107.95 off publishers' prices.

Dear Reader,

AND IF WE HEAR FROM YOU SOON, THERE'S A LITTLE SOMETHING EXTRA FOR YOU...

NO POSTAGE NECESSARY IF MAILED IN THE UNITED STATES

COMFORTABLE? GOOD. INSIDE ARE 106 OF TODAY'S BEST BOOKS. TAKE YOUR TIME AND CHOOSE 4 OF YOUR FAVORITES, FOR ONLY $2.
You simply agree to buy 4 books within the next two years.

TAKE YOUR TIME AND CHOOSE YOUR FAVORITES FOR ONLY $2.
You simply agree to buy 4 books within the next two years.

B□MC BOOK-OF-THE-MONTH CLUB®
America's Bookstore® since 1926

Title:	Browse Through Our Largest Selection of Today's Best Books
Art Director:	Sherry Scharschmidt
Copywriters:	Rose Marie Miksis, Rob Earl
Design Agency:	Wunderman, Ricotta & Kline
Client:	Book of the Month Club

A strong graphic and creative approach was needed to pitch book club membership to lists that had already been mailed extensively with the same offer.

Result:
Responses to this package were 16% more than for the standard control package, significantly lowering the cost per order.

Title: Harlequin Heart Package
Art Director: Ed Blas
Copywriter: Peter Maher
Design Agency: Ayer Direct
Client: Harlequin Books

The excitement of romance and adventure were emphasized in this mailing in order to create a strong loyalty between readers and Harlequin romantic novels.

Title: Royal Harvest Mailing
Art Directors: Michael Campbell, Len Sherman,
                    and Barbara Scholey
Copywriters: James Overall, Robert Culver
Design Agency: Scali, McCabe, Sloves Direct
                    Response
Client: Scandinavian Laboratories

Product samples and a mail order catalog sales approach
were used for these natural vitamins. The offer emphasized the cachet of an "imported" product.

Result:
The size of the order was higher among those who
received the mailing than similar consumers responding
to print ads in health-oriented magazines.

SONATOL™

S onatol is our "flagship
product." This
pleasant-tasting,
sugar-free liquid
multi-vitamin
preparation was invented by the
founders of our company over 50
years ago. While it was initially
designed as a vitamin A & D
supplement, we have constantly
improved Sonatol so that today's
preparation is a complete dietary
supplement for children of all
ages, supplying a full range of
vitamins.
    Sonatol is not only popular in
Norway. Today people in more than
40 countries take Sonatol as an
important supplement to their diet.
    Sonatol's worldwide success
can be attributed to its delicious

taste, stability of flavor, and the
high bio-availability of its active
ingredients.
    In Scandinavia, Sonatol has
come to mean good health and
good taste. It is not only one of the
most complete liquid multi-vita-
mins available, but also the most
enjoyable one to take. It's part of
our philosophy that improving
your health should be a pleasure,
not a chore.
    This Sonatol formulation has
been designed to specially fit the
nutritional needs of Americans.
And in introducing Sonatol to the
U.S., we are offering it for a limited
time at a special lower price.
    You may not live in a climate as
harsh as Norway's, but it's reas-
suring to know that Sonatol can
protect your health year-round.
1101   8.4 fl. oz. (250 ml) $3.95
1102 16.8 fl. oz. (500 ml) $5.95
                    (Regularly $6.95)

For complete potency information, refer to the chart on back flap of catalog.
— 12 —

You may use this form to order Royal
Harvest Products.
    Or if you prefer, you may order by
telephone using a credit card for faster
service. For complete information on
telephone ordering see inside.

ROYAL HARVEST™
OSLO · NEW YORK

For complete potency information...
— 13 —

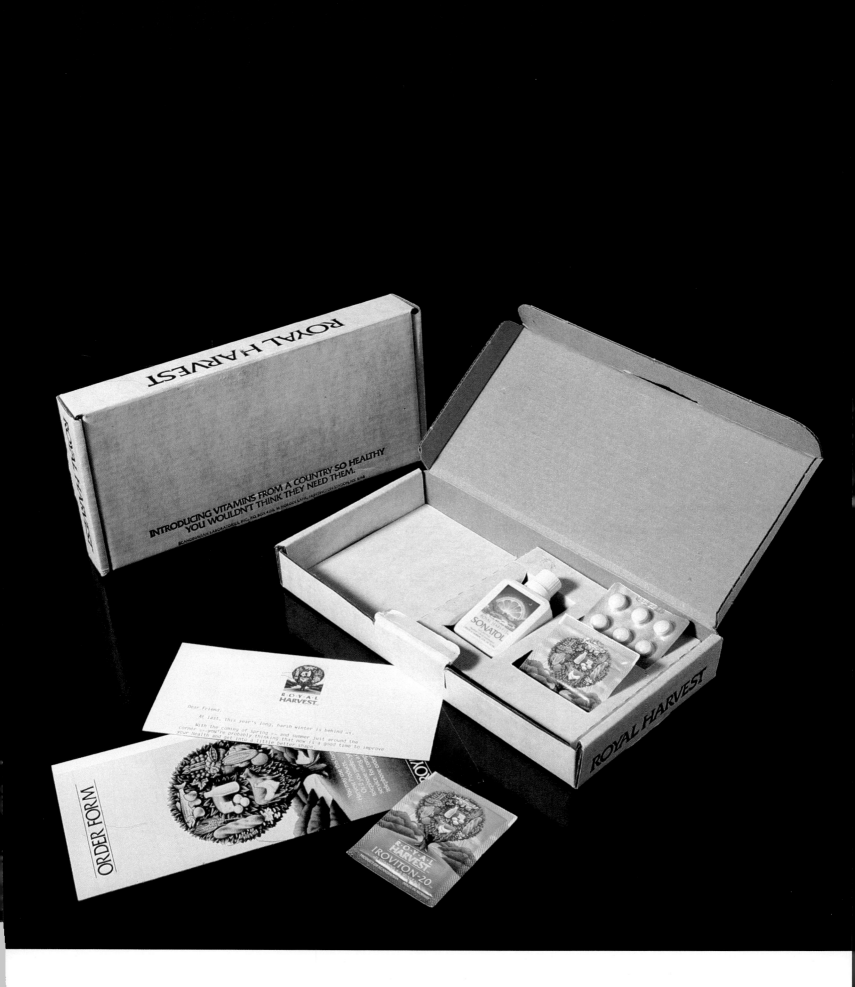

Initial response was 10% higher than projections, with
revenues exceeding projections by 50%.

Important information for new Cardmembers enclosed

JOHN W WILLIS
32 DAVIS ST
TYNGSBORO MA 018

AMERICAN EXPRESS TRAVEL RELATED SERVICES COMPANY, INC.
AMERICAN EXPRESS PLAZA, NEW YORK, NY 10004

s E. Isenberg
President
mer Marketing

r Cardmember:

the few weeks since you received the American
ress® Card, I hope that you've had an opportu-
y to "try it out" and see how it adds an extra
sure of convenience to your life.

you're no doubt aware, the Card is among the most
ely accepted and respected financial instruments
ilable for travel and entertainment -- your assur-
e of charge privileges worldwide.

more than a
sive benefits
urity while

Getting the most from your Cardmembership

Credit Card Registry

Expressphone —
low-cost long-distance telephone s

AMERICAN EXPRESS

AMERICAN EXPRESS

AMERICAN EXPRESS

ican Express
age Tags

THE
AMERICAN EXPRESS
GIFT CERTIFICATE

The American E

Additional Cardmembers

AMERICAN EXPRESS

AMERICAN EXPRESS

3712 345618 95006

58   AX

C F FROST

Getting the most from your Cardmembership

AMERICAN EXPRESS

tomatic Flight Insurance Plan

Title: Best Looks—Vogue
Art Directors: William Whitney, Tiia Sahni
Copywriter: Claire O'Brien
Design Agency: Rapp & Collins, Inc.
Client: Conde Nast Publications, Inc.

Potential new subscribers to Vogue magazine were
offered four free issues instead of the customary
discounted price. A combination letter/brochure was
used to convey the style and excitement of the four-color
fashion publication.

Title: Discover Silver Mylar Package
Art Director: Stas Mirek
Copywriter: Regina Kolbe
Design Agency: Time, Inc.
Client: Discover Magazine

Discover magazine offers its readers information on the
latest developments in science and technology. Silver
mylar gave this premium-loaded subscription offer a high-
tech appearance.

THE DISEASE DETECTIVES:
Workers in protective gear study exotic germs in the Center for Disease Control's maximum-containment lab.

—Handsome black "flex" band.

—Quartz digital accuracy.

—Liquid crystal readout.

—Full 1-year limited guarantee.

—Stopwatch function.

...eggs with gold dust, a photographer ...t occur at the very moment of conception.

...SSION: TO CATCH COMET DUST:
...met is only three years out of sight, but scientists can't wait. Already they are catching comet ...wings of specially equipped U-2 spy planes to study in the lab. What they find may reveal ...has ever been known about the orbiting gas masses.

...-FRILLS TRIP ...SPACE
...aid de-regulation is bad?
...maverick company, backed
...by Texas oil money pushes the
...frontiers of private enterprise
...beyond the atmosphere. And
...proves that anyone can do it.

EXPLORING THE EDGE OF THE UNIVERSE
Astronomers crouched within giant telescopes ...n the edges of the universe for the energized sources known as quasars.

...y say YES to the FREE Calculator/Watch.
...losed card to DISCOVER today.

The DISCOVER Calculator/Watch Is The Slimmest "Micro-Chip" Quartz Calculator/Watch In The World.

You'll never have to wind this amazing timepiece. Because it's governed by a micro-chip and powered by a mini-battery.

The 16-pad-keyboard calculator quickly computes all basic math functions—from simple addition to percentages.

The precision timepiece—accurate to within seconds per year—reads out the hour, minute and second in a clear crystal digital display.

And one quick push of a button calls up the calendar function to give you a look at the month, the date and the day.

Whether you're computing important data...or just checking the time of day—you'll find the DISCOVER Calculator/Watch is DEPENDABLE, PRACTICAL, and INDISPENSABLE!

YOUR DISCOVER CALCULATOR/WATCH HAS THESE SPECIAL FEATURES...

CALCULATOR Mode:
• Performs all standard math operations—addition, subtraction, percentages and more...
• Accurate up to 8 places...
• Sophisticated 16-pad-keyboard...
• Plus a full computer memory.

WATCH Mode:
• Shows the hour, minute and second...
• Displays the year, month, date and day of week...
• Has a built-in alarm that can be preset to sound every hour on the hour...or to go off at a predetermined hour.

Your DISCOVER Calculator Watch comes with a striking flexible wrist ...band and is distinguished by the ...handsome DISCOVER logo.

See inside for a look at ...VER'S ...Watch. ...REE!
...OR/WATCH ...EK.

Title: Le Picnique Lunch
Art Director: Lesley Singer
Copywriter: Carol Milam
Design Agency: Ogilvy & Mather Direct
Client: American Express Company

Picnic boxes are a high-profit item for the Brasserie
Restaurant. The mailer targeted American Express card
holders in the restaurant's area.

Result:
Sales volume of picnic lunches doubled in the first
weeks of the effort.

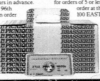

The Water Lily Clock—yesterday's heritage, today's treasure, tomorrow's heirloom.

Distinction fills your home the moment you place this replica of a classic Victorian clock on your wall. An authentic re-creation of a 19th century time-piece, it enriches any room with its charming reference to a gracious era. In a hallway, your clock will welcome your family and guests; in your living room, it will reflect the finest traditions of the past; wherever you decide to hang it, it will be the focus of admiration.

A trellis of water lilies, carved entirely by hand, floats on the glass surface of the door panel, defined by partially fluted pilasters and gently rounded finials. Lovingly crafted of solid Indonesian walnut, the case has been sanded, rubbed, and stained by expert woodworkers. The lily-white enamel face is ringed with gleaming, solid brass.

You'll enjoy the gentle chime, itself an echo of the past, as it counts the hours and strikes the half-hour. A solid brass pendulum bears decorative initials on its enameled surface: an "R" for "retard" and an "A" for "advance"—the means by which you govern the accuracy of the clock. The convenient, 31-day movement is meticulously crafted of solid brass to give you years of reliability.

Beautiful clocks occupy a unique place in the world of art. They are prized as much for their decorative aspects as for their timekeeping. From its graceful pediment to its clockwork movement, the Water Lily clock is among the finest, offering both beauty and accuracy. Why not make it yours! Order this masterful copy of a late 19th century masterpiece, today. Some-day, it may be a treasured heirloom.

It's Yours to Enjoy for 15 Days Absolutely Free!

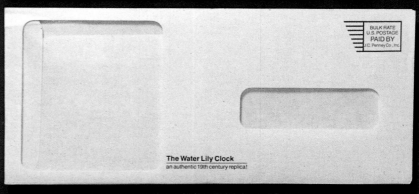

JCPenney

Order Your Water Lily, 31-Day, Hand-Crafted Clock Today!

Yes! Please send me the clock(s) as indicated for my 15-day FREE HOME TRIAL. I understand that I may examine it in my own home for 15 days and, if not completely satisfied, I may return it and owe nothing. JCPenney will pay return postage. Otherwise, add the purchase price (plus $7.95 transportation and handling, and applicable local tax) to my JCPenney Charge Account as a Regular Charge purchase. Pay as little as $20 per month as a Regular Charge purchase!

Fill in completely including signature.

How Many	Item Number	Description	Price
	LA994-3218FH	Water Lily Clock	$149.95

Print name desired

Year purchased

Phone Number (   )
area code   phone number

Your Signature Required   all charge orders must be signed to ship item(s)

72 83-35 414

The Water Lily Clock
an authentic 19th century replica!

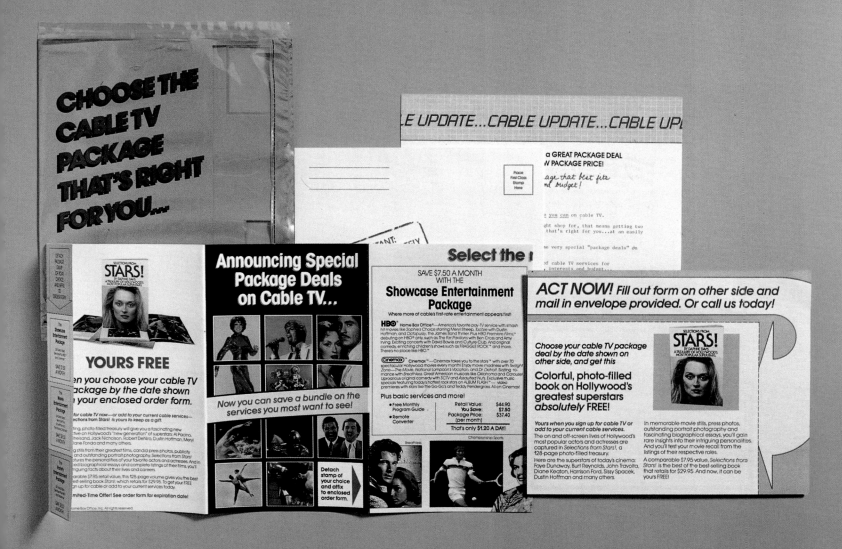

Title: Cable TV Package Deal
Art Director: Derek Karsanidi
Copywriter: Jeff Ostroth
Design Agency: Kobs & Brady Advertising
Client: Home Box Office

To allow local cable affiliates to promote individualized packages of pay TV services, Home Box Office had this package designed so that the back of the brochure and the order card could be customized through surprinting.

◄

Title: The Water Lily Clock
Art Director: Leo Lobell
Copywriter: Barbara Bragg
Design Agency: JC Penney Company
Client: JC Penney Company, Inc.

The water lily clock offer was geared to take advantage of Penney's customers' high response to previous period-replica clock promotions.

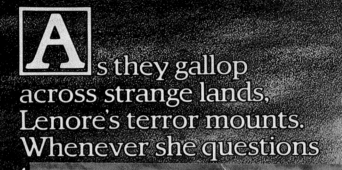

A s they gallop across strange lands, Lenore's terror mounts. Whenever she questions

Like thunder, the Wild Hunt roars across the midnight sky. Astride demonic horses charge the skeletal riders, their sunken faces seething fury. Behind them race the monstrous hellhounds, whose bloodcurdling howls pierce the dark clouds.

Sparking terror, these dreaded hunters of souls portend death or unspeakable evil for any unfortunate mortal who sees or hears them.

THE ENCHANTED WORLD

Dear Rea

If
tales of
off the
secrets

Her
world.
gnomes..
and evil
Magical
mermaids
appear t
of encha
and spir

Nev
unveiled
time, TI

THE ENCHANTED WORLD

Discover its magic and mystery with Ghosts FREE for 10 days!

Immerse yourself in a primeval realm of power, illusion and darkest sorcery in this introduction to THE ENCHANTED WORLD. Thrill to beloved and little-known tales from Celtic, Norse and Slavic folklore... dramatically retold, exquisitely illustrated!

Just mail attached order card today!

Ghosts

TIME
LIFE
BOOKS

Detach here before mailing.

FREE QUARTZ DESK CLOCK

Yours as a bonus gift when you purchase Ghosts.

ORDER CARD

YES! Please send me Ghosts for a 10-day FREE examination as my introduction to THE ENCHANTED WORLD. Also send me future volumes of this new series under the terms described in the enclosed letter. The handsome quartz clock will be mine to keep as a special gift—absolutely FREE-when I purchase Ghosts.

Send no money now.
Just mail this postage-paid card today!

Please initial here _____

EWL

Enter the spellbinding realm of legend, myth and magic!

Snatched by a ferocious dragon, a damsel might be swept away to an underground lair and made to sleep on mounds of hoarded gold. For in the days when dragons roamed free throughout Europe and Asia, maidens were commonly sacrificed to appease the menacing beasts.

Dragons, you'll discover, come in various sizes, forms and temperaments. Some sport huge wings, many several heads and several rows of deadly teeth. Others breathe scorching flames or pestilence. Still others can be helpful to humans.

You'll meet the dreaded Drac who lives under water and dines on French peasants...Tiamat, the powerful she-dragon who spawned Babylonian gods...noble dragon slayers such as Sigurd and Saint George...and more in Dragons!

Camelot's Sir Galahad summons all his skill and daring in his mystical quest for the Holy Grail. Legendary chalice of the Last Supper, the Grail was said to possess miraculous powers of feeding and healing. But the sacred vessel could be revealed only to the purest knight...the one most chaste in thought, word and deed.

Share action-packed trials of valiant knights and virtuous ladies. See a great chieftain single-handedly vanquish an army of foes. Thrill to tales of hairbreadth rescues, poison rings, cloaks of invisibility, mysterious weapons and more in Legends of Valor.

Troops of golden fairies glide through the forest in unearthly light, searching for human infants to strengthen their dwindling race. At greatest risk of being kidnapped are unbaptized children, for they have no name to tie them to the mortal world.

Watch anxious mothers surround their newborns with charms in hopes of deterring a fairy raid. Encounter elfin warriors engaged in ferocious battle. Meet the shimmering Snow Queen...beguiling Morgan le Fay, said to have lured the defeated King Arthur away to her enchanted island...and scores of other seductive creatures in Fairies and Elves.

The elusive unicorn, pure white with a single magical horn, has captured the human imagination since the Middle Ages. Unveil the colorful legends that surround this rare and fanciful creature. Savor artists' visions of its proud and graceful form.

Then chance upon soaring pegasus...strange centaurs...and that fabulous half-lion, half-eagle creature-the Griffin...all waiting for you in Magical Beasts!

Ulysses resists the sirens, escaping their deadly lure through ingenious measures. These mythical sea nymphs inhabit a rocky island in the Mediterranean. So sweet is their song, that sailors who hear it are drawn ever closer, and fatally shipwrecked. Forewarned of this danger, Ulysses has himself lashed to the mast of his ship, and the ears of his crew stopped up with melted wax.

Succumb to the spell of rapturous mermaids, magical sea horses, and other strange spirits that lure unwary mortals to their kingdom beneath the waves in Water Spirits.

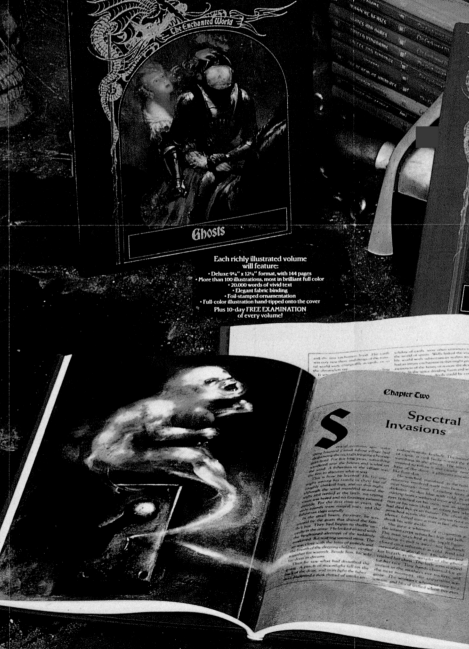

Captivating stories in every volume!

Charming story essays await you in every chapter of every volume. Laced with enticing border designs, they retell classic tales, like young Janet's rescue of handsome Tam Lin from the grasp of captor fairies.

"The knight appeared before her in the leafy shade, tall and pale and cloaked in silk."

"With jingling bridles and pealing bells, the fairy troop came into view. At its head, riding tall on a black horse, was the Queen...At last, Janet saw Tam Lin."

"Janet found herself holding the cold scaly coils of a serpent that flexed and twined about her arms and neck."

"From the well stepped a naked man—Tam Lin, reborn into the mortal world. Janet wrapped him in her cloak.... their thoughts were only for mortal love."

Stunning art that spans the centuries!

British illustrator Wayne Anderson, winner of the American Society of Illustrators' Gold Medal, created this seven-headed beast especially for our "Field Guide to Dragons."

N.C. Wyeth, one of America's most revered illustrators, envisions King Arthur with Merlin behind him, receiving the magical sword, Excalibur.

To evoke the vibrant beauty of THE ENCHANTED WORLD, TIME-LIFE BOOKS has gathered masterworks of art from many eras and many nations. Each magnificent volume brings you more than 100 illustrations, most in vivid full color. Included are images from Byzantine times, the Middle Ages and the Renaissance ...Oriental and Scandinavian classics...favorite works of such renowned illustrators as Ivan Bilibin, Arthur Rackham, Harry Clarke and Edmund Dulac. Plus outstanding contemporary paintings and drawings, many commissioned exclusively for this new series.

Title: Dare To Unmask The Illusion
Art Directors: Ron Wilcox
Copywriters: Marueen Palmedo
Design Agency: Time-Life Books
Client: Time-Life Books

This mailer was geared to position the Time-Life Enchanted World book series as a product for adults, rather than children.

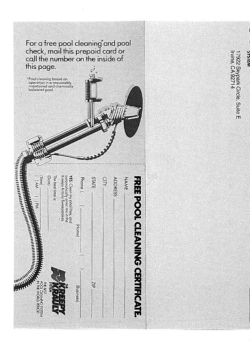

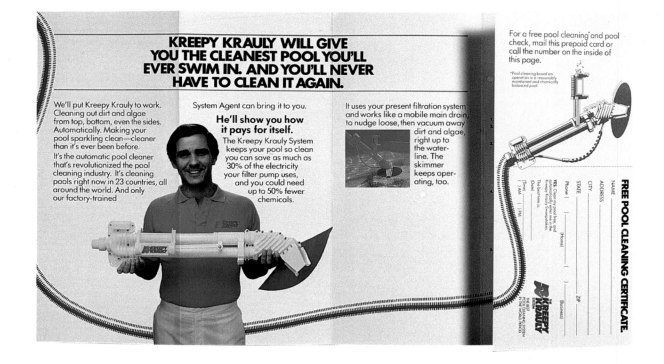

Title:	Your Chance
Art Director:	Gerry Ulrich
Copywriter:	David Wesolowski
Design Agency:	Keller Crescent Advertising
Client:	The Kreepy Krauly System

Using lists that had received five previous mailings over 18 months, this package was designed to produce a steady, but manageable, flow of sales leads for offices selling the Kreepy Krauly swimming pool cleaning system.

Result:
Approximately 450,000 pieces were mailed, and 1% of the qualified recipients responded, reversing a decline in response from these lists.

Title: Free Round Trip
Art Directors: Tom Miano, Karin L. Lihmroth
Copywriter: Richard Sprano
Design Agency: Ogilvy & Mather Direct
Client: American Express Company

A free trip was offered to travelers on the New York Air airlines' northeastern shuttle routes when they used the American Express card to pay for tickets.

Result:
The use of American Express Cards on this shuttle route increased dramatically.

PACKAGING DESIGN

Large format—9" x 12"
hardbound
256 pages, over 450
illustrations, most in full color
Price: $45.00
ISBN: 0-86636-000-X

Package Designers ▪ Product Manufacturers ▪ Art Directors ▪ Advertising and Marketing Executives—anyone involved in creating and manufacturing product packaging needs this guide to the best in package

EXHIBIT DESIGN

Large format—9" x 12"
hardbound
256 pages, over 500
illustrations, most in full color
Price: $45.00
ISBN: 0-86636-001-8

Trade Show Exhibitors and Coordinators ▪ Exhibit Designers ▪ Graphic Artists ▪ Art Directors ▪ Architects ▪ Marketing Executives—everyone involved in the planning and production of trade show exhibits will find this

PRODUCT DESIGN

Large format—9" x 12"
hardbound
256 pages, over 500
illustrations, most in full color
Price: $45.00
ISBN: 0-86636-002-6

Industrial Designers ▪ Product Manufacturers ▪ Artists ▪ Engineers ▪ Consumers—anyone involved in creating or using equipment for the home or office will find this collection of award-winning designs an essential guide to contemporary products.

Equipment and furnishings for home, office and industrial use have undergone an extraordinary revolution in the past two decades. New kinds of equipment and tools and advances in construction techniques, materials and designs have transformed the way we work and live. PRODUCT DESIGN presents a compendium of the best of these innovations. Hundreds of full color illustrations cover the excitement of the new visual style in:

- Appliances, houseware and tools
- Home electronics and entertainment
- Lighting
- Contract and residential furnishings
- Business equipment
- Medical equipment
- Industrial equipment and transportation
- Recreational and sports equipment
- Textiles
- Designs for the handicapped

Each photograph is accompanied by details on the client, designer and design firm, construction and materials, and awards received.
Product design is written, compiled and edited by Akiko Busch with the assistance of the editors of Industrial Design magazine. A resident of New York City has written e

POINT OF PURCHASE DESIGN

Large format—9" x 12"
hardbound
256 pages, over 500
illustrations, most in full color
Price: $45.00
ISBN: 0-86636-003-4

Retail Merchandisers ▪ Retail and Marketing Executives ▪ Display Designers ▪ Packagers ▪ Builders—or anyone involved in point of purchase marketing should have this unique major reference work.

The battle for the consumer's dollar may very well be won in the aisles of the retail store. Studies done in outlets where point-of-purchase displays are most widely used, such as supermarkets and drugstores, show that between 60% and 65% of purchase decisions are made in the store at the time of purchase. Successful merchandisers recognize the high volumes that can be generated by point of purchase displays. POINT OF PURCHASE DESIGN illustrates hundreds of these displays in full color, with a text explaining why they are effective and how point of purchase displays can best be used.
POINT OF PURCHASE DESIGN features over 400 display units for products including:

- Food and paper goods
- Beverages
- Health and beauty aids
- Household goods
- Jewelry, toys, greeting cards and other personal products
- Hardware and building materials
- Farm and garden supplies
- Automobiles, trucks and other vehicles

Information accompanying each illustration details the designer, advertiser/client, the producer and the display plus other important

PBC International, Inc.

I D E A   B O O K S

FOR ▪ GRAPHIC ARTISTS
▪ PROFESSIONAL DESIGNERS
▪ MARKETING AND SALES EXECUTIVES
▪ DESIGN ENGINEERS

Title: Double Pleasure/Double Treasure
            Flight to Fancy
Client: Doubleday Book Club

A travel sweepstakes was offered as an incentive to get new members to join the Doubleday Book Club.

Title: 4-Book Flyer
Art Director: Richard Liu
Copywriter: Herb Taylor, Steve Blount
Design Agency: PBC International, Inc.
Client: PBC International, Inc.

This 4-page flyer was conceived to make consumers aware of the quality design books produced and published by PBC International, Inc. The flyer uses four-color photography and descriptive copy to promote the design books, and is used as a self-mailer. This flyer was not entered in the John Caples Award Program.

Title:	PCP Test-Mature Market Program
Art Director:	Sam Woo
Copywriters:	Gil Bob, W. Kendall Brown
Design Agency:	W. Kendall Brown
Client:	Continental Insurance Company

Backed by a modest telemarketing program and local co-op advertising with insurance agents, this mailing tested a national program to solicit inquiries and insurance policy expiration dates from homeowners 50 years of age or older.

Result:
From a mailing of 150,000 in two states, the piece drew a response of 1.5%, generating $5 million in incremental sales. The test was considered successful and was scheduled to be rolled out in 25 more states in 1985 with projected revenues of $80 million.

Hello.

You should take a few minutes to learn about a unique insurance policy that in one package protects your home, your car, and your personal property. This policy is particularly right for you if you happen to be fifty or older.

It's called PCP--Personal Comprehensive Protection--from Continental Insurance. As you may know, Continental is one of the largest insurers in the world, and we've developed and refined PCP to make it the outstanding protection for people who own both a home and a car.

What is PCP? It's a "package" of vital insurance coverages that most people like you need, consolidated into a single policy. By grouping home, auto and personal liability insurance together in one product, Continental is able to give you greater value for your insurance dollar than the several standard policies you probably have now.

PCP is a simple, easy-to-understand policy that was designed to sell itself to you through the good, old-fashioned technique of giving you more for your money.

Continental Insurance
Property/Casualty Operations
2 Corporate Place South
Piscataway, NJ 08854

"Take the first step toward PCP peace of mind."

PCP offers you more coverage for your insurance dollar. Act now to learn more. Mail this pre-paid reply card today.

For Georgia residents —
Even more savings with PCP!

In addition to the economical comprehensive pr____ for home and auto owners, PCP offers even mor__ with these discounts:

For the property portion of your premium —
- *2% credit* for a smoke alarm
- *5% credit* for an alarm connected to a fire or police station
- *10% credit* for burglar & fire alarm connected to police & fire station with back-up capability

For the auto ___ of your prem__
- *15% credit* fo__ more motor ve__
- *10% credit* if v__ exclusively for __ farm use
- *10% credit* if d__ 65 or older

Take advantage of PCP's protection and disco____
Call Continental's TOLL-FREE telephone num___
1-800-345-8540, ext. 143
Or mail the enclosed pre-paid reply card today!
A local independent agent will contact you shortly.

Continental Insurance
180 Maiden Lane, New York, NY 1003_

Continental Insurance

YES, I'm very interested in Continental's PCP policy. I understand there is no obligation on my part.

	Expiration Date	Company
My current auto policy		
My current homeowners policy		

☐ Please contact me for more information about PCP.

"We've got good news for you, if you're 50 or older!"

PRINTED IN U.S.A.

INSIDE:
A special offer to give grad students a running start....

DIANE SHAIB
VICE PRESIDENT
MARKETING

AM

Gary Raiczyk
615 Wayne Ave.
Haddonfield, NJ   08033

Dear Gary Raiczyk:

You face a virtual bridge, the one that takes you from graduate school to the next plateau in your career.

The crossing can be easy, provided that you're prepared. And
provided that you carry the decided advantage of an American
Express® Card.

You may think it's too soon to get the Card. You may not have
a job lined up. In fact, you're still in school. But I'm
writing to let you know, that doesn't matter.

We're ready to accept you almost solely on the
basis of your future potential!
    So apply now. It may never again be this
easy to get the Card.

Special American Express Card Application for Graduate Students   PLEASE
                                                                         PRINT

Your next step
from graduate school
has just been
made...

Title: This Easy
Art Director: Bob Adamec
Copywriters: Aurelio Saiz, Kathi Stark
Design Agency: Ogilvy & Mather Direct
Client: American Express Travel Related
Services Company, Inc.

A special program was created to encourage college
students enrolled in post-graduate degree programs to
apply for an American Express card. Many consumers
consider this credit card hard to qualify for. The mailer
had to show how easily students could qualify under this
program.

Result:
In combination with a letter mailing, the package
generated a total response rate of 13%.

This easy.

Get an
American Express Cardmembership.
Now, when you need it most.

Title:	Please Don't Discard
Art Director:	Herb Ackerman
Copywriter:	Ellen Kahn-Piderit
Design Agency:	Ogilvy & Mather Direct
Client:	AT&T

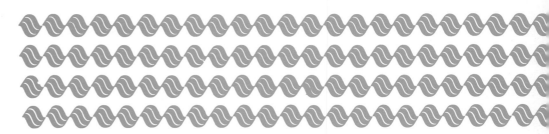

Consumers, confused by the effects of the break up of AT&T, were unaware that they needed to actively choose a long distance telephone service. The effort sought to explain the available choices to the consumer and position AT&T long distance service as necessary and not overly expensive.

Result:
The initial response rate averaged 60%.

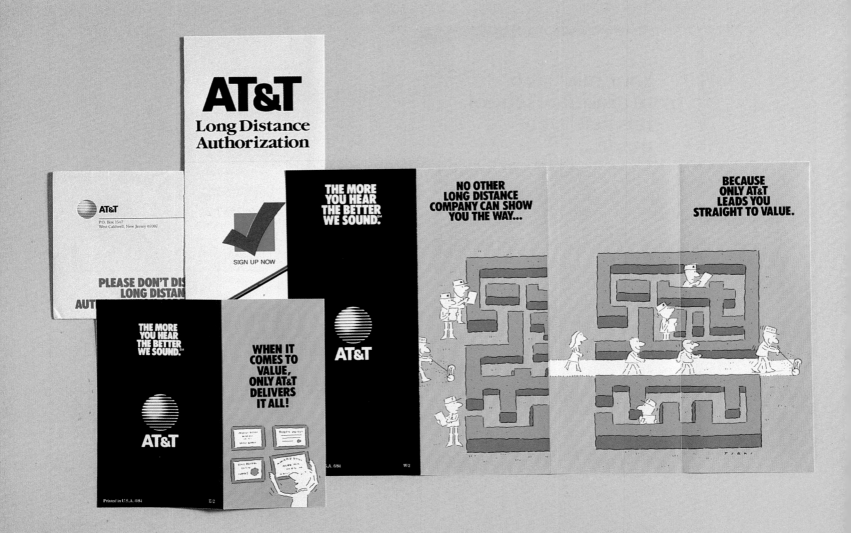

ONLY ONE LONG DISTANCE COMPANY CAN LEAD YOU STRAIGHT TO VALUE...

AT&T: THE CLEAR-CUT CHOICE

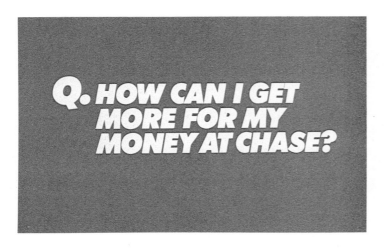

Q. HOW CAN I GET MORE FOR MY MONEY AT CHASE?

Title: Chase CD Cross-Sell
Art Director: Lucia Barrientos
Copywriters: Gina Bruce, Mike Morehead
Design Agency: Rapp & Collins, Inc.
Client: The Chase Manhattan Bank

Through competitive interest rates and saturation advertising, Chase Manhattan Bank had attracted a large group of Cash Deposit customers, most of whom did their basic banking at other banks. Chase wanted to keep these customers after their CDs matured, by transferring the proceeds of the CD to other programs and perhaps selling them additional banking services.

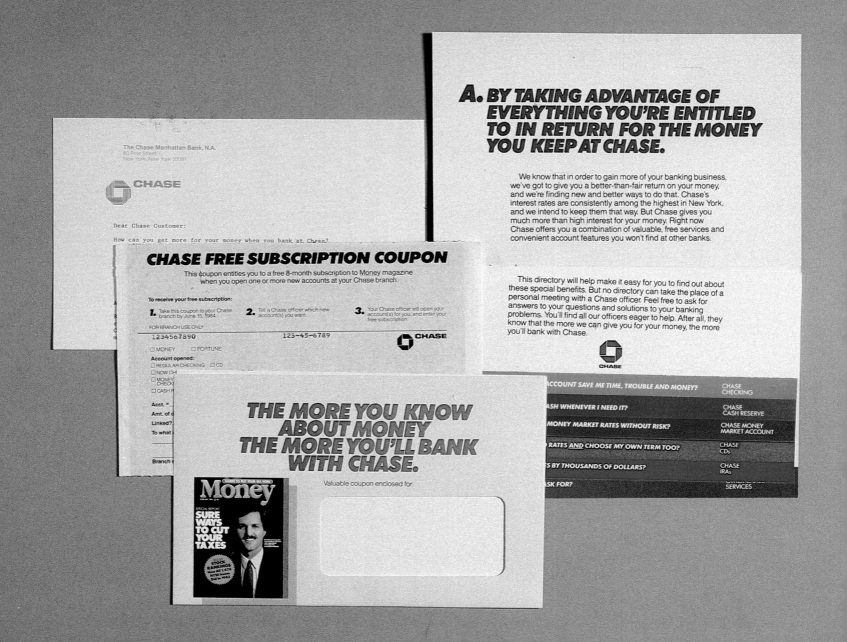

An Extraordinary Concept.

Imagine the luxury and prestige of owning a private residence in the south's fastest growing city, Atlanta. During your frequent visits to Atlanta, consider the convenience of living, entertaining and conducting business as you wish within the privacy and comfort of your own home. That's the concept and that's exactly what American Home Equities had in mind when they designed a limited number of unique one-bedroom homes at The Plantation at Lenox. Uniquely priced as well, at just $67,900, these elegantly appointed one-bedroom condominiums offer all the amenities and quality construction that has made The Plantation at Lenox one of Atlanta's premier residential communities. Privately secured behind impressive brick and wrought-iron gates, the beautifully manicured grounds, hardwood forests and natural lake and waterfall create a sublime setting for the exquisitely rendered traditional Williamsburg architecture.

The Privacy and Prestige of Ownership:
The luxury one-bedroom, professionally decorated to your individual taste, offers the ultimate in uptown Atlanta living. Spacious living/dining areas with standard features such as gas-log fireplaces, mirrored doors and built-in bookcases, adjoin a gardenroom overlooking a peaceful forest view. Efficiently designed kitchens with lattice pass-through, adds the perfect ingredient for entertaining or simply dining at home. Enter the bedroom through the gardenroom or through the dressing vanity/bath area designed to maximize space and privacy. As an added bonus, the unit even comes complete with a washer and dryer. But the luxury doesn't stop here. Enjoy the convenience and security of garage parking and glass-enclosed elevator service and the leisure activities at the antebellum-styled clubhouse and olympic-size pool. All of this in a one-bedroom residence at The Plantation at Lenox for only $67,900, you're asking? Well, here is the best part. The investment potential.

The Investment:
Owning a private one-bedroom residence in Atlanta at The Plantation at Lenox provides the frequent Atlanta visitor an outstanding potential investment, tax-shelter opportunity and an important hedge against spiraling hotel room rates:

		Today's Hotel Costs*	
Cost of a Luxury One-Bedroom Unit = $67,900			
Monthly mortgage (including taxes) = $679./mo.	Daily Cost	= $80/day	
Monthly income tax deduction – $284./mo.	Times 5 Days		
(based on 50% tax bracket)	per month	x 5	
Total Monthly Expense $395./mo.		$400./mo.	
*based on average near-by superior room rates.

The Appreciation:
Of course the ultimate long-term benefit of owning a one-bedroom home at The Plantation at Lenox will be the significant appreciation potential in the value of your property. Owners in Atlanta have consistently enjoyed increases well above the national averages.

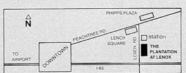

The Location:
Sharing one of uptown Atlanta's most sought after addresses, The Plantation at Lenox is conveniently located on Lenox Road within walking distance to the south's most exclusive restaurants and shopping at Lenox Mall and Phipps Plaza, the homes of Saks Fifth Avenue, Lord & Taylor, Gucci and Neiman-Marcus to name but a few. With easy access to Atlanta's rapid transit system with its soon to be completed Lenox Road Station, and Interstate 85, the pulse of the city's downtown business district and Atlanta International Airport are just minutes away.

For more information on The Plantation at Lenox, call Gail Myhand at **(404) 262-3711** or simply mail this card and one of our sales representatives will contact you.

☐ **YES**, I am interested in learning more about the benefits of owning a residence at The Plantation at Lenox.

NAME
COMPANY   TITLE
ADDRESS
CITY   STATE   ZIP
HOME PHONE   BUSINESS
☐ I plan to be in Atlanta _____ dates _____ and would like to arrange an appointment to see a model.

THE PLANTATION AT LENOX

Marketing by Plantation Brokers Inc. • Developed by American Home Equities Inc. • 3033 Lenox Road, Atlanta, GA. 30324 (404) 262-3711

Title: Frequent Traveler
Client: American Home Equities, Inc.

To spur sales of 10, one-bedroom units at a condominium community, The Plantation at Lenox, 20,000 mailers were sent to doctors, lawyers and Georgia legislators who might stay in Atlanta on business at least 60 days a year. Potential investors were advised of the cost savings between paying for a hotel room and owning a condominium.

Result:
All 10 units were sold within one week.

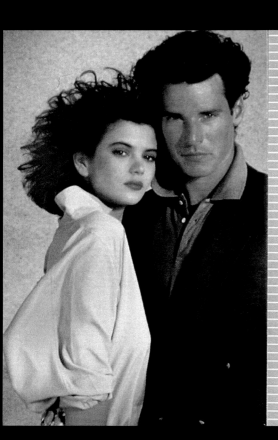

GQ. The Magazine
For The Modern Man.
The Magazine For You.
Month After Month
GQ Brings You All The Best...

FASHIONS

LOOKS

DESIGNERS

SIGHTS

SOUNDS

CARS

FOODS

DRINKS

PERSONALITIES

IDEAS

TRENDS

Title: A New Look
Art Director: Jim Pastena
Copywriter: Jim Consolantis
Design Agency: Rapp & Collins, Inc.
Client: Conde Nast Publications, Inc.

This piece stressed Gentleman's Quarterly's editorial
quality in an effort to reposition the fashion publication
as a guide to good living.

3
Space

Magazine and Newspaper Advertising

They don't drop neatly into your hand from the mailbox, slam into your head with shouts or a thumping good tune, or idly ease into your consciousness in the middle of a good television program.

No, space ads are inert little things. They just lie there, buried on a page somewhere in a publication, performing no real function other than breaking up the editorial matter.

Print ads don't shout, sing, wriggle, or pop-up. To be noticed at all, they must somehow pull the mind and eye away from the other ads; away from the editorial content. They must capture the readers' attention no matter what mood they're in or how pressed they are for time.

So far, there's no problem. A big dot in the middle of a blank page will get noticed. But to be *read* an ad has to immediately show that it contains information that pertains to the reader's self-interest or curiosity.

These points encapsulate what *all* print ads are supposed to do. But attracting attention and getting read are only the means for a direct response space ad.

They have to go one crucial step further than most general advertising: Direct response ads must compel the reader to get a pen, fill out a coupon, dig out a credit card or checkbook, transpose the necessary information, find an envelope, address it, stamp it, and mail the whole assemblage to the sponsor. While the inclusion of a toll-free telephone number can make responding easier for the customer, the direct response ad must still produce immediate *action* on the part of the reader.

While that mission is no different from the job done by other direct response vehicles, it is more difficult using space. Aside from having to compete with other ads and editorial matter, space is limited, restricting the amount of copy that can be used. The size of other vehicles, such as direct mail, can be adapted to the amount of copy needed. The benefits of purchasing the product or service have to be summed up in sentences in a space ad, where direct mail pieces may offer paragraphs or even pages on the subject. There's little room to romance the reader. And compared to the dramatic effects and product demonstrations available through the use of television, the space advertiser is at a distinct disadvantage.

To produce a successful direct response space ad today requires more than just great copy. The graphic concept and execution must not only support the copy theme, but act as a strong catalyst to move the reader to act. The ads must be layered to give them more than one or two dimensions, and to present the reader with a number of decisive selling points.

The copy for direct response ads is subject to much more scrutiny today. The attention of government agencies and consumer advocates makes it almost impossible to create a "winning" space ad through sensational, unsupported claims.

Even in this tough environment, it is possible to succeed. The pieces that follow are surely winners. They've been judged so by some of the best creative minds in the direct response field. As a group, then, these space ads are a tribute to the creators of direct response space ads, who have sold so much with so few natural advantages to work with.

July 14, 1861

My Very Dear Sarah,
2,000 men are sleeping
around me, many of them
enjoying the last sleep
before that of death

NO PLANES. NO TANKS. JUST MEN, MUSKETS AND CANNONS IN THE DEADLIEST U.S. WAR OF ALL.

Major Sullivan Ballou wrote the poignant letter to his wife Sarah predicting his own death at Bull Run.

Their letters capture an unforgettable personal picture of men in battle. Their diaries—all too often unfinished—record life on the march, on the run, in battle.

In their own words they tell the stories of their personal war, of action as they saw it at places like the Devil's Den at Gettysburg. The Hornet's Nest at Shiloh. The devastation at Antietam with over 20,000 dead and wounded.

Never before such stirring personal accounts of pivotal events and battles.

The editors of TIME-LIFE BOOKS have gathered the most

vivid of these eyewitness accounts to create an unprecedented picture of the most awesome war in America's history.

An account all the more real because you see it through the eyes of the men who fought it. Through classic battle paintings. Drawings made on the spot. Maps that pinpoint the action and the tactics. And rare photos—many never before published—by some of the world's first battlefront photographers.

You can almost smell the gunsmoke.

From the first cannon shot that smashed into Ft. Sumter to the last pistol shot that killed Lincoln, here is the full sweep

as well as the pers took one of every

Examine the firs

THE CIVIL WAR fr is an unsurpassed unstintingly accur absorbing.

Mail the coupo volume, *Brother A* Examine it for 10 satisfied, send it b Otherwise keep it plus shipping and volumes will com

THE CI
As close as
the exper

ignettes of the war that
ho fought it.

me for 10 days FREE.
ME-LIFE BOOKS
nal library,
vealing and

ceive the first
t Brother.
f you aren't
d owe nothing.
ay just $12.95
ing. Future
about every other

L WAR
an come to
e today.

month. Same free trial. Keep only
the books you want. Cancel any time
simply by notifying us.
          Send no money.
      Just mail the
      coupon today.

© 1984, Time-Life Books, Time & Life Bldg., Chicago, IL 60611

EXAMINE BROTHER AGAINST BROTHER FOR 10 DAYS FREE.

YES! I would like to see *Brother Against Brother* as my introduction to THE CIVIL WAR series. Please send it to me for 10 days' free examination. Also send me future volumes under the terms described in this ad.

Name_____
            (Please print)
Address_____

_____

City_____

State_____ Zip_____

TIME
LIFE
BOOKS

All orders are subject to approval.
Price subject to change.

Title: My Very Dear Sarah
Art Director: Jerry Lawrence
Copywriter: Mel Bruck
Design Agency: Wunderman, Ricotta & Kline
Client: Time-Life Books

This multi-volume chronicle of the U.S. Civil War, primarily marketed in the Southwestern U.S., was nearing the end of its life cycle. An earlier ad that had appeared in TV Guide magazine was adapted for use as a pre-printed magazine insert.

SEE THEM LAUGH, PLAY AND TICKLE BABIES WHILE THEY PLAN MASS MURDER.

Hitler with Goering. (UPI/Bettmann Archive)

dared to disobey evil. They're all in *German High Command*, your introductory videocassette to WORLD WAR WITH WALTER CRONKITE.

The German High Command 90-minute documentary of evil in chapters: I—*Goering*; II—*Ministe Hate* (Goebbels); III—*The Strange Case of Rudolf Hess*; and IV—*The Plots Against Hitler*.

It's yours at the special price of just $9.95 (plus $2.45 shipping and handling)—a full $40 off the regular subscription price! As a subscriber, future cassettes will be shipped to you, one every other m always for 10 days' free examina You'll see actual combat footage take front-line cameramen of *both* s Here's a partial list of contents:
• Anzio Beach
• B

Hermann G front some

WORLD WAR II with WALTER CRONKITE
The German High Command

WORLD WAR II WITH WALTER CRONKITE

Narrated by Walter Cronkite.

NOW ON VIDEOCASSETTES EXCLUSIVELY FROM THE CBS VIDEO LIBRARY.

They were perfect Nazis. Hermann Goering, who charged fees to spectators at his own wedding, and who told his Gestapo: "Better to shoot the wrong man than not to shoot at all!" Joseph Goebbels, a failure as a writer who found in Nazism the ideal outlet for his fierce hatred. And Rudolf Hess, Hitler's alter ego, whose life took the most bizarre twists and turns of all.

See the men around Hitler...cavorting one moment, planning mass destruction the next. And then see the few who dared plot against Hitler and his madmen...who

Joseph Goebbels

Title:	See Them Laugh, Play, and Tickle Babies
Art Director:	Rodger Minyard
Copywriters:	Bill Keisler, Jim Infantino
Design Agency:	Wunderman, Ricotta & Kline
Client:	CBS Video Library

A series of documentaries chronicling the events of World War II was promoted by creating curiosity about the leaders of Germany's Third Reich. The headline, "See them laugh, play, and tickle babies while they plan mass murders" was used to broaden the appeal of the series beyond its natural market—those who lived through the war—to younger consumers.

Title: Every Secret Passion
Art Director: Don Swanson
Copywriter: Roz Cundell
Design Agency: Doubleday Creative Services
Client: Doubleday Book Clubs

Candlelight Ecstasy, a continuing series of romantic novels from Doubleday, was promoted to female readers using photos featuring satins, furs, and pearls. A coupon offered four free books to new subscribers, plus two more free books after payment for the subscription was received.

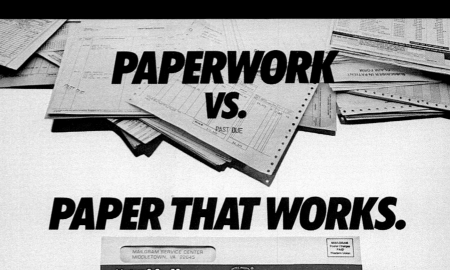

PAPERWORK VS.

PAPER THAT WORKS.

MAILGRAM SERVICE CENTER
MIDDLETOWN, VA. 22645

Western Union **Mailgram**

JEANNIE TOBIA
482 W. 45TH ST.
NEW YORK, N.Y. 10036

If your hospital's paperwork is piling up, what you need is paper that works better: Western Union's Overnight Mailgram.®

It works miracles on your bills, forms, and notices. All right from your own computer terminal.

Take collections. In just moments, you can create hundreds of highly itemized bills that arrive with Mailgram's "open-me-first" impact—helping your bills really pay off.

You can send hundreds of Overnight Mailgrams as easily as one—which makes quick work of your social service notices and payment schedules.

And as the name promises, Overnight Mailgram arrives the next business day—to get faster action on bad check notices or to track vendor orders.*

There are so many more ways Overnight Mailgram can save your hospital time and money, it would take a kit to tell the whole story. And we have one for you.

Among other things, our free kit has samples of how other hospitals are actually using Overnight Mailgram.

For your free kit, call 1-800-336-3797 Ext. 513. Or just return the attached card or coupon.

Every day, it's you vs. a stack of paperwork. Overnight Mailgram helps you come out on top.

SEND FOR A FREE INFORMATION KIT.

Call 1-800-336-3797 Ext. 513 (in Virginia call 703-448-8877) or mail this coupon to: Western Union Electronic Mail Inc., P.O. Box 1037, McLean, VA 22101 Attn: E.M.R.C.-513.

☐ I would like a free Overnight Mailgram information kit ASAP.

☐ My paperwork is *really* piled up. Have an Overnight Mailgram representative trained in hospital administration call my office immediately for an appointment.

Name_____
Title_____
Hospital_____
Address_____
City_____
State_____ Zip_____
Phone (   )_____

*The vast majority of Mailgram messages are delivered in the next day's mail. Mailgram service is subject to provisions and restrictions of Western Union's F.C.C. Tariff #260.

WESTERN UNION'S OVERNIGHT MAILGRAM. It takes the work out of paperwork.

© 1984 Western Union Corporation.

SPEND A TRANQUIL WEEKEND WATCHING TWO MEN ARGUE.

This November 18–20, don't go to the movies. Go into the movies with Siskel and Ebert.

Television film critics Gene Siskel and Roger Ebert will spend the entire weekend critiquing five modern classics including some of the best work of Brando, DeNiro, Bertolucci, Malle, Scorsese, and others.

This exclusive weekend engagement will take place at the Arrowwood conference center, situated on 114 wooded acres in Westchester County.

There, movie fans will attend private screenings followed by in-depth discussions with the contentious critics themselves. When they're not watching movies, guests can enjoy Arrowwood's outstanding cuisine, as well as an indoor pool, sauna, tennis, racquetball, and squash.

Only a limited number can attend, so call for reservations.

The price of admission for this weekend is $295 per person double occupancy, $325 single occupancy. Including meals and, of course, unlimited popcorn.

For reservations or information call Ms. Sally Dininny at 914-939-5500, Ext. 7849.

 **Arrowwood** OF WESTCHESTER

Anderson Hill Road • Rye Brook, New York 10573

Arrowwood is located next to The State University of New York at Purchase. Convenient from Manhattan by train. Complimentary transportation to/from the Rye Station. Arrowwood of Westchester and the Arrowwood design are registered service marks of Citicorp.
© Arrowwood of Westchester 1983

ARW-4

Title:	Spend a Tranquil Weekend Watching Two Men Argue
Art Director:	Michael Campbell
Copywriters:	Bruce Lee, Robert Culver
Design Agency:	Scali, McCabe, Sloves Direct Response
Client:	Arrowwood of Westchester

To solicit reservations for a special weekend of movie viewing and criticism with newspaper film critics Gene Siskel and Roger Ebert, this one-third page ad was run in the *New Yorker* magazine. A full page version was run in *New York* magazine.

Result:

Although the price of the package at this exclusive conference center was high, $295 to $325 per person, the weekend sold out after just one insertion of each ad.

"Mommy, why did the dinosaurs die?"

For generations, children's imaginations have been captivated by the awesome size and power of the dinosaurs; and their minds have been intrigued by the mystery of why they died.

Now, they can unravel the secrets of the prehistoric world in *T-Rex*, a scientifically-accurate computer simulation game that brings the age of the dinosaurs to vivid life.

T-Rex is the first program in SciSoft's *Adventures in Science*, a new series of role-playing science games that introduces children to all the "whys" and wonders of natural science.

An advanced new concept in educational software

While most educational software programs rely on routine drill-and-practice formats, *T-Rex*—like all games in the series—is a state-of-the-art interactive simulation with superb, lifelike graphics and arcade-quality excitement.

Based on the most current learning concepts in both science and education, it's designed to develop critical thinking *and* problem-solving skills as it teaches the player about one of the most fascinating ages the world has ever known.

Build a complete home science library

Other programs in the *Adventures in Science* series include *The Honey Factory*, *Life on the Coral Reef*, *The Gardener*, *Migration* and *Mountain Gorillas*. Together, they reveal, as never before, the wonderful world of science to young, inquisitive minds. Said noted education expert Herbert Kohl, "The SciSoft scientific simulations ... provide an entire new way in which computers can be used to develop sophisticated thinking."

Begin the adventure today!

Simply mail the attached coupon for a 10-day, no-risk examination of *T-Rex*. If you decide to keep it, you'll receive future programs one at a time, about every other month, and always on the same no-risk trial basis. Keep only the programs you want; cancel at any time.

If you should decide not to keep *T-Rex*, simply return it within 10 days for a full refund. Your subscription will be canceled, and you will be under no further obligation.

Begin the adventure with a 10-day, no-risk examination of T-Rex!

SciSoft™ Adventures in Science

Each program in this exclusive mail-order edition includes:
1. *Substantial savings* off the suggested retail price.
2. *48-page guide book* with complete instructions and educational background material. 3. *Sturdy library case* to store the program and guide book. 4. PLUS, a *free* computer-graphic poster!

Free poster with every program!

© 1984 Keron Productions Inc. All rights reserved. "Apple", "Atari" and "IBM" are registered trademarks of Apple Computer, Inc., Atari, Inc. and International Business Machines Corp. respectively. "Commodore 64" is a trademark of Commodore Business Machines, Inc. SciSoft, T-Rex, The Honey Factory, Life on the Coral Reef and The Gardener are all trademarks of Keron Productions Inc.

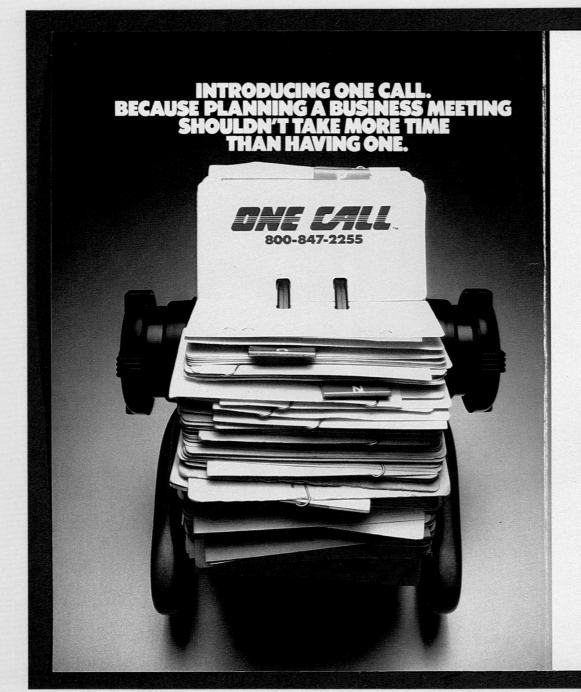

INTRODUCING ONE CALL.
BECAUSE PLANNING A BUSINESS MEETING
SHOULDN'T TAKE MORE TIME
THAN HAVING ONE.

ONE CALL™
800-847-2255

If you've ever planned a business meeting, you know it's possible to spend half your life on the phone getting information, and the other half waiting for your calls to be returned.

But now there's a service that can help you plan meetings for more than twenty-five people with just one call.

It's called One Call.™ And it saves an enormous amount of tedious work.

It's the biggest thing in travel since the wheel.

WE REDUCE PLANNING A BUSINESS MEETING TO MANAGEABLE PROPORTIONS.

One Call is easy to use. You just call our toll-free number and give us the details of the meeting you're planning.

We'll electronically transmit this information to hotels, airlines, ground transportation companies, and more.

Naturally, we're flexible about taking special requests. You might be looking for a conference center with sophisticated audiovisual equipment. A motorcoach that's specially equipped for the Board of Directors. Or a place to meet that's also convenient for post-meeting trips.

We'll communicate what you're looking for, wherever you're looking.

WE GET YOU COMPETITIVE BIDS FROM HOTEL, AIRLINE, AND GROUND TRANSPORTATION COMPANIES.

In five days we send you a Mailgram® containing all the information you asked for, including competitive bids

and the phone number of the person to contact when you ready to finalize arrangement

If you're really in a hurry, te We'll get back to you in 48 h

Because there are thousa properties in the One Call ne we can get back to you with wider selection of bids than could have gotten yourself.

Which saves you more th time. It saves you money.

WE GIVE YOU AL THE INFORMATION NEED TO MAKE A INFORMED CHOIC

One Call has several big adv First, it gives you all the ir tion you requested. Availability. Prices. Special services. All in an inform- ative, well- organized format.

Second, it eliminates hours of repetitive phone conversations needed to give the same requirements to many different people.

Third, it's simple. The on equipment you need is a ph

But we've saved the best

WE GUARANTEE YO LIKE THE PRICE. WE EVEN GUARAN YOU'LL LIKE ONE C

One Call is amazingly inexp

Plan your next meeting
Or mail this coupon or th

☐ I'd like to subscribe to One
☐ I'm not planning a meeting

NAME

COMPANY

ADDRESS

CITY

STATE

(   )
If you'd like us to call you, please give

© 1984 WESTERN UNION TRAVEL INDUS

After a one-time subscription fee of $75, it costs $25 if you select a hotel, airline, or ground transportation supplier. Only $15 if you select any two kinds of suppliers. And only $10 if you select all three kinds.

In other words, the more you use it, the less it costs.

The reason One Call is inexpensive is that Western Union doesn't need to charge you for setting up a telecommunications network.

We already have one that reaches around the world.

What's more, we guarantee you'll like One Call. If you don't think it makes planning a meeting a lot easier after you've tried it, we'll refund your subscription fee.

WE'RE AS CLOSE AS THE NEAREST PHONE.
Reaching One Call is as convenient as a toll-free phone call.

For people who plan business meetings, it's simply a better form of communication between supply and demand. And it eliminates the monotonous task of getting basic information and soliciting bids.

If you'd like to subscribe, or would like more information, mail the coupon below.

Or call 800-847-2255, ext. 109. It's the one call to make, if you don't want to make more than one.

Title: Introducing One Call
Art Director: Michael Campbell
Copywriter: Robert Culver
Design Agency: Scali, McCabe, Sloves Direct Response
Client: Western Union

One Call, a service for travel agents and others who occasionally plan meetings for 25 or more people, was introduced with two four-color print ads. The copy emphasized the convenience and time-saving features of One Call.

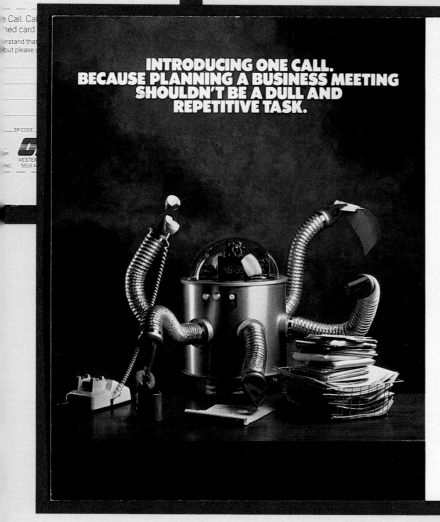

SANTA'S DEADLINE COMES BUT ONCE A YEAR. CHANCES ARE YOU'RE NOT SO LUCKY.

That's why Muse Air freight meets your toughest deadlines every single day.

Some people seem to have all the luck. Granted, Santa's annual push is quite an ordeal, but at least it's seasonal. Your need for a quick, reliable air delivery service continues day-in, day-out every day of the year.

Lucky for you there's Muse Air freight, offering a convenient schedule of departures to and from Austin, Dallas, Houston, Los Angeles, Lubbock, Midland/Odessa and Tulsa every business day. Of course, there's an equally convenient schedule of

arrivals, and our counter-to-counter charges are the lowest rates to be found (see attached reply card).

So every time your package is going our way, you'll find that you're in luck — because nobody delivers like Muse Air freight when your deadlines are nip and tuck.

Muse Air ®
makes flying beautiful.

MUSE AIR FREIGHT OFFERS THE LOWEST RATES AVAILABLE.

0-50 pounds	$30
51-100 pounds	$40
over 100 pounds	$40

plus 41¢ per pound over 100 pounds

For more information on Muse Air freight, complete and mail the attached card, or call your Muse Air Freight office.

Austin	512/473-8307
Dallas	214/559-5700
Houston	713/643-5484
Los Angeles	213/670-5598
Lubbock	806/765-7225
Midland/Odessa	915/563-5378
Tulsa	918/832-1754

Muse Air
makes flying beautiful.

Title:	Santa's Deadline
Art Directors:	Celesta T. Segerstrom, Chuck Bua
Copywriter:	Chuck Coursey
Design Agency:	Keller Crescent Company, Southwest
Client:	Muse Air Freight Service

Muse Air's new air freight service was introduced through this print ad in the airlines' in-flight magazine.

Title:	Good News, Bad News
Art Directors:	Joe Cupani, Vincent Chieco
Copywriters:	Vincent Chieco, Joe Cupani
Design Agency:	Ogilvy & Mather Direct
Client:	TWA Cargo

A unique service was created to help distinguish TWA air cargo in the crowded air freight field. TWA Express allowed shippers to reserve space aboard specific flights for their cargo, and these shipments were loaded first. The ad had to emphasize the benefit to shippers, whose cargo would not be left behind in the event of overbooking, and attract attention in magazines already carrying many ads from competing air freight companies.

The good news is the flight left on time.
The bad news is your freight wasn't on it.

You should've used TWA's Priority Express. Priority Express assures that your valuable freight will fly on the flight that you choose. Even in this busy season.

Whatever the size of your urgent shipment, all you have to do is get it to the airport 90 mins. before flight time. Or if you prefer, TWA can provide pick-up and delivery services.

Either way, we'll call you within 2 hours after your special freight is loaded, just to let you know it's on its way. And with TWA's computerized tracking system we can pinpoint the exact location of your freight at any time.

So give your valuable freight the top priority it deserves—call TWA's Priority Express: **1-800-TW-CARGO.**   You're going to like us   **TWA**

Priority Express. Get the freight you want, on the flight you want.

OUR TELEX, TWX AND DDD TERMINALS COME WITH MORE THAN JUST OPERATING DIRECTIONS.

Joe Boyd
Maintenance Service

Valerie Hynes
Customer Care Service

Eric Matthews
Relocation Service

Lynn Carpenito
Product Coordinating Service

Ed Lyons
Consultation Service

George Tanaka
Installation Service

Gail Stevens
Instruction Service

Face it. You have better things to do than worry about your communications terminal. That's why Trans-Lux doesn't just supply equipment. We offer a full line of special support services to make certain you get the most for your dollar—now, and in the years ahead. From the selection of your Trans-Lux terminal, through installation, training and on-going use, we stand ready to serve you in every way.

We pay as much attention to you *after* you lease or buy a Trans-Lux teleprinter as we do before. All of the valuable services shown above are

yours with any teleprinter you choose.

When it comes to teleprinters, you can rely on Trans-Lux—whether your office's communications are domestic or international; whether you use the Telex, TWX (Telex II), DDD or EasyLink networks; whether you require one terminal or twenty. You'll receive high performance equipment that's designed, engineered and manufactured by Trans-Lux—and backed by our full line of valuable support services.

FREE CONSULTATION

Without charge or obligation, we'll evaluate your needs to make sure you're getting the most out of your current teleprinter. Call TOLL-FREE now:

1 800 243-5544

IN CONNECTICUT, CALL 203 853-4321

Yes, I want a Free Teleprinter Consultation and Evaluation. I understand there is no obligation for this service.

Name _____ Title _____

Company _____

Address _____

City _____ State _____ Zip _____

Business Telephone _____ (Area Code)

TRANS-LUX
CORPORATION

110 Richards Avenue • Norwalk, Connecticut 06854
Telex 965863 • TWX 710-468-0241

EXECUNET

THE TROUBLE WITH TRAVEL AGENTS:

PROMISES, PROMISES.

Remember that sweet talking travel agent who told you not to worry about a thing? She'd take care of it, she said. She promised. She promised. You ended up with tickets to Pittsburgh when your meeting was in Philadelphia. Your hotel reservation mysteriously vanished. And your luxury rental car turned out to be a pick-up, stripped. So much for promises.

THE EXECUNET SOLUTION:

GUARANTEES, GUARANTEES.

Execunet Travel Systems has the solution to the empty promises most travel agents make. 24-Hour Problem-Free Guarantees.
Hotel. If for any reason a hotel won't honor our reservation, call our 800 number, night or day. We'll use our clout to get you in. Or, we'll find you a comparable room instantly. And we'll award you a hotel night for personal use, and your company an additional hotel night, both absolutely free.
Car Rental. Execunet guarantees any reservation we confirm will be honored. If our 800 desk can't solve a problem, you and your company receive a complimentary car rental day.

Airline. Any ticket we provide is guaranteed correct. If you can't get on a flight we've confirmed for you, and you've met advance check-in requirements, then the next available flight will be free of charge.
THE END OF "THE CALL OF THE WILD."
If you've ever tried to reach your favorite reservationist and had your call bounced around the entire agency, you know why we created the Reservation Team.
You're assigned not one, but a group of agents, who know how you like to travel. All your calls will go directly to your Team, so there's always a familiar voice at the other end of the line.

LIONS AND SHRINERS AND ELKS, OH MY!
To solve problems that your reservationist can't, we assign you a Service Representative. He or she is there to help you get on a flight that's sold out, or to free up hotel space during convention time.
Execunet's list of services goes on and on, from 24-hour ticket delivery, to a special global travel department for help with the international tariff system, foreign currencies, exchange rates and travel regulations. There's even a separate vacation planning department that provides corporate rates for personal use.
Execunet. It isn't simply the smartest way to travel on business. It's simply smart business.
For complete information, call us at 312-SMARTER.

EXECUNE

✳ THE SMARTEST DISTANCE BETWEEN TWO POI

Title: Promises, Promises
Art Directors: Troy Hayes, Linda Schweikert
Copywriter: Eric Olson
Design Agency: Dawson, Johns & Black
Client: Execunet Travel Systems

Execunet, a new competitor in a field with a reputation for poor service, sought to build awareness and credibility through this print execution.

Result:
Execunet received 100 inquiries within one week of the first insertion.

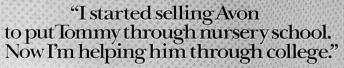

"I started selling Avon to put Tommy through nursery school. Now I'm helping him through college."

Avon and you. It's a partnership which can grow right along with you and your family.
It's the pride and satisfaction of putting a child through school. The security of putting money in the bank. The thrill of taking that dream vacation or that first ride in a new car.
You'll work at your own pace. At your convenience. Have your own business and still be home for the kids' lunch.

Naturally, the more you work, the more you earn. But Avon is right there behind you, if you need help. We'll teach you the ropes. Guarantee you at least 100 homes to call on. And an opportunity to make even more by sponsoring other Representatives.

Avon gives you the highest potential earnings of all major direct-selling companies. Our top Representatives now earn an average of $6 to $10 an hour. How much you earn is up to you. You're the boss.
Send for our FREE booklet, *How to Earn the Extra Money You Need Working the Hours You Want.* There's no obligation. But it will open your eyes. And show you how you can have a business of your own. One that fits your family life perfectly. Isn't it time *you* called on *Avon?* Call now for your FREE booklet: 1-800-251-AVON

Mail to:
Avon Products, Inc.
P.O. Box 5037
Clifton, NJ 07015
Avon and me—it's worth considering! Send me your booklet, How to Earn the Extra Money You Need Working the Hours You Want. I understand it's FREE and without obligation.

Name
Street
City   State   Zip
Phone (   )
Or call toll-free: 1-800-251-AVON
Applicant must be 18 years or older and be a resident of the continental U.S., Alaska or Hawaii.
Offer expires December 31, 1984.

SELLING AVON NOW. WOW!
MC 1

Title: Tommy
Art Director: Don Tom
Copywriter: Peggy Tomarkin
Design Agency: Ayer Direct
Client: Avon, Inc.

Avon sells its cosmetics and other products exclusively through field representatives. These women often join Avon for a short time, to earn money for a specific use. The ad was created to emphasize the long term benefits of remaining with Avon. The primary audience was mothers who would like to earn money without interrupting family life.

Gotten a speeding ticket lately? Read this.

This...

instead of these.

Last year, more than 8 million* citations were issued for driving over 55 mph on US highways.

If you were unfortunate enough to receive one of these tickets, maybe it's time to protect yourself. With the Whistler® Spectrum™ radar receiver.

Gives you earliest possible warning of police radar.

MAX RANGE TEST

1	2	3	4	5	6	7

5.6

3.2

WARNING DISTANCE IN MILES

OVER HILL TEST

10	20	30	40	50	60	70	80	90

80.0

12.7

WARNING DISTANCE IN SECONDS

© Motor Trend, Aug. 1983

When Direct Response, Inc. started looking for a radar detector to offer our customers, we went to the experts first: car magazines.

Their opinion was nearly unanimous. **Motor Trend, Autoweek,** and **BMW Roundel** had all recently completed independent, comprehensive tests of all the leading radar detectors. And all had picked a winner: the Whistler Spectrum. **Motor Trend** said "The Whistler Spectrum resides at the top of the list. A world-class radar detector."

Whistler is also first choice of truckers and other professional drivers. Whistler

Spectrum detects all kinds of speed radar. Stationary – moving – trigger – even pulsed radar. On the straightaway – from behind – over hills and around curves. If there's police radar in the area, Spectrum lets you know. Long before radar can lock onto you.

Spectrum cuts down on annoying false alarms.

Filter Mode for city driving.

Unfortunately, the FCC authorizes some security systems and traffic signals to also operate on police frequencies. And any sensitive radar detector will report these signals.

That's why Spectrum developed two features not available in any other radar detector: The **Filter Mode™** and **Pollution Solution.™** Both features cut down on false alarms.

For city driving (where microwave intrusions are frequent) switch to the **Filter Mode.** You'll get the same early warning – but it will be quieter, less urgent. When the microwave signal reaches a critical speed radar level, you'll see the amber warning light switch to a flashing red. And hear the soft tone gear up to a high-frequency, geiger-effect sound.

Most other radar detectors give off false signals. Spectrum's **Pollution Solution,** built into each unit, can tell the difference between these signals and real police radar. Spectrum automatically screens the polluters out – you'll never even hear them.

Dash/Visor or Remote model.

You have your choice of two top-line Spectrum models – both reliable performers.

The Spectrum **Dash/Visor** model is portable and compact. It plugs into the cigarette lighter socket, and mounts easily on dash or visor. It's quickly removed for use in another car, or to prevent theft.

Remote receiver hides behind car grille.

The Spectrum **Remote** gives you the same great radar protection. But it's hidden from view. The weather-proof receiver installs behind your car grille. And the small console fits handily in, on, or under the dash. You can install the Remote in about 30 minutes. After that, you're in operation every time you turn on the ignition.

No-risk trial. Free gift.

Order your Whistler Spectrum – **Dash/Visor or Remote** – from Direct Response, Inc., for just **$255 complete.**

Call toll-free, **1-800-824-2408.** (In NH, 603-886-1310.) Use your VISA, MasterCard, or American Express.

Write to Direct Response, Inc., at 472 Amherst St., Nashua, NH 03063. Send us your credit card account number, expiration date, and your signature. Or enclose a check or money order. (Allow an additional 15 days for personal checks.)

Or visit Direct Response, Inc., in Nashua, and pick up your Spectrum in person.

Satisfaction guaranteed.

We tested it. Now you can test it yourself. Use your Spectrum for 30 days. If not completely satisfied, return for a **full refund.**

Free, Rand McNally Road Atlas & Travel Guide, with map light, if you order now.

DIRECT RESPONSE, INC.
1-800-824-2408
Ask for Operator 0

Dash/Visor

FILTER   VOLUME   POWER   SPECTRUM WHISTLER

FILTER   VOLUME   POWER   SPECTRUM WHISTLER

Remote console

*Source: Speed Limit Enforcement Certification Data. October 1, 1982 through September 30, 1983.

Title:	Gotten a Speeding Ticket Lately?
Art Director:	Jory Sutton Mason
Copywriters:	Constance McCabe, Michael Nemetz
Design Agency:	Ingalls Direct Response
Client:	Direct Response, Inc.

In order to cut down on speeding tickets the ad offers a device to detect police radar. A no-risk, free gift offer is included with a toll-free number to order the dashboard device.

Title:	Volvo Parts Make Customers Last Longer
Art Director:	Len Sherman
Copywriters:	James Overall, Bruce Lee
Design Agency:	Scali, McCabe, Sloves Direct Response
Client:	Volvo of America Corporation

Addressed to auto parts buyers for foreign car repair shops and service stations, this ad was designed to convince them that using replacement parts manufactured by Volvo, rather than independents, would increase repeat business from Volvo owners.

VOLVO PARTS MAKE CUSTOMERS LAST LONGER.

Everyone knows Volvos last.

And with genuine Volvo parts, you can make Volvo customers last, too.

That's because surveys show Volvo owners overwhelmingly prefer genuine Volvo parts. Naturally, they prefer shops that install them.

Using Volvo parts also puts you in a position to provide even better service.

For example, your Volvo dealer usually has the parts you need immediately. Plus our full line of over 30,000 part numbers on call. So you can finish repairs sooner.

Volvo parts are designed to fit perfectly right out of the box, so there's no costly downtime re-ordering. And good fit means good repairs that last.

A car that lasts this long means longer-lasting customers.

And nothing but nothing lasts longer than Volvo's free replacement limited warranty: 12 months, <u>unlimited</u> mileage.* So you can guarantee your work longer than shops using jobber parts.

But Volvo parts are expensive, right? Hardly. You'll find our suggested prices very competitive.

We've put all these exclusive advantages together for

you in The Genuine Volvo Parts Program.

We'd like you to have a kit that shows how The Genuine Volvo Parts Program can actually help build your business.

There's no obligation. It's simply a smart way to help make your shop more profitable.

In America, the average Volvo lasts over 16 years.** Think of it: You could <u>retire</u> on servicing Volvos.

A FREE KIT FOR INDEPENDENT MECHANICS.

Send this coupon or the attached card for a valuable kit containing Volvo's 88-page Quick Reference Parts Catalog, a plan for building your business, and more.

CC

Mail to: The Genuine Volvo Parts Program,
Volvo of America Corporation, P.O. Box 930, Rockleigh, NJ 07647

NAME_____

BUSINESS NAME_____

STREET_____

CITY_____ STATE_____

ZIP_____ PHONE # (   )_____

THE GENUINE VOLVO PARTS PROGRAM
A genuine commitment to you and your business.

* See a Volvo dealer for complete details. ** Based upon an actuarial analysis of 1981-82 U.S. Registration Data conducted by Ken Warwick & Associates, Inc. © 1984 Volvo of America Corporation.

4

Great success
in stores
like yours!

.3.

Small investment.
Big earnings!

Our Donut
Shoppe program's
ready-made!

.2.

The $2 billion
donut market.

Bag your share!

.1.

It's in
the bag.

BUSINESS REPLY MAIL
FIRST CLASS   PERMIT NO. 1180   BUFFALO, NEW YORK

Postage will be paid by addressee:

RICH PRODUCTS CORPORATION
ATTN
P.O. Box 245
1150 Niagara Street
Buffalo, New York 14240

NO POSTAGE
NECESSARY
IF MAILED
IN THE
UNITED STATES

Title:	It's In The Bag
Art Directors:	Dennis Domkowski, Ron Pike
Copywriter:	Nancy A. DeTine
Design Agency:	Healy-Schutte & Comstock Advertising, Ltd.
Client:	Rich Products Corporation

This preprinted insert was used to sell Rich's Donut Shoppe program to convenience store operators and food retailers. Donut-shaped sales pieces were packed inside an actual donut bag. The entire unit was then bound into trade magazines.

Result:
After one insertion, more than 600 reply cards were returned. Rich's converted 45% of the resulting leads into sales.

We'll even pay you to forget Sears Bank.

To help you forget our old name and remember our new one, we're offering extra interest on one-year Certificates of Deposit ($1,000 minimum).

They currently earn 9.8%.

But if you call 876-4308 or send us the attached coupon to open a one-year Certificate of Deposit before January 13th, we'll pay you 10.5%. Compounded daily that's an 11.07% effective annual yield. The additional interest is yours just for knowing what to call us.

◊ UnibancTrusT

Yes, I'm willing to forget Sears Bank.
☐ Please send me more information.
☐ Enclosed is a check in the amount of $_____ for a one-year CD earning 10.5% interest, compounded daily and insured up to $100,000.
Preferred Interest Payment: ☐ Monthly   ☐ Quarterly   ☐ Upon Maturity
Name(s)_____ Soc. Sec.#_____
_____ Phone_____
Address_____
City_____ State_____ Zip_____

Mail to: Marketing Dept., UnibancTrust, Sears Tower, Chicago, IL 60606.   Substantial penalty for early withdrawal.

Member FDIC

Title: We'll Even Pay You To Forget
Art Director: Bev Martin
Copywriters: Jeanne Shorter, William Waites
Design Agency: Ogilvy & Mather Direct
Client: UnibancTrust

When Sears Bank & Trust changed its name to UnibancTrust, print ads were prepared to create awareness for the institution and encourage new deposits. An order form allowed readers to open a cash deposit account through the mail.

Result:
The ad generated over $22,000,000 in new deposits, 700% more than had been projected.

Here's why your first bite at Fuddruckers tastes

We grind fresh sirloin steak into hamburger patties in our butcher shop.

Everything's fresh at Fuddruckers. The burgers are fresh. The buns are fresh. The fixin's are fresh.

Why even our decor is fresh. The minute you walk in you'll see crates and crates of lettuce and tomatoes.

Sacks of flour for our bakery.

Butchers grinding meat in our butcher shop and cooks grilling burgers in a big, open kitchen.

It's all these ingredients that make Fuddruckers the freshest, most delicious burger you ever put in your mouth.

Everything's fresh, fresh, fresh at Fuddruckers.

like your burger cooked: Wonderfu rare, medium or well done.

We've got lots of dough.

You're gonna love our buns.

That's because we make th from scratch and bake them fresh all day long. Starting at 6 o'clock every morning in the bakery that right next to the butcher shop.

We give you plenty of green st

At Fuddruckers, we believe everyo should build their hamburger just the way they want it.

So we give you truckloads of farm fresh lettu tomatoes, pickles and sweet onions that you can pil on to your heart's content.

We also have crocks of hot melted cheese. Ar on every table, our very own brand of mustard, a bo of salt, can of pepper and your very own bottle of ketc All to help you top off the world's greatest burger.

Here's how to cash in on a free burger.

We're so sure that you're going to love our burgers that we'll give you one absolutely free.

All you have to do is clip the coupon on the ot side of this mailer, present it when you order, and v fork over a free burger.

It pays to have fresh beef.

At Fuddruckers, our meat is ground fresh every single day. In fact, you can watch butchers cut fresh fore-quarters of beef and grind patties right before your eyes, in our very own butcher shop.

So, instead of plain hamburger meat, Fudd-ruckers gives you a half-pound of fresh ground steak that's pure and additive-free.

The way we cook makes sense.

The best way to cook a burger is the old-fashioned way on a black iron griddle. The patty is seared on both sides and all the natural juices are sealed in the middle.

All you have to do is to tell us exactly how you'd

We cook your burger any way you want — rare, medium or well done.

Title: We're Changing
Art Director: Charles Hively
Copywriter: Julie Harrigan
Design Agency: The Metzdorf-Marschalk Company
Client: Fuddruckers

A family restaurant in Southern California, Fuddruckers, ran this full page ad to inform area customers of the quality of its meals. A coupon for a free hamburger and a map showing the restaurant's location were included.

ike a million.

We make our buns from scratch in our on-premise bakery every day.

To top off your burger we give you loads of farm fresh vegetables.

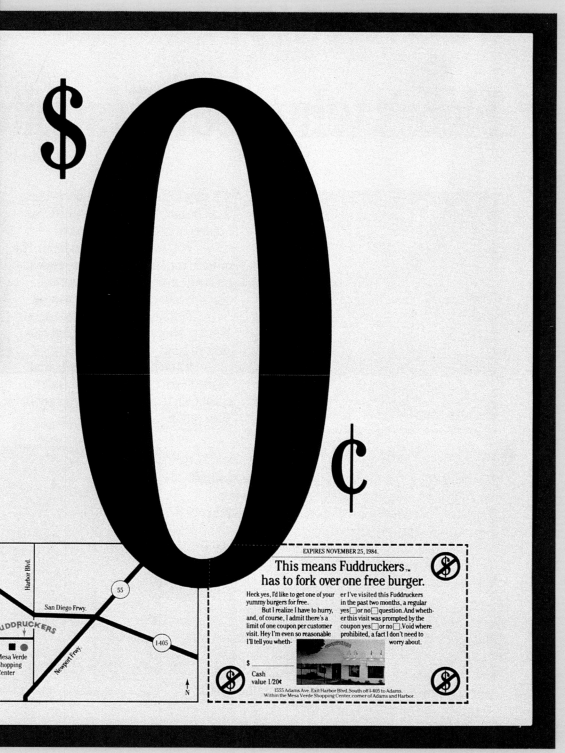

$0¢

EXPIRES NOVEMBER 25, 1984.

This means Fuddruckers™ has to fork over one free burger.

Heck yes, I'd like to get one of your yummy burgers for free.

But I realize I have to hurry, and, of course, I admit there's a limit of one coupon per customer visit. Hey I'm even so reasonable I'll tell you wheth-

er I've visited this Fuddruckers in the past two months, a regular yes☐ or no☐ question. And whether this visit was prompted by the coupon yes☐ or no☐. Void where prohibited, a fact I don't need to worry about.

$ Cash value 1/20¢

1555 Adams Ave. Exit Harbor Blvd. South off I-405 to Adams.
Within the Mesa Verde Shopping Center, corner of Adams and Harbor.

Brookhurst
Harbor Blvd.
San Diego Frwy.
55
Adams
FUDDRUCKERS
Mesa Verde Shopping Center
Newport Frwy.
I-405
N

GREAT RESULTS ARE IN YOUR FUTURE!

Results are what we take pride in delivering for our clients. *Results* have earned us numerous top honors, often over competition from the largest and most prestigious agencies in the country! *Results* are our number one goal for every client. And *Results* are in store for you when you become a client of The Chrystal Direct Marketing Group.

What kind of results?

If you are like one of our banking clients, you may have a *500% increase* in loan applications. We might introduce a technique that could increase your customer base by 25%, as we did for a cable client. Maybe you would like to have a *10% response* to your new subscriber offer, like one of our publishing clients or have the President of your company say that yours is the *best promotion* ever developed by the corporation, as happened to one of our

Fortune 100 clients. Or, perhaps you would be happy with a test which pulls *20% better* than the control, such as the one we created for an insurance client.

Let us be part of your future.

Return the "Chrystal Ball" coupon, or call Gail Chrystal at 1-312-398-5560 to learn how our techniques and special service can lead to a bright successful future for your company's promotions.

The Chrystal Direct Marketing Group, Inc.
3227 N. Frontage Road
Suite 2703
Arlington Heights, IL 60004
312-398-5560

A full-service advertising agency specializing in direct response.

Yes, Gail,
I want to know how Chrystal Direct can produce great results for my company. Contact me right away via the medium I have selected!

☐ phone   ☐ mail   ☐ spirit

Name _____

Title _____   Phone _____

Company _____

Address _____

City/State/Zip _____

Type of Business _____

Title: Great Results are in Your Future
Art Directors: Jan Szabo, Chuck Strausser
Copywriter: Gail Chrystal
Design Agency: Chrystal Direct Marketing Group, Inc.
Client: Chrystal Direct Marketing Group, Inc.

Creativity and results were promised in this self-promotional print ad by Chrystal Direct Marketing. Copy linked the use of unusual graphics with the agency's practice of solid marketing techniques.

Title: Bent Knife
Art Director: Chris Quillen
Copywriter: Eric Steinman
Design Agency: Allen and Dorward
Client: Castle & Cooke Inc.

As the major supplier of pineapples in the U.S., Castle & Cooke found that consumers felt it was difficult to prepare fresh pineapple. To encourage sales, this ad offered 20 cents off on a fresh pineapple and a reduced price on a specially-shaped knife that simplifies pineapple preparation.

A Gift for Advertisers On People's Birthday

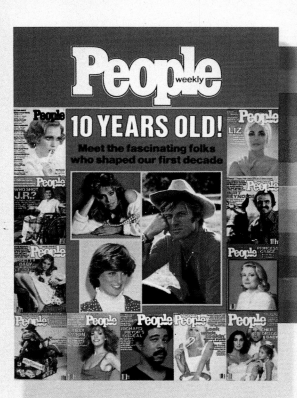

The Biggest Editorial Issue Ever

Special Photo Gallery Section

Circulation Rate Base: 3,000,000

Projected Circulation: 3,200,000

Total Adult Readers: 26,880,000

Coverage of U.S. Adults: 16.3%

Big Teen Audience: 8,288,000

Efficient CPM: $2.11*

4-Color Page: $56,800

B&W Page: $44,000

4-Color Closing: January 16, 1984

B&W Closing: February 13, 1984

Surprise! PEOPLE, believe it or not, is about to celebrate its 10th birthday. And for all the advertisers who appear in our spectacular 10th Anniversary Issue on March 5, 1984, we have a gift.

For that issue, we are projecting a circulation of 3,200,000, an increase of 600,000 over our existing circulation. But our rates are based on a circulation of 3,000,000, providing you a bonus circulation of at least 200,000. The estimated total audience for this issue is 26,880,000 adults and another 8,288,000 teens. It is our Birthday Present to advertisers for contributing so much to PEOPLE's success.

We are thanking our readers, too, with a very special Anniversary Issue. It will be a showcase of the PEOPLE decade, 1974-1984, reflecting the past and, in some cases, anticipating the future. Among the wide variety of editorial features, there will be a sixteen-page photo gallery, printed on special stock, devoted to the best pictures from PEOPLE over the past 10 years. It will be an issue to save and enjoy over and over again.

Editorially, this will be the biggest issue of PEOPLE ever—packed with memorable pictures, wit and observations in celebration of the first decade of the magazine that "has changed the soul of modern journalism."

Don't miss this exceptional advertising opportunity available in the 10TH ANNIVERSARY ISSUE of PEOPLE. For more details, contact your PEOPLE representative, or Bill Myers, Advertising Sales Director, at (212) 841-4536.

THE FIRST DECADE

Sources: 1983 SMRB, 1981 STARS Teen Study (Audiences adjusted to reflect increased circulation for this issue.)

*Based on adults. 1-time P-4C

Title:	A Gift For Advertisers
Art Directors:	Arthur Beckenstein, Dick Martell
Copywriter:	Harry Welsh
Design Agency:	People Promotion
Client:	People Magazine Time, Inc.

To solicit advertising for People Magazine's tenth anniversary issue, this ad was placed in Advertising Age magazine.

Result:
The tenth anniversary issue carried more ads than any single issue in the magazine's history.

Title: Civilization
Art Director: Steve O'Neill
Copywriter: Michele Paccione
Design Agency: Soskin/Thompson Associates
Client: Bloomingdale's

This special ad was created to test the combination of a four-color support page with a self-mailer insert against the use of a four-color page alone.

Title: How to Look Like a Breeze . . .
                    When it's Ninety Degrees
Art Director: Karen O'Neill
Copywriter: Laurie Meltzer
Design Agency: RoyalVision
Client: Royal Silk

A page from a four-color catalog for magazine insertions by Royal Silk, a mail order clothing retailer.

Result:
From two insertions, orders for 4,600 units were received, generating $134,000 in sales.

TEE
$22

PANTS
$60

How to look like a breeze...
when it's ninety degrees.

Presenting our pure silk separates — fresh new looks with cool snap and feel-good fit. Taking it from the top, our Japanese Tee of pure *Soie de Chine*, canvas-crisp and wonderfully wearable. With square neck, kimono sleeves, slit sides — and loose, alluring contours. Cream, raspberry, or dusty blue. Hand washable. Sizes 4-20. Style #132701. $22. For double the glow, our Classic Pants of pure *Silk Crêpe de Chine*. With pleated front, slash pockets, and side zip. Fully lined. Taupe, ruby, cinnamon, navy, black, grey, purple, white or olive. Dry clean. Sizes 4-16. Style #123801. $60. Our pure silk separates are unavailable in any store, except our own catalog showroom in Clifton, NJ. Yours, with a full money-back guarantee, and complimentary silk-care guide.

ROYAL SILK
Clifton, NJ

In the long run, performance is best judged at the finish line.

The strategy for running the marathon is vastly different than for the 100-yard dash.

A successful pension fund has a different investment strategy, too. Far different than the quick return, end-of-quarter performance goals of many investment funds.

While many financial service companies are racing to offer higher risk investments with the hope of higher returns, TIAA and CREF continue to achieve steady growth with broadly diversified portfolios of retirement-oriented investments.

This balanced, long-term investment philosophy is the foundation for building lifetime retirement incomes.

Maintaining the highest yields over 40 years would be comparable to maintaining the speed of the 100-yard dash over the 26-plus miles of the marathon. Highly unlikely.

The key to successful retirement funding is consistency over long time periods, because the investments must provide annuity payments throughout a staff member's entire retired life. A very real reason why over 100,000 retired educators enjoy the rewards of having participated in a TIAA-CREF retirement plan.

When the results are in at retirement, you will find that TIAA-CREF retirees are far ahead.

Send for a free copy of our recent survey among staff members retired from educational institutions. Simply write on your letterhead.

TIAA-CREF. You can count on us today... and for tomorrow.

Teachers Insurance and Annuity Association
College Retirement Equities Fund

730 Third Avenue, New York, NY 10017

Title: In The Long Run
Art Director: Neil Wagner
Copywriter: Larilee Frazier
Design Agency: Ogilvy & Mather Direct
Client: TIAA

To position the TIAA Basic Retirement Plan more aggressively, this ad was created to run in a periodical targeted to educational administrators.

Title: A Handgun Can-Take Away Your Innocents
Art Director: Ron Hartley
Copywriter: Vanessa Levin
Design Agency: Wunderman, Ricotta & Kline
Client: National Alliance Against Violence

This print ad was one of two prepared to convince handgun owners and those considering buying a handgun that there are other ways to protect themselves and their families. The ad points out that children are often the victims of handgun accidents in the home.

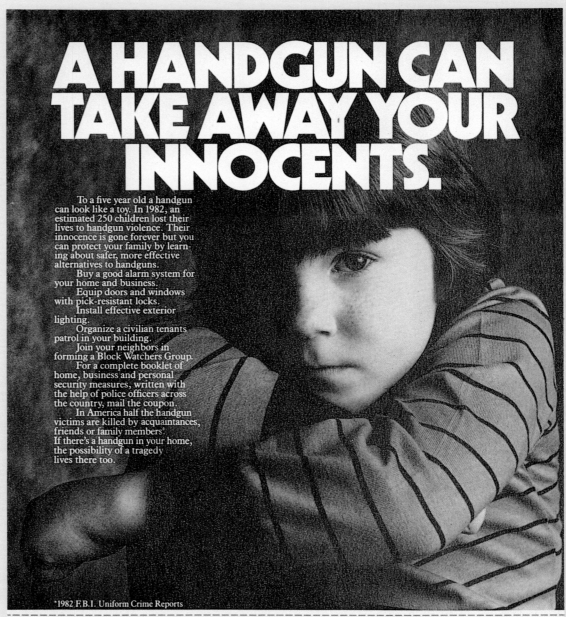

4

Catalog

Telephone or Mail Home Shopping

While no one knows for certain how many different catalogs were published and mailed in the past year, estimates run as high as 7,500. These catalogs purveyed everything from computer software to do-it-yourself airplane kits.

Not all of those catalogs were well done. Unfortunately, the creative teams involved in catalog production tend to underestimate the effort required to produce a good one. Clients tend to think simplistically that success with a catalog depends solely on the product, the price, and the market niche sought.

There was a time when potential customers received one or perhaps two catalogs for a specific product—such as cosmetics—each year. The copy, photography, and layout weren't critical because competition was scarce. Today, consumers may receive a half dozen catalogs offering the same merchandise at virtually the same price simultaneously. The chances are, they won't buy from each catalog, but will confine their purchases to one, or possibly two.

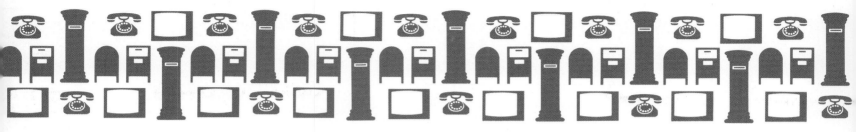

Those two will be the ones they "trust" most; that give the most information on the products and services offered; that show the clearest photos.

Their purchases will also be strongly influenced by the attractiveness of the catalog, by the ease with which they can associate the photos with the appropriate copy, and by the benefits they'll get by making a purchase.

There will be appeals to their vanity. Are they smart to save money through this catalog; are they smart to buy the best, eliminate unnecessary work, or for some other reason?

The buying decision will also be affected by how easy it is for them to visualize in their minds the product or service being offered. The way the art director designs the photographs, showing the product or service in use rather than just floating on the page with no surrounding context, can improve the catalog's sales performance.

Even little details, such as the way code numbers and prices are handled, can affect the results.

The sheer number of catalogs being produced makes it inevitable that, unless a conscious effort is made, many of them will look alike. Clients publishing catalogs are beginning to realize that it pays to buy the best creative services available. Cheap, formula-driven copy and an average lay-out normally produce no more than average sales and profits.

The pieces that follow in this chapter are a testimony to the ability of some writers, artists, and photographers to make an appreciable difference in the success of a catalog effort.

A. No girl ever had too many sweaters, especially when they're 100% pure wool classic crewnecks, full fashioned by Crazy Horse in heavenly shades of Red(83), Grey(88), Lavender (55), Natural (5) or Blue (40). S(7-8), M(10-12), L(14), girls size 7-14. #A502-2800 $22.

B. Five classic autumn colors from Barrel...Navy (42), Grey (88), Plum (66), Hunter (34) or Camel (11)...in a soft 70% acrylic/30% wool Shetland crewneck sweater. An easy care, machine wash pleasure. Sizes 4-7 unisex. #A505-6210 $16.

C. Here, you have a choice of blends, textures and colors in a handsome, Jersey stitched crewneck sweater by Robert Bruce. In Donegal Navy (42), the blend is 70% wool/21% poly/9% acrylic. In the solid colors the blend is 70% wool/30% poly in Grey (88), Wine (67), Cream (2), Hunter (34). And, happily all of them are machine washable. 8-14 sizes. #A543-0135 $25.

D. These well shaped corduroy pants? Brittania, of course. They have European scoop front pleated pockets, two back pockets, and the seams are flat felled for easy wash and wear. Purple (57), as shown, and also Grey (88). In 14 wale weight: Toddlers 2-4T #A501-2163 $12. Size 4-6x. Reg. #A501-6163 $13.50. Slim. #A501-6164 $13.50. In 16 wale weight: Size 7-14. Reg. #A501-7163 $16. Slim. #A501-7164 $16. Her pretty lavender sweater shown on in item A.

E. In a lively broad stripe of Grey/Burgundy/Royal(88), a khaki collared Donmoor shirt with 2 snap placket, twill collar with taping and banded knit bottom. Easy care blend of 50% cotton/50% poly jersey. Also in Jade/Royal (35), Stripe. See page 3. Toddlers' 2-4T. #A508-4543 $15. Toddler corduroy pants ½ elastic pieced back pocket in Royal (43), Grey (88), or Tan (14). Size 2-4T. #A501-4163 $12.

F. The shoulder tied sweater is shown in item C. Under it, a Donmoor heavyweight knit of Charcoal/Cream/Steel Blue stripes on soft Grey (88). Grey twill collar, finished snap buttons. 50% cotton/50% Fortrel® poly. Machine washable. Sizes 8-14. #A508-4666 $21. His cord jeans and all the boys' cord jeans shown on these 2 pages are by Brittania. Straight leg style with full waistband, they have 4 pockets, snap closure, brass zipper and pieced back pockets. Side seams are non-pucker stitched, seat seams and back yoke are flat felled. All points of stress have bar tacs plus hems are lockstitched to prevent raveling. Navy (42), Grey (88), or Tan (14). Size 4-7. Slim. #A501-3424 $13. Reg. #A501-3524 $13. Size 8,9,10,11,12,14. Slim. #A501-3624 $15. Reg. #A501-3724 $15.

G. Shadow striped Burgundy/White/Turquoise on Navy (42), this Donmoor pullover has a burgundy fashion collar and placket. 50% cotton/50% Fortrel®poly, machine washable. Sizes 4-7. #A508-4658 $12. Sizes 8-12. #A508-4668 $14.

His charcoal grey cords are described in item F.

H. Her soft blue sweater is described in item A; and her Brittania corduroy pants in item D.

J. The Plum (66) sweater by Barrel is described in item B; her Grey Brittania cord pants in item D.

K. His crewneck sweater by Barrel is a versatile combo of Navy/Grey/Burgundy (65) framed in Tan. 70% acrylic/30% wool to machine wash and dry with ease. Size 4-7. #A505-6211 $18. Size 8-14. #A505-7211 $20. His Navy cord jeans are described in item F.

PREMIER EDITION

Title: My Child's Destiny
Art Directors: Jo-Von Tucker, Diana Chase
Copywriters: Kathleen Bonifield, Roy Raymond
Design Agency: Jo-Von Tucker & Associates
Client: Roy Raymond

A new venture offering children's products through the mail was geared to parents concerned about the quality of their children's lives. The catalog presentation emphasized quality and the credibility of the company.

"here's
looking
at you,
kid!"

Spiegel

$2.00

A Oshkosh B'Gosh® baggie overalls for kids
come in hot colors as well as the favorite blue
denim. With five pockets and adjustable shoulder
straps. All cotton drill; machine wash.
Sizes: 4, 5, 6, 6X. State size.
A3028 8989—Hot Turquoise.
A3028 8988—Fuchsia.
A3028 8990—Maize. (12 oz.)   17.00
A3028 8991—Cotton Denim. (1 lb.)   18.00

B Everything's coming up tulips on a
screenprinted top from Oshkosh B'Gosh. Round
ruffled neck with short sleeves and gathered
shoulders. Buttons in back. Polyester/cotton
interlock; machine wash. White/Multi.
Sizes: 4, 5, 6, 6X. State size.
A3028 8993—(6 oz.)   14.00

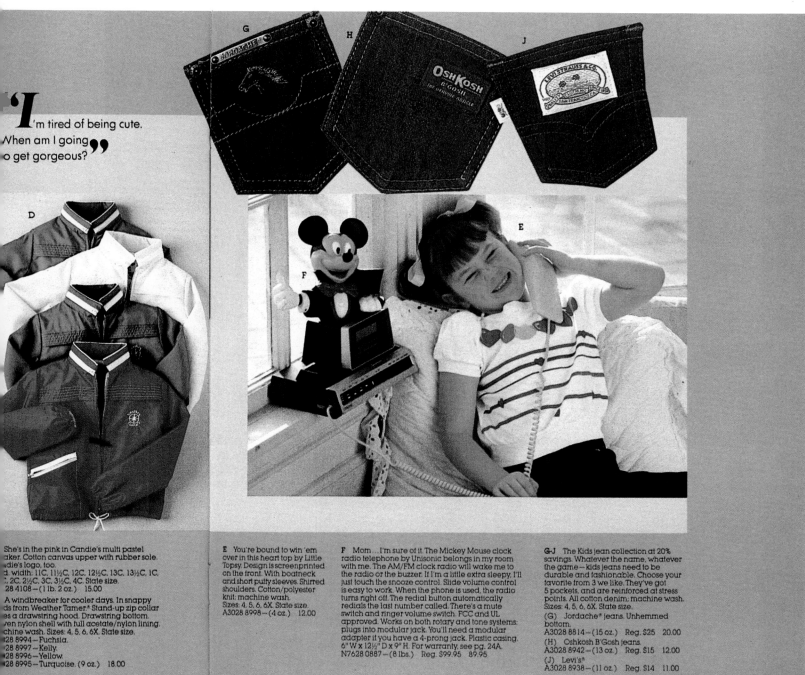

"I'm tired of being cute. When am I going to get gorgeous?**"**

She's in the pink in Candie's multi pastel
[sne]aker. Cotton canvas upper with rubber sole.
[Can]die's logo, too.
[...]d. width: 11C, 11½C, 12C, 12½C, 13C, 13½C, 1C,
[...], 2C, 2½C, 3C, 3½C, 4C. State size.
28 4108 — (1 lb. 2 oz.) 15.00

A windbreaker for cooler days. In snappy
[col]ds from Weather Tamer.® Stand-up zip collar
[mak]es a drawstring hood. Drawstring bottom.
[Wov]en nylon shell with full acetate/nylon lining.
[Ma]chine wash. Sizes: 4, 5, 6, 6X. State size.
[#]28 8994 — Fuchsia.
[#]28 8997 — Kelly.
[#]28 8996 — Yellow.
[#]28 8995 — Turquoise. (9 oz.) 18.00

E You're bound to win 'em
over in this heart top by Little
Topsy. Design is screenprinted
on the front. With boatneck
and short puffy sleeves. Shirred
shoulders. Cotton/polyester
knit; machine wash.
Sizes: 4, 5, 6, 6X. State size.
A3028 8998 — (4 oz.) 12.00

F Mom... I'm sure of it. The Mickey Mouse clock
radio telephone by Unisonic belongs in my room
with me. The AM/FM clock radio will wake me to
the radio or the buzzer. If I'm a little extra sleepy, I'll
just touch the snooze control. Slide volume control
is easy to work. When the phone is used, the radio
turns right off. The redial button automatically
redials the last number called. There's a mute
switch and ringer volume switch. FCC and UL
approved. Works on both rotary and tone systems;
plugs into modular jack. You'll need a modular
adapter if you have a 4-prong jack. Plastic casing.
6" W x 12½" D x 9" H. For warranty, see pg. 24A.
N7628 0887 — (8 lbs.) Reg. $99.95 89.95

G-J The kids jean collection at 20%
savings. Whatever the name, whatever
the game — kids jeans need to be
durable and fashionable. Choose your
favorite from 3 we like. They've got
5 pockets, and are reinforced at stress
points. All cotton denim; machine wash.
Sizes: 4, 5, 6, 6X. State size.
(G) Jordache® jeans. Unhemmed
bottom.
A3028 8814 — (15 oz.) Reg. $25 20.00
(H) Oshkosh B'Gosh jeans.
A3028 8942 — (13 oz.) Reg. $15 12.00
(J) Levi's®
A3028 8938 — (11 oz.) Reg. $14 11.00

Charge by phone toll-free 24 hours a day 1 800 345-4500 • 35

Title:	Here's Looking at You, Kid
Art Director:	David Shearon
Copywriters:	Rob Longendyke, John Galante, Debra Kanter and Diane Strand
Design Agency:	Spiegel, Inc. In-House
Client:	Spiegel, Inc.

Action wear for play and formal attire are showcased in
this children's catalog by Spiegel. Four-color photography
illustrates the style, and color varieties, while copy
details the quality.

a. GRAFFITI 25333
45% DACRON® POLYESTER/
45% COTTON/10% LYCRA
SIZES: S, M, L
COLORS: GREEN MIST STRIPE
ROSEBERRY STRIPE

b. SLEEK 25363
45% DACRON® POLYESTER/
45% COTTON/10% LYCRA
SIZES: S, M, L
COLORS: BLACK, CORAL, GREEN MIST

c. FIT 25373
45% DACRON® POLYESTER/
45% COTTON/10% LYCRA
SIZES: S, M, L
COLORS: BARK, BLACK, GREEN MIST,
LEMON, ROSEBERRY, TEAL,
VIOLET, WHITE

d. CURL 25313
45% DACRON® POLYESTER/
45% COTTON/10% LYCRA
SIZES: S, M, L
COLORS: BLACK, ROSEBERRY, TEAL

e. MARYANNE 25153
45% DACRON® POLYESTER/
45% COTTON/10% LYCRA
SIZES: S, M, L
COLORS: BLACK, TEAL BLUE,
AEROBIC RED, JADE GREEN, LILAC,
WHITE

13

f. ATRIUM 21231
50% DACRON® POLYESTER/
50% COTTON
SIZES: S, M, L, XL, XXL
COLORS:
BLACK/POPPY RED, WHITE
CLEAR BLUE/POPPY RED, WHITE
GUNMETAL/ROYAL, WHITE
HONEY YELLOW/ROYAL, POPPY RED
NAVY/TURQUOISE, SILVER
POPPY RED/ROYAL, WHITE
ROYAL BLUE/SILVER, WHITE
SILVER/BLACK, POPPY RED
WHITE/ROYAL, POPPY RED

h. JAZZ 25343
45% DACRON® POLYESTER/
45% COTTON/10% LYCRA
SIZES: S, M, L
COLORS: BARK, LEMON, VIOLET

g. PAT 25123
45% DACRON® POLYESTER/
45% COTTON/10% LYCRA
SIZES: S, M, L
COLORS: AEROBIC RED, BLACK,
CORAL, GREEN MIST, JADE,
LEMON, LILAC, ROSEBERRY,
TEAL, VIOLET

DACRON
DUPONT POLYESTER

Title: Nautilus Apparel Spring '85
Art Director: Kevin Cea
Design Agency: Tultex Design Services
Client: Tultex Corporation

To showcase its spring line of sports clothing, Tultex
created this catalog. The piece was designed to generate
individual sales and to serve as a reference for dealers.

SLEEK AND SHAPELY BODYWEAR

FOR A SENSATIONAL WORKOUT

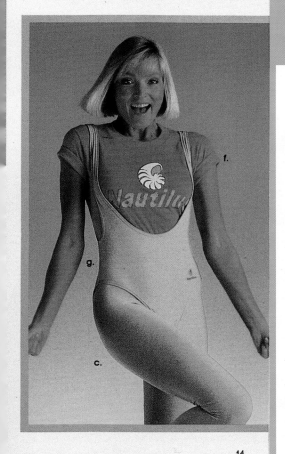

14

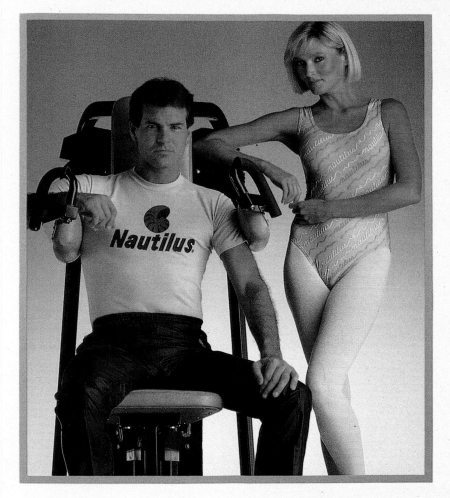

NAUTILUS APPAREL SPRING '85

Nautilus

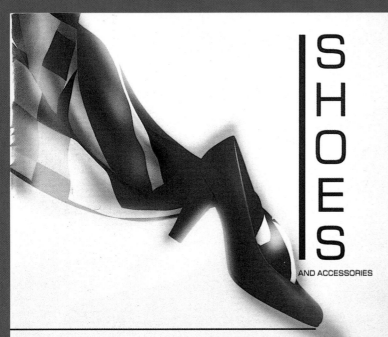

S H O E S

AND ACCESSORIES

Spiegel

$2.00

A

B

36

W IDE BA
NEW TEXTURE
INSPIRATION FOR

BEENE
BAG
MADE IN ITALY

福

Title: Shoe/Accessory Catalog
Art Director: Marty Moran
Copywriters: Martha Grush, Cindy Patterson
Design Agency: Spiegel Design
Client: Spiegel, Inc.

An accessories catalog was developed to mail to Spiegel customers who had shown an interest in these items in the general catalog. The colorful brochure included new styles not shown in the general catalog, and was designed to showcase the merchandise in a clean environment.

Result:
Orders from the accessories catalog were 25% over projections, 71% over in profits, and 37% over in value of average order.

A Straps go bigger, bolder; neutrals go deeper . . . we're wild about the safari trend! Sand Dancers™ ankle-wrap is what you'll be wearing with cropped pants, longer shorts. It has a leather upper, man-made sole.
Medium: 4B, 4½B, 5B, 5½B, 6B, 6½B, 7B 7½B, 8B, 8½B, 9B; 10B; 11B.
A2426 3723—Luggage (tan).
A2426 3725—Black.
A2426 3724—Plum.
A2426 3726—Dark Khaki.
State size. (1 lb. 4 oz.)   30.00

B For wrapping at head, neck or waist Liz Claiborne's silk scarf adds a subtle, primitive presence. In a batik-look print of rust, khaki and royal. 17x58 in. long. Dry clean.
N2626 7173—(5 oz.)   25.00

C Anne Klein's very civilized safari look The little flat has sleeker lines and great lacing. All leather.
AA(Narrow): 7, 7½, 8, 8½, 9; 10.
B(Medium): 5½, 6, 6½, 7, 7½, 8, 8½, 9; 1
T2026 0247—Red.
T2026 0248—Natural.
T2026 0249—Khaki. (1 lb. 2 oz.)
State size, AA or B.   75.00

D Anklets from Hue are wild, fun jung prints. Essential for urban safaris! Mostly cotton with nylon. Machine wash. One size fits 9-11.
N2126 0642—Beige (ocelot).
N2126 0641—Mahogany (streak).
Not shown:
N2126 0643—Gray (splatter).
Shpg. wt. 4 oz.   Pr. 7.50

Charge by phone toll-free
24 hours a day 1 800 345-4500

The skimmer and accessories
are sold on pg. 2.

5

B

C

D

39

Title: Shoe/Accessory Catalog
Art Director: Marty Moran
Copywriters: Martha Grush, Cindy Patterson
Design Agency: Spiegel Design
Client: Spiegel, Inc.

An accessories catalog was developed to mail to Spiegel
customers who had shown an interest in these items in
the general catalog. The colorful brochure included new
styles not shown in the general catalog, and was
designed to showcase the merchandise in a clean
environment.

Result:
Orders from the accessories catalog were 25% over
projections, 71% over in profits, and 37% over in value of
average order.

22B

Pantcoats with plenty of panache
make a real fashion statement.
22A. Jill Jr.'s trapunto-stitched coat,
5-13, regularly 180.00, sale 149.99.
22B. Debutog's one button coat, white,
5-13, regularly 90.00, sale 69.99.
22C. From Jill Jr., tweed coat, black/white,
5-13, regularly 180.00, sale 149.99.
22D. Debutog's stand-up collar coat,
black, regularly 90.00, sale 69.99.
Jr. Outerwear (D. 373), all stores.

Turn on the neon brights with
our oversized beret by Fedora.
22E. Leather-trimmed beret, kelly,
royal, red, fuchsia, gold, 20.00.
Hats (D. 411), all stores.

Snap-up fall with our red
cobra pin. 22F. Renaissance bar
pin with multi-color gemstones
in golden metal, 40.00.
Jewelry (D. 141), Downtown, Westgate,
Severance, Parmatown, Belden,
Beachwood, Summit only.

22C

22D

Title: Junior Back to School
Art Director: Judy Loyd
Copywriter: Toby Wietzke
Design Agency: Higbee Company Adversiting
Client: The Higbee Company

Back-to-school fashions are a major addition to any fall
line. The Junior Back-to-School catalog showcases
formal and informal clothing for young, college age,
adults.

22A

Handsome is as handsome does—
just like these handsomely tailored
sportcoats and dress pants by E. Joven.
23A. Sportcoats from a group
of Donegal tweeds, herringbones,
tic weaves, solids, patched and
unpatched elbows, 36-42, reg. 72.00 to 85.00.
Solids, sale 59.99; fancies, sale 69.99.
Dress pants, plain or pleated front,
brown, grey, black, tan, navy, 29-36,
regularly 25.00 to 28.00, sale, 21.99.
New Breed (D. 554), all stores.

Title: Junior Back to School
Art Director: Judy Loyd
Copywriter: Toby Weitzke
Design Agency: Higbee Company Adversiting
Client: The Higbee Company

Get the bright Esprit de corps
of fall...right here with Esprit's
very spirited sportsters. From top:
2A. Geometric sweater,
grey/eggplant, S,M,L, 48.00.
Corduroy jeans, eggplant,
French blue, grey, teal,* 5-11, 37.00.
2B. Striped shirt, grey/multi, S,M,L, 34.00.
Canvas jeans, French blue,
grey, teal,* 5-11, 37.00.
2C. Geometric sweater, eggplant
or teal* combinations, S,M,L, 42.00.
Corduroy jeans, grey, French blue,
eggplant, teal,* 5-11, 37.00.
Jr. Collections (D. 375), all stores.
* Teal and teal combinations not
at Severance, Midway, Euclid, Summit.

Take a Santa Cruz into the new
season and you won't wait long
for the good times to roll.
3A. Featuring our quilted vest, 33.00;
pant, 38.00. Funnel neck sweater
in fuchsia or grey, 37.00.
Dolman sleeve shirt in blue
or fuchsia, 26.00.
3B. Also from our media mix
by Santa Cruz of vests, pants,
shirts, sweaters — all in grey
sparked with fuchsia in solids,
checks and stripes, S,M,L,
and 5-11, 26.00 to 37.00.
Jr. Tops (D. 372), all stores.

Call 579-2500 anytime
in Cuyahoga County;
elsewhere in Ohio, call
toll free 1-800-362-2945.

A. **Spellbound by this glass lantern,** I can easily envision a real forest of snow covered trees through which the warm candlelight warms and welcomes. Add an aura of mystery and beauty to any setting while dining- in the boudoir or as window lights with these unusual candleholders. Includes pewter holder and white taper. 5" x 5" D x 8½" H.
#A1200 Trees Lantern $28.00 each
#A1220 Trees Lanterns $54.50 set of 2

B. **Here's one wreath that does much more than welcome visitors**—it says "why be ordinary, when you can be extraordinary!" Made of naturally appealing fabrics and charmingly rustic straw, it's decked out in the holiday's finest satin, moiré taffeta and lace ribbons, gold lamé and silk flowers, baby's breath and a scattering of leaves, all artfully arranged on a sturdy frame. Give your home (or someone else's) a last-a-lifetime Christmas present—hang our handmade wreath on the front door, over the fireplace, in the kitchen, anywhere! Ecru and mauve. 16" dia.
#A8202 Satin & Straw Wreath

C. **Frederick and I share thoughts, jokes and secrets but not our supple** leather portfolio. Made of the finest Italian leather, it has a full-length outer pocket to store glasses; inner zippered compartment holds folders, important briefs, and manuscripts for when your trip doesn't warrant a briefcase but you still want to make a striking impression. A leather tassle makes zippering easy. For men and women. In burgundy only. 10½" x ...
#A5101 Italian Leather Portfolio

D. **Three thousand years of exacting craftsmanship helped create this unusual** necklace. Each precious jade bead, interspersed with black onyx and extra... is hand-strung. It looks delicate, but don't be fooled; you'll find it wonderfully ind... versatile. I enjoy the necklace so much, I gave my mother one (we promised not... we go out together!). Share this traditional gemstone of the East with someone y... corners of the world. 18" L.
#A3307 Rare Jade Necklace

POSTMASTER: If addressee has moved please deliver to current resident.

Nostalgia Shop, Inc.
1200 Everman Parkway
Ft. Worth, Texas 76140

Ashley D. Adams

Title: Ashley D. Adams
Art Directors: John Lauricella, Norman Rich
Copywriters: Katie Muldoon, Barbara Plotkin
Design Agency: Muldoon Direct, Inc.
Client: Ashley D. Adams Nostalgia Shoppe
                  Limited

The competition among luxury gift catalogs is fierce. To establish a unique identity for this catalog targeted to upscale, affluent, working females, the agency created a fictional character, Ashley D. Adams, and followed it up with "storybook" style copy. Customers were asked to find and count hidden "masks" representing catalog exclusives to qualify for a free gift.

THE BRIDE'S COLLECTION™

A lingerie catalog from Creations by *Elaine*

Title: The Brides Collection
Art Director: Liz Nickels
Copywriter: Mary Ann Rood
Design Agency: D'Arcy MacManus Masius
Client: Creations By Elaine

To showcase a special collection of lingerie designed to appeal to new brides, this catalog used photographs of men and women posed together, showing how they related while wearing the lingerie.

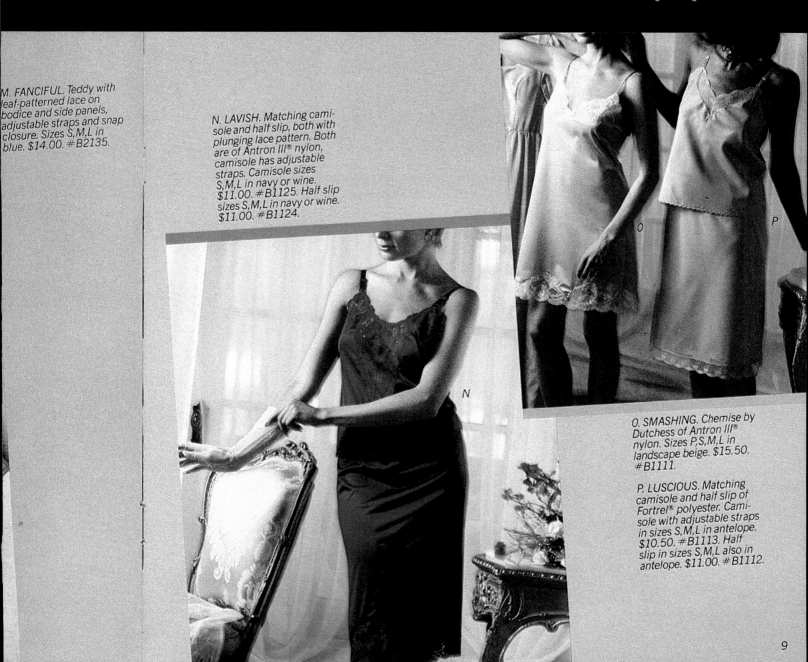

M. FANCIFUL. Teddy with leaf-patterned lace on bodice and side panels, adjustable straps and snap closure. Sizes S,M,L in blue. $14.00. #B2135.

N. LAVISH. Matching camisole and half slip, both with plunging lace pattern. Both are of Antron III® nylon, camisole has adjustable straps. Camisole sizes S,M,L in navy or wine. $11.00. #B1125. Half slip sizes S,M,L in navy or wine. $11.00. #B1124.

O. SMASHING. Chemise by Dutchess of Antron III® nylon. Sizes P,S,M,L in landscape beige. $15.50. #B1111.

P. LUSCIOUS. Matching camisole and half slip of Fortrel® polyester. Camisole with adjustable straps in sizes S,M,L in antelope. $10.50. #B1113. Half slip in sizes S,M,L also in antelope. $11.00. #B1112.

Atlanta's PERIMETER ✦ MALL

So much more to love.

C H R I S T M A S   1 9 8 3

Title: Atlanta's Perimeter Mall
Art Director: David Mimbs
Copywriter: Barbara Gabor
Design Agency: Three Score
Client: Perimeter Mall

This catalog was a joint venture by the stores in Atlanta's Perimeter Mall. The catalog was designed carefully to allow each store to retain its own unique identity.

Result:
A number of items promoted in the catalog sold out and the mall has committed to producing the joint catalog annually.

What's in a name? Everything, when it's Morninglory

Morninglory...razzle dazzle dressing for the woman of impeccable style. Come see our holiday separates, sparked with all the prettiness that goes with this special season.
6A. High fashion glitter and glamour in sequins and bugle beads on silk. Each, a piece of wearable art. The group, from **$290.** Shown: turquoise, silver and gunmetal sparkle on an easy-fitting cocoon with a V-neckline. One size fits all.
6B. Classic black silk pants with soft pleats and set-in waistband with elastic back. Sizes 4-12, **$95.**
Morninglory 399-5415

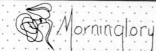

Morninglory

Luxurious boudoir dressing for private times and places

The Lingerie Coll

$2.00

Spiegel

IRELAND—THE MAGIC IS HERE

Title:	Ireland, The Magic Is Here
Art Director:	Patt Parker
Copywriter:	Kit McCracken
Design Agency:	Spiegel Design
Client:	Spiegel, Inc.

A travel theme was selected to give mail retailer
Spiegel's fall catalog the flair and excitement of an i
store import fair sale.

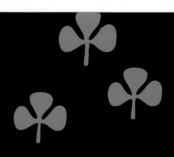

HANDMADE VASE. Kilkenny is a community of the crafts spirit, out of which comes Nicholas Mosse's creative handthrown pottery. The whiskey

T he loom teaches Muriel Beckett something new every time she works at it. The noted Dublin weaver doesn't hold with hand-craftsmanship looking hand-crafted: "I can spend a week on one (wall hanging), getting it as perfect as I can." Numerous awards attest to her design and technical brilliance.

A Now Muriel Beckett and her studio produce "The Window Box," a wall hanging made espressly for you. Handwoven of Irish wool and cotton, with wood rod for hanging, leather patch bears your name (and Muriel Beckett's). 28½" wide, 40" high. State name up to 10 characters. Allow 30 days for delivery plus transit.
X6669 4247T. (12 lbs.) 600.00

We're happy that the woven rugs by Muriel Beckett Studio, too—see pg. 33.

NOTHING IS MORE CENTRAL to life (and warmth) in the Irish house than the fireplace. Our solid brass, handmade-in-Ireland accessories bring a little of the glow home, to your own hearth.
Firetools, 3-pc. set: shovel, tongs, poker. Each 29½" long.
N7769 6218T. (14 lbs.) .... Set 99.95
Fire grate extends to 45" wide.
N7769 6219T. (18 lbs.) 139.95
Andirons, each 5½"Wx6¼"Dx9½"H.
N7769 6221T. (8 lbs.) .... Each 19.95

THE PURE IRISH WOOL RUG—what attracts you is the creamy color, the interesting weave—the same things that attract you to an Aran sweater. Designed by Eileen Ellis for County Mayo's Tintawn Carpets. Commercial dry clean.
4x6' rug.
N6769 2296T. (16 lbs.) 449.00
6x9' rug.
N6769 2297T. (35 lbs.) 899.00
9x12' rug. Freight shipped. Allow 2 to 3 weeks transit.
N6769 2298F. Plus $50 delivery 1899.00

THE WHISKEY JUG TABLE LAMP is from Stoneware Jackson's studio in Kilkenny—with the same cork and wood spout you might see on a jug of poteen. Hand-thrown gray stoneware with an earthy blue-and-brown stripe; natural muslin shade. Three-way switch; use 150-watt max. bulb (not incl.). 110-120V, AC.
N6669 2517T. 24" high. (15 lbs.) 99.95

CHARGE BY PHONE DAY OR NIGHT
TOLL-FREE 1-800-345-4500

B The quintessential luxury of imported, pure Irish linen sheets: nothing—no indulgence—surpasses their. Woven by Creative Crafts in Cork, Ireland—immaculately finished with a two-row corded hem. White. Machine wash.
Twin sheets. (1 lb. 8 oz. each)
N6969 9990. Flat, 66x96".
N6969 9991. Fitted, 36x75" .... Each 99.00
Full sheets. (1 lb. 12 oz. each)
N6969 9992. Flat, 81x96".
N6969 9993. Fitted, 54x75" .... Each 119.00
Queen sheets. (2 lbs. each)
N6969 9994. Flat, 90x102".
N6969 9995. Fitted, 60x80" .... Each 139.00
King sheets. (2 lbs. 8 oz. each)
N6969 9996. Flat, 108x102".
N6969 9997. Fitted, 78x80" .... Each 159.00
Pair pillow cases, standard size.
N6969 9998. (8 lbs.) .... Pair 69.00

C The bedshawl, new and important in American decorating, has been an Irish fixture for ... well, forever. "Annie's Ribbons," from Tapestries Ireland, is the essence of Country Irish—a wool/acrylic shawl with misty, pastel acetate ribbons loomwoven throughout; knotted fringe ends. Dry clean.
N7369 0378. Twin, 60x90" (4 lbs.) 89.00
N7369 0379. Full/Queen, 80x90" (5 lbs.) 149.00
N7369 0380. King, 108x90" (6 lbs.) 179.00
N7369 0381. Pillow sham, std. (1 lb.) .... Each 39.00
Toss pillow, polyester filled, 12x12".
N7369 0382. (1 lb.) 24.00

BEDRUFFLE. Exceptional in 200-countestim/polyester percale. Platform top. Machine wash.
1-White.   2-Bone.   State color number.
C7369 2825. Twin. (1 lb. 8 oz.) 35.00
C7369 2826. Full. (1 lb. 12 oz.) 39.00
C7369 2827. Queen. (2 lbs.) 49.00
C7369 2828. King. (2 lbs. 4 oz.) 59.00

"I think people are into the country feeling of any sort. Particularly in a world of tremendous trauma, people like home better. They want to be home."
—Carleton Varney

D

E

A We had seen the multitude greens of the land, the subtler greens of the sea—but when we saw these crystal weights, the color went straight to our hearts all over again. Kerry Glass blowers show their skill and Irishness in handmade paperweights, each as individual as the maker.
40 Shades of Green. 5" diam.
N7769 6211. (4 lbs. 2 oz.) **14.95**
Bit O'Blarney, embedded with a magical shard. 2½" high.
N7769 6210. (2 lbs. 2 oz.) **13.95**

B We couldn't track down the wine-and-cheese gathering in Irish rural tradition, but Stoneware Jackson convinces us it must have been. Handthrown ceramics are dishwasher and microwave safe. Gray, with honey and blue trim.
Wine jug, 7½" high.
N8069 4143. (3 lbs. 9 oz.) **29.95**
Goblets, in set of 2. Each 6" high.
N8069 4141. (1 lb. 4 oz.) . . . Set **12.95**
Cheese plate, 9¼" diam.; 5½" high.
N8069 4142. (3 lbs.) **19.95**

C There is nothing so humble that can't be made beautiful with Irish lace. Lynda Carroll handmakes her aprons of cotton the color of wheat tops, trims them with cotton/polyester lace. (You'll recognize the plaid cotton blouse and skirt from pg. 14.) Machine wash.
Pinafore style, 37½" long.
N8069 4915. (12 oz.) **35.00**
Half apron, 27¾" long.
N8069 4916. (8 oz.) **24.00**

D Anyone with an eye for crafts can spot a Puckane: jigsaw-fitted country scenes that always, always carry the artisan's signature on the back. Paddy Walsh, who runs the Puckane Community Crafts shop, introduced us to this wooden pub board—your menu or message slides into the grooves. 9¼" wide, 15" high.
N6669 4342T. (5 lbs.) **29.95**

E Irish tradition has it that an ounce of Irish whiskey is larger than an ounce of any other whiskey. From Irish Pewter Mill, two handsome jiggers, entirely handcrafted, with Irish pence for handles and the maker's personal touchmark impressed in each.
2½ oz. size.
N8069 4581. (2 oz.) **12.95**
1¼ oz. size.
N8069 4582. (2 oz.) **9.95**

BRAD BENNETT, noted watercolorist, is a native of Kenosha, Wisconsin. Charmed by his four series on American cities, we commissioned him to capture a bit of the magic of Ireland.

F Quiet reminders of the chimerical solitude of Ireland, recreated here by artist Brad Bennett. The fine quality, limited edition prints, each hand-numbered and signed, are from original watercolors created especially for Spiegel. Framed behind glass in brass-finished aluminum; each 18" high, 24" wide. A narrative description of subject is included.
O'Donoghue's Pub (top, left).
N6669 4345T. (5 lbs.) **99.95**
Dingle at Low Tide (top, right).
N6669 4343T. (5 lbs.) **99.95**
Adare Cottages (center).
N6669 4344T. (5 lbs.) **99.95**
The Creamery (bottom).
N6669 4346T. (5 lbs.) **99.95**
Portfolio: one of each print described above (unframed, centered on 18" high, 24" wide paper).
N6669 4347T. (10 lbs.) **229.00**

G The right serving pieces for a strong Irish party punch. Pewter punch set handwrought by the craftsmen of Irish Pewter Mill, with medieval tradition's touchmarks stamped into the heart of it. Seven pieces: 5" high x 6" diam. bowl, six 2¾" high cups (2⅔ oz. cap.).
N8069 4580. (2 lbs. 6 oz.) **199.95**

G

Title: Ireland, The Magic Is Here
Art Director: Patt Parker
Copywriter: Kit McCracken
Design Agency: Spiegel Design
Client: Spiegel, Inc.

FINE · JEWELRY · AT · BEAUTIFUL · PRICES

Cover merchandise also shown on page 20.

LAPIS, PEARLS & SODALITE

Timeless elegance...classic blue lapis lazuli contrasts with lustrous pearls. Enhanced by settings and accents of polished 14K gold.

Lapis and Pearls with 14K Gold:
4A. 30" bead necklace.   #1000-447
Compare at $389.00   **Our price $249.00**
36" bead necklace.   #1000-454
Compare at $469.00   **Our price $298.00**
4B. Round pierced earrings.   #1000-116
Compare at $298.00   **Our price $229.00**

Lapis and 14K Gold:
4C. Braid trimmed ring.   #1001-031
Compare at $599.00   **Our price $349.00**
4D. 14K gold shrimp ring.   #1001-163
Compare at $498.00   **Our price $299.00**
4E. 16" lapis necklace.   #1640-093
List $149.95   **Our price $109.00**
4F. Shrimp pierced earrings   #1000-017
Compare at $149.00   **Our price $99.95**
4G. Lapis shrimp ring.   #1000-348
Compare at $275.00   **Our price $189.00**
4H. Lapis/gold bangle.   #1639-707
Compare at $450.00   **Our price $299.00**

Etc.
4J. Sodalite encircled with 14K gold
pierced earrings.   #1000-355
List $99.95   **Our price $49.00**

4H

4

Title: Loves
Art Directors: Steve Pelkey, Ron Starke
Copywriter: Barbara Gabor
Design Agency: Three Score
Client: Loves Jewelry

Using a combination of photos of models and still lifes solved the problem of how to effectively showcase fine jewelry. Special attention was given to the separations and printing to ensure that the gold and gems would appear the correct color.

Lapis or sodalite to mix or match with the gleam of 14K Gold.

14K Gold Jewelry:
5A. ⁷⁄₁₆" gold bangle.   #1631-746
Compare at $649.00   **Our price $389.00**
5B. Sculptured dome ring.   #1000-405
Compare at $395.00   **Our price $249.00**
5C. Dome pierced earrings.   #1640-697
Compare at $190.00   **Our price $129.00**

Lapis and 14K Gold:
5D. Fancy pierced earrings.   #1643-386
List $59.95   **Our price $34.95**
5E. Oval lapis ring.   #1640-036
List $315.00   **Our price $229.00**
5F. Round pierced earrings.   #1000-330
Compare at $219.00   **Our price $139.95**
5G. Lapis dome ring.   #1643-485
List $179.00   **Our price $119.95**

Blue Sodalite with 14K Gold:
5H. Shell pendant.   #1640-192
List $169.95   **Our price $129.95**
5J. Shell pierced earrings.   #1640-184
List $69.95   **Our price $49.95**

Call toll free: 1-800-845-6151.
In South Carolina call 803-366-8391.
All jewelry 14K gold except where noted.

5

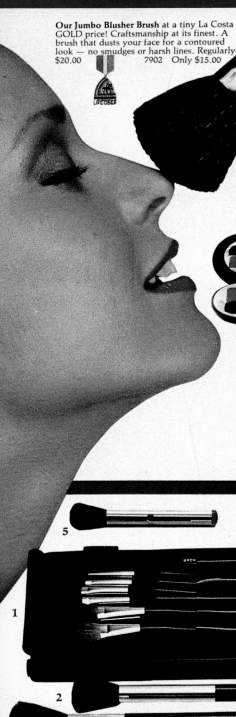

Our Jumbo Blusher Brush at a tiny La Costa GOLD price! Craftsmanship at its finest. A brush that dusts your face for a contoured look — no smudges or harsh lines. Regularly $20.00   7902   Only $15.00

BEAUTIFUL EXPRESSIVE EYES...
LUCIOUS LIPS...
THAT LOVELY LA COSTA FACE!

Our Italian Color Experts Turn Their Eyes to Your Beauty in These Magnificent Color Compacts!

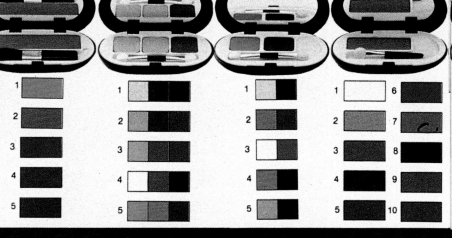

Glow-Blush Powder. Sexy subtle colors glide onto your cheekbones and contour your face. Specify color. 7515 $8.50

Triple Eyeshadow Compact. Sensational trios to shape, highlight and define the sensuous curves of your eyes. Select color combinations that are you! 7514 $12.50

Double Eyeshadow Compact. Creamy colors with lustre in today's coordinated combinations. Choose your favorites. 7513 $10.00

Single Eyeshadow Compact with ultra-creamy eyeshadow in colors for eyes that hypnotize. Specify color from color chart. 7512 $7.50

Foundation Face Powder. A feather-light powder that diffuses facial shine, minimizes pores and keeps you looking fresh and natural all day. Specify color. 7516 $8.50

CALL NEW TOLL-FREE NUMBERS
1-800-LA COSTA (522-6782)
IN CALIFORNIA 1-800-772-5665

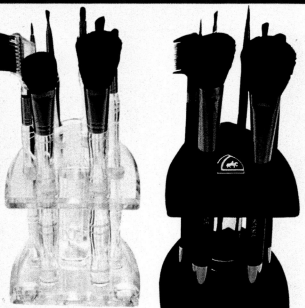

Globe Trotter Travel Brush Kit. Complete brush set for when you're out and about includes: A Contour Brush, Rouge Brush, Angle Shadow Brush, Brow Brush, Eyeliner Brush, p Brush and Lash Brow Comb. 7579 $22.50

Three-in-One Brush. So unique! So practical! Three brushes in all, one fits inside the next d all are contained in one handle. A brush for cheeks, eyes and lips. 7577 $15.00

Our Four-in-One is the same idea as our Three-in-One plus a brush for brows! 7578 $18.50

New! Mini-Purse Make-Up Brush is compact, light as a feather, perfect for touch-ups on e go. Slides in and out of stylish gold casing. Haven't seen this anywhere else.
00   Regularly $5.00   La Costa GOLD priced $3.50

Our Medium Purse Blusher Brush is great for cheeks and powders. Pops out of casing th decorative lever and bottom. A La Costa Spa find! 7901   Regularly $10.00
Costa GOLD priced $7.50

The Professional Brush Collection in a Sophisticated Stand. Eight exquisite make-up brushes in our custom stand. Includes: Powder Brush, Lip Brush, Eyeliner Brush, Diagonal Shadow Brush, Brow Brush, Blusher Brush, Domed Shadow Brush and Lash Brow Comb.
7568   Clear Sculptured Bamboo Set $40.00
7569   Deluxe Polished Black Lucite® Set $42.50

New! Suede Like Purse Sized Make-U You'll Love The Look...the feel! "Be on your block to own one," as they sa really it's very special and it's going to you looking very special with eyeshad blushes, lip gloss and applicators. Wh color clears the price will be $17.50. F — For you — A La Costa GOLD Special $12.50 7563

Perfume/Cologne Spray Atomizers. A elegant refillable pump-mist spray bot take your favorite fragrance whereve Nestled inside a soft suede-like case w La Costa Spa emblem embossed on to Arrives in its own pretty pouch! A be addition to your boudoir or purse. Ch your color: 1) Black 2) Brown 3) Burg 0995 $15.00

...LLIANT COLORS, MOODY COLORS, ...RVELOUS COLORS — OUR COLOR ...LISTS IN ITALY PUT THEM ALL ...GETHER IN THE LA COSTA SPA'S MAKE-UP KITS.

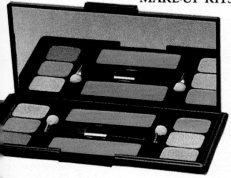

...urse Perfect ...Up Kit. Slimmer than Slim in △ ...Black Case. You're going to love to flash this Purse ...Make-Up Kit at him — and wait til he sees you look-...ra elegant with your choice of six sensuous shadows ...o blushes and three different applicators to apply ...Aren't La Costa products fun and wonderul too! $18.50

And a Make-Up Classic...Our La Costa Spa Paint Set. It's marvelous! Everything you need for That La Costa Look! Open it up to 8 velvety Eyeshadows, 2 Applicator Wands, Mascara and Eyeliner Pencil. And there's more! The trays slide apart to reveal Blush Powder, Lip Gloss and Creamy Rouge. All in a sleek compact kit. What fun!
7528 $22.50

△

The Paint Set Lip Colors. An artist's palette of magical shades that glide on evenly and stay on shining for hours. For moist, wet, luscious lips. Choose your favorite colors from our 21 beauties!   7705 $6.50   ▷

△
More La Costa GOLD! When you buy a Paint Set Lip Color — you can receive our $6.50 Black Thai Silk Case with mirror '0409   for only $3.00!

THE PAINT SET NAIL GEMS FROM THE LA COSTA SPA .45 FL.OZ.

The Paint Set Nail Colors. An array of colors that stroke on smooth and stay on long. Our priceless finish is made from actual diamond fragments for the hardest nail protection! Pick a color for your every mood.
7850 $6.00

---

23 Chinese White Glace	24 Clear Double
2 Burnt Sienna	15 Sandy-Glace
3 Apricot Nectar	16 Indian Gold G
4 Sage Honey	17 Peach Melba
5 Hot Chocolate	18 Red Hot Glac
6 Coffee Au Lait	19 Sherry Glace
7 American Rose	20 Bronze Glac
8 Plum Pretty	21 Copper Glac
9 Marvelous Mauve	22 Mauve Glacé
10 Ramblin Rose	31 Tickled Pink
11 Strawberry Parfait	33 Island Coral
12 Sunset	34 Very Berry Glacé
13 Fire Engine Red	35 Capuccino Glacé
1 Indian Red	14 Nearly Pink Glacé	36 Cinnamon Glacé

3 Rosalon	31 Tickled Pink
7 Bonita	33 Island Coral
8 Plum Pretty	34 Very Berry Frost
9 Marvelous Mauve	36 Cinnamon Frost
11 Strawberry Parfait	37 Ripe Raspberry Frost
12 Sunset	38 Burgundy Cherry
17 Peach Melba Frost	39 Marmalade Frost
19 Sherry Frost	40 Sangria Frost
21 Copper Frost	41 Bella
1 Indian Red	22 Mauve Frost	42 Diosa

15

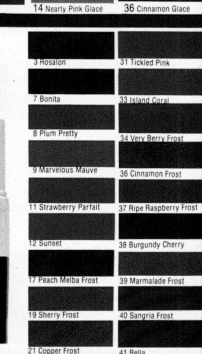

THE LA COSTA SPA
1984 SPRING SUMMER CATALOG

That La Costa Look

Title: That La Costa Look
Art Director: Sahad Baghdassarian
Agency: La Costa In-House
Client: La Costa

This catalog was produced to incorporate new product lines and present a cross section of La Costa spa products. Special values were tied into Olympic marketing awards.

Title: Sir Thomas Lipton Collection
Art Director: Richard Nelson
Copywriters: Suzanne Taliaferro, Marilyn Siegel
Design Agency: Tolliver, Inc.
Client: Thomas J. Lipton, Inc.

As part of an effort to encourage hot tea consumption, Lipton created a catalog of tea accessories, the Sir Thomas Lipton Collection. The items were photographed in a holiday setting, and the catalog released in time for the Christmas season.

. In-
as in
agnifi-
e pre-
cludes:
. Yun-
jeeling, Earl Grey and English Breakfast. The foil-lined bags
seal out moisture and seal in flavor.
132 cups of tea for the leaf tea lover
to enjoy!
#6006L Leaf Sampler Chest (six
1.77 oz. samplers) **$22.00**

The Legacy of Sir Thomas Lipton
(1850-1931)

Here for your pleasure, are some of the finest teas in all the world, selected using uncompromising standards and a commitment to excellence.

B. CURRIER & IVES COOKIE ASSORTMENT. Tea and cookies — what could be better? 2 lbs. of fancy cookies, mouth-wateringly good. Topped with delicious almonds, pecans, rich chocolate, and colorful non-pareils. Comes with our Special Assortment canister of 30 tea bags: 5 each of Darjeeling, Earl Grey, English Breakfast, Golden Assam, Finest Ceylon, and Yunnan.
#3010C Cookie and Tea Set (2 lbs.) **$19.50**

Call Toll-Free
1-800-932-0488
In New Jersey, call 1-800-624-0793
7 days a week, 24 hours a day,
Credit card orders only

C. PRETTY TEA-FOR-ME. When
othing is more welcome than a cup
f tea . . . alone. A 10 oz. porcelain
up, saucer, and lid with charming
norning-glory pattern. Comes with
ur 12-Tea Bag Sampler: 2 each of
ur six favorite varieties.
#7059B Tea For Me Set $16.50

D. IRISH WHISKEY CAKE. Truly
crumptious! An unbelievably
elicious 2½ lb. cake thoroughly
renched in 10 oz. of the finest
mported Irish whiskey and turned
very other day allowing whiskey to
ermeate the entire cake. Sublimely
ood with any tea. Anytime!
#5201W Irish Whiskey Cake $23.00

E. DELUXE TREASURE CHEST.
jive the most elegant introduction to
ir Thomas Lipton's world of tea. We
Ter eight of our exclusive varieties.
40 tea bags in a handsome wooden
hest ready to present to guests. There
re 28 tea bags each of our Earl Grey
nd English Breakfast varieties and 14
ea bags each of: Finest Ceylon,
Darjeeling, Golden Assam, Yunnan,
asmine and Nuwara Eliya. Each tea
ag is individually foil-wrapped to
reserve freshness and flavor.
6140B Deluxe Treasure Chest
(140 Tea Bags) $32.00

E

Title: Balducci's Catalog
Art Directors: Diane Meier, Darcey Lund
Copywriter: Diane Meier
Design Agency: Meier Advertising
Client: Balducci's

Balducci's, an exclusive gourmet food shop in New York's
fashionable Greenwich Village, wanted to position itself as a resource for fine foods and open a gift market
for the store. This direct mail catalog expanded the
store's reach beyond Manhattan to a national audience.
The illustrations, copy, colors, and papers were chosen to
make the store appear exclusive without losing the
shop's unique, homey feeling.

Result:
Over 8% of those who received the catalog responded.

SPARKLING SAVINGS

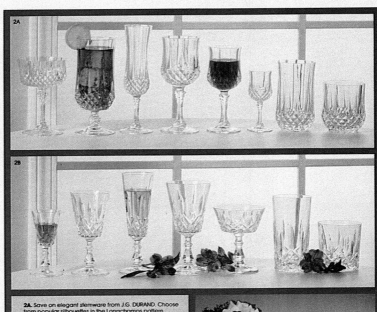

2A. Save on elegant stemware from J.G. DURAND. Choose from popular silhouettes in the Longchamps pattern.

	ORIG.	SALE
Goblet, wine, cordial, flute or saucer champagne, each	$6.50	$2.99
On-the-rocks or hi-ball, each	8.50	3.99
Ice tea, each	10.00	4.99

2B. Handsome ROYAL CRYSTAL ROCK stemware, at special savings. In the Shannon pattern choose cordial, wine, flute champagne, goblet, saucer champagne, hi-ball or double old fashioned. Each, orig. $10.00, **$6.99**

2C. Save on beautiful MIKASA Carmen serveware. Fine serving pieces accented with a frosted grape motif.

	REG.	SALE
Serving bowl	31.50	15.95
Footed cake plate	50.00	24.95
Set of 4 fruit bowls	31.50	15.95
Not shown:		
13½" round server	32.50	15.95
Canape tray	31.50	15.95

SAVE 40% TO 50% ON ARITA AND

3A. MIKASA Sea Mist stemware. Choose from all sizes. Shown are jade, coral and clear. Each, reg. $24.95, **$14.95**

3B. Save 40% on 20-piece sets of ARITA Contours dinnerware. Quality china that sets a pretty table for company or for your family. Your choice of three lovely patterns: Rapture, Freesia or Tiger Lily. Each 20-piece set (for all ARITA dinnerware shown) contains four each: dinner plate, salad plate, cereal bowl, cup and saucer. Also, save 33% on all of our ARITA Contours open stock pieces. Contours 20-piece set. Reg. $150.00, **$89.99**

China and Glassware, not in Working Wonders, Riverside, Han

SPECIALTIES OF THE HOUSE

Revereware® 14-piece set, $99.99. See page 10 for details.

Thalhimers

Sale begins July 1 and ends July 28, 1984.

Title: Specialties of the House
Art Directors: Mary Pat Nanney, Ron Starkey
Copywriter: Robin Wills
Design Agency: Three Score
Client: Thalhimers

Housewares items were promoted through an oversized catalog. The hard-sell quality of the large "savings" headlines was softened through the use of color.

Title: The Tinsmith's Craft
Art Directors: Michael DeBrito, Billy Jean Csapo
Copywriter: Charlotte Cook Box
Design Agency: Gregory & Clyburne, Inc.
Client: ACP Enterprises

To launch a new venture in direct mail, ACP Enterprises created a catalog of attractive gift items. Decorative tin boxes were used as the focal point and theme for a catalog to help launch this new venture. Folksy settings were used for the photographs, calling up nostalgic images of the old-time Yankee peddler.

ACP Enterprises, Inc., 1921 Fairmount Avenue, Philadelphia, PA 19130 215-232-0666

5
Collateral

**Bill Stuffers, Posters, and
Other Auxiliary Material**

Ordinarily, when people think of advertising, they think of magazines, newspapers, radio, television, billboards, car cards, and mail. They do *not* ordinarily think of the printed sales material enclosed with a bill, tucked inside a package shipped to a home or office, or found inside of an egg carton, washing machine, or pack of paper napkins.

Of course, all of this, and more, is advertising. These pieces, such as the brochures for credit cards displayed in airports, hotel lobbies, and restaurants, are all collateral advertising. If that credit card brochure falls out of the Sunday newspaper, it's still collateral. If it arrives at the office or home inside a package of postcards, if it is tucked inside of a photo finishing envelope; or if it is displayed on a shelf in the supermarket, it's still collateral advertising.

In general advertising, these extra devices for influencing consumers are called sales promotion. But in direct response advertising, which asks for action *now,* these vehicles are lumped together under the single heading of collateral advertising.

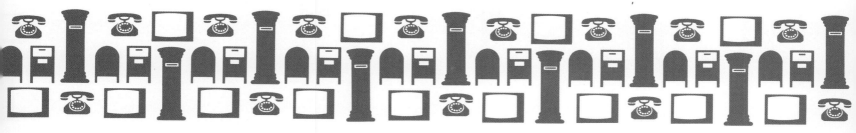

Collateral is used both to acquire new customers and to increase sales to current customers. It's an enormously powerful generator of business. The costs of delivery are usually low, so that the percentage of profit yielded by one sale made through collateral can be much higher than for one sale made through a more conventional advertisement. Collateral is powerful and is practically invisible to the consumer.

Collateral is also practically invisible to many direct response advertising agencies. For some reason, collateral doesn't often get discussed when an advertising campaign is being planned; the agency doesn't include it in the creative or media budgets submitted to the client; it's almost never given to freelancers outside of the agency as a creative assignment. Therefore, collateral is most often conceived and produced by the client's in-house advertising manager.

Collateral is a swan disguised as an ugly duckling.

A change in this attitude is beginning to take place. Some very intelligent corporate marketing executives are exploring the staggering diversity of ways in which direct marketing can increase sales. And some of them are demanding that their direct marketing agencies participate in conceiving and producing collateral promotions. Suddenly, creative directors, art directors, and copywriters at these agencies are discovering a whole new world. A handful of the many outstanding examples appears on the following pages.

Title:	Stouffer Hotels Club Express	A fulfillment package including baggage name tags and
Art Director:	Stefanie Palermo	Stouffer Hotel information was sent to American Express
Copywriter:	Laura Buoncuore	credit card holders who responded to a newspaper ad
Design Agency:	Ogilvy & Mather Direct	inviting calls to Stouffer's reservation telephone number.
Client:	American Express Company	The campaign was designed to build loyalty for Stouffer
		Hotels and American Express credit card holders who
		travel frequently.

Title: Mother-Get-A-Mother
Art Director: Robert Cesiro
Copywriters: Fred Lida, Bill Trembath
Design Agency: Ogilvy & Mather Direct
Client: Kinder-Care Learning Centers

The strongest advertising for a child care facility is word
of mouth, the recommendation of a satisfied parent.
Kinder-Care's package was designed to be given to
parents picking up children from the company's facilities.
Information inside the package encouraged them to pass
the material to a friend who was a prospective Kinder-
Care client.

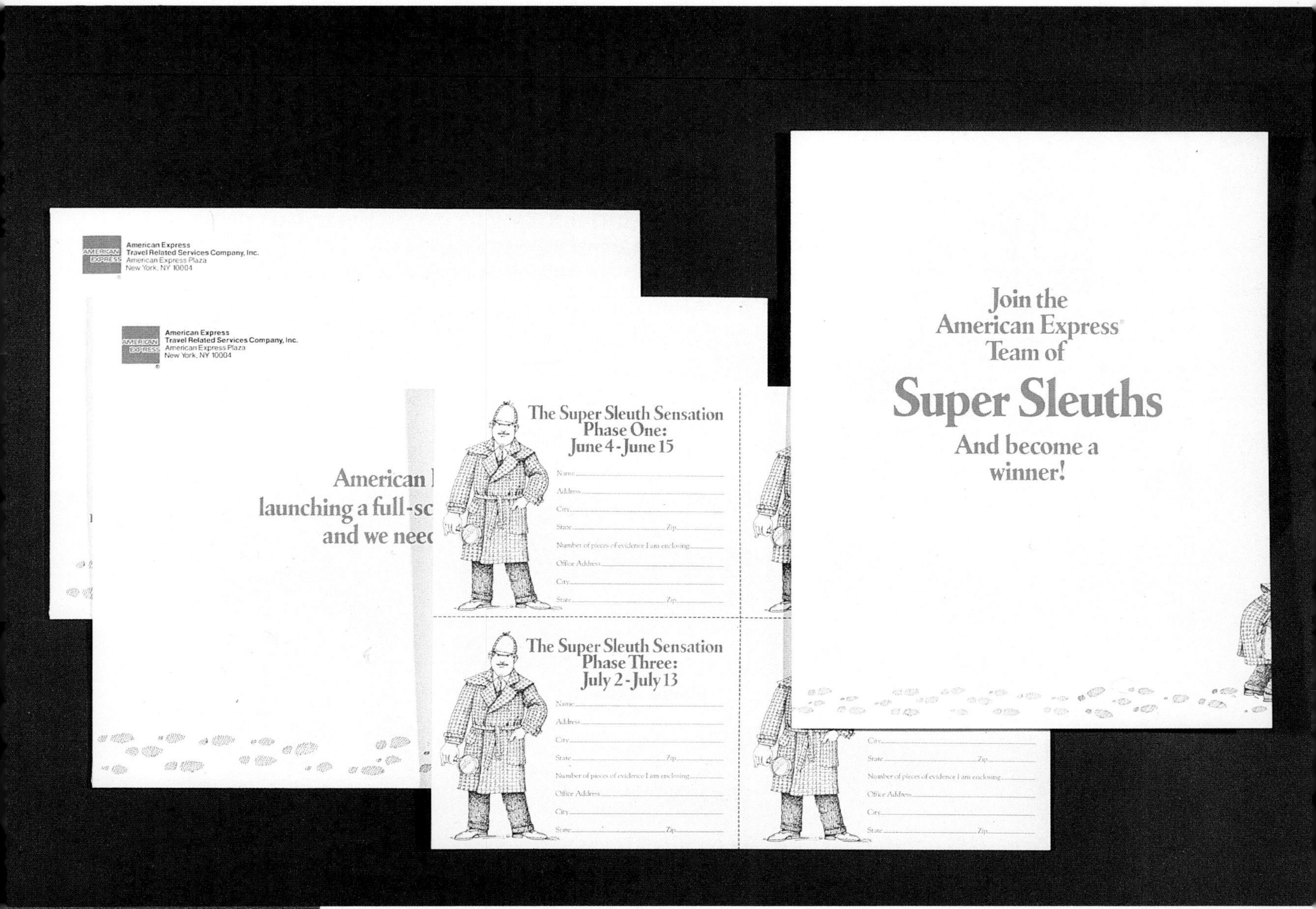

American Express
Travel Related Services Company, Inc.
American Express Plaza
New York, NY 10004

American Express
Travel Related Services Company, Inc.
American Express Plaza
New York, NY 10004

American E
launching a full-sc
and we nee

The Super Sleuth Sensation
Phase One:
June 4 - June 15

Name
Address
City
State   Zip
Number of pieces of evidence I am enclosing
Office Address
City
State   Zip

The Super Sleuth Sensation
Phase Three:
July 2 - July 13

Name
Address
City
State   Zip
Number of pieces of evidence I am enclosing
Office Address
City
State   Zip

Join the
American Express
Team of

Super Sleuths

And become a
winner!

City
State   Zip
Number of pieces of evidence I am enclosing
Office Address
City
State   Zip

OUR EXPERTS
ANSWER THE
0 QUESTIONS
PARENTS
MOST OFTEN
ASK ABOUT
KINDER-CARE

Title: Super Sleuth
Art Director: Candi Schaefer
Copywriter: Betsy Sloan
Design Agency: Ogilvy & Mather Direct
Client: American Express Company

This contest mailing was sent to American Express
cardmembers. Clues were hidden in the mailings and
cardmembers had to return the dated cards detailing the
evidence they found.

The Smiths: (sample data)

Male Head of Household: Bob Smith	Mortgage Amount: $58,000
Drivers License Renewal Date for Bob Smith: 4/28/84	Make of Car: Ford Econowagon
	Dog Ownership: Yes
Number of Members in Household: 3	Propensity For Ownership of VCR, Personal
Youngest Household Member's Year of Birth: 1/12/71	Computer or Related Equipment: Low

Introducing a revolution in targeted marketing services from a revolutionary new information company.

ADVANCED INFORMATION MARKETING

The Smiths: (sample data)

Male Head of Household: Bob Smith	Mortgage Amount: $58,000
Drivers License Renewal Date for Bob Smith: 4/28/84	Make of Car: Ford Econowagon
	Dog Ownership: Yes
Number of Members in Household: 3	Propensity For Ownership of VCR, Personal
Youngest Household Member's Year of Birth: 1/12/71	Computer or Related Equipment: Low

Before AIM, you couldn't tell the difference between the Smiths and the Johnsons.

Title: Advanced Information Marketing
Art Director: Jerry Lawrence
Copywriter: Alan Ishar
Design Agency: Wunderman, Ricotta & Kline
Client: Advanced Information Marketing

To introduce a new business, Advanced Information
Marketing (AIM) to the U.S. direct marketing industry,
colorful fold out was created showcasing AIM's data
targeting abilities. The piece was distributed at a dire
marketing convention in New York.

Result:
In less than two months, the piece generated 50 majo
accounts.

The Johnsons: (sample data)

Male Head of Household: John Johnson Sr.	Mortgage Amount: $22,000
Drivers License Renewal Date for John Johnson Sr: 10/28/84	Make of Car: Toyota Supra, Dodge Maxima.
Number of Members in Household: 3	Dog Ownership: No
Youngest Household Member's Year of Birth: 3/15/71	Propensity For Ownership of VCR, Personal Computer or Related Equipment: High

When you stop looking at clusters and start looking at people, you get the prospects you want without the waste.

For most information companies, looking at the Smiths and looking at the Johnsons is like looking at the same family.

Clustering systems can't tell the difference. Sure, they're better than traditional segmentation techniques, but even for them, a zip code is a zip code and a neighborhood is a neighborhood. As a direct marketer you're told that whatever products the Smiths buy are the same products the Johnsons are using.

Problem is, this theory's often wrong.

If you treat the Johnsons and the Smiths as one, it's costing you money.

Fact is, the Johnsons and the Smiths, and everyone else on the block, are very different families... with different tastes, different buying patterns, and different ways of responding to your product.

Send a financial offer to both Smith and Johnson, for instance, and there's a good chance one of them will have no interest in it at all. A 40% chance, in fact, based on industry statistics. This means that every time you launch a direct marketing campaign you risk throwing away as much as 40% of your money on people who have a very low probability of buying your product.

But, now there is an alternative. Because, now, there is AIM® — Advanced Information Marketing.

For the first time, AIM is able to offer direct marketers 100% information efficiency, 100% of the time. How? With a revolutionary system that recognizes far more than the diversities of neighborhoods, or even households — we can look at individuals. Yes, individuals.

When we focus on small differences, you get big results.

With exceptional accuracy, we're able to focus on multiple attributes and use them to mirror your customer profile. We can measure differences between MR. Smith and MRS. Smith, for instance, or tell you what kind of car Mr. Johnson bought recently. We can determine how long the Smiths have owned their home, or whether the Johnsons are likely to buy a new television this year. Our targeting efficiencies are so precise, in fact, you can actually direct your marketing efforts to the very individual making the purchasing decisions.

More importantly, at AIM we not only give you an ability to see information more clearly, we can help you use it to dramatically increase response. Instead of simply grouping same-zip households into pre-set clusters, we'll give you customized targeting tools that will help you find the most efficient prospects every time... and build your maximum potential universe with less waste than ever before. You get the prospects you want... one by one.

All the information the other guys have, and more.

Advanced Information Marketing has access to the exact sources of information as the major direct marketing consultants, database compilers and geo-demographic targeting suppliers. All of it. Plus we've added several proprietary data sources that give us a definitive edge.

But the real magic in our service is the creative ways in which we can use this information. Operating with the most powerful database equipment available today, we can access more than 150 billion bytes of data on a relational basis... in a matter of minutes. Our unique software and fully-customized services will help you plan, create, implement, and successfully execute a direct marketing program that is vital to the growth of your business. We do much more than support your program... we build it.

There's more, of course. AIM has recently designed and constructed a large, totally new computer facility. We have developed software so revolutionary and so sophisticated, it currently has no competition. We have a huge database capable of carrying 513 billion records on line at all times. We have an expertly skilled staff of marketing consultants, statistical analysts, application programmers, and system developers. And we have a diverse line of products and services designed to meet your immediate and future needs.

Never in direct marketing history has one company been able to do so much for its clients.

The Johnsons: (sample data)

Male Head of Household: John Johnson Sr.	Mortgage Amount: $22,000
Drivers License Renewal Date for John Johnson Sr: 10/28/84	Make of Car: Toyota Supra, Dodge Maxima
Number of Members in Household: 3	Dog Ownership: No
Youngest Household Member's Year of Birth: 3/15/71	Propensity For Ownership of VCR, Personal Computer or Related Equipment: High

It's knowing the essential difference between the Smiths and the Johnsons, that will make the big difference in your direct marketing program.

With Advanced Information Marketing, helping you build the most efficient direct marketing program possible means much more than finding the right prospects. It means you'll enjoy the advantages of six innovative marketing services that no other company can offer:

LINKAGE ONE℠ Customer Identification Service

LINKAGE ONE is a powerful segmentation technique that can identify high potential prospects at the individual or geo-demographic level. This prospect selection method is custom modelled for specific businesses and client objectives. It can also be used to analyze individual attribute data in conjunction with developing precise custom-clusters, or for predicting promotional results.

VISTA℠ List Enhancement Service

VISTA enables the client to dramatically improve the usability of an inhouse list. You can effectively identify non-responsive names on your list, improve deliverability of addresses mailed, and overlay required data such as telephone numbers, car ownership, or any other matchable attribute existing on the AIM information file.

RAINBOW℠ Prospect Identification Service

An extraordinary ability to isolate key information on file allows RAINBOW to generate data quickly and with extreme accuracy. You can rent the individual names associated with the data for promotional mailings, or use the RAINBOW service for precise statistical analysis.

HORIZON℠ Marketing Support Systems

The diversity of direct marketing businesses requires insight into the unique needs of each client. The skilled staff of our HORIZON service can provide consulting in the design, development and implementation of marketing support systems. We can assist you in the creation of support services as abstract as goal establishment or as immediate as your method of product fulfillment.

FOCUS IV℠ Custom Database Creation

In conjunction with your HORIZON representative you might determine that your business objectives would best be served through the creation of a custom database. FOCUS IV has

developed many such custom files to support the specific marketing programs of diverse companies. These custom databases have proved extremely cost-effective and have accelerated business growth.

EYEVIEW℠ Custom Analyses

Established direct marketers may have efficient marketing programs already in place, but still be lacking in one or more key areas of service. EYEVIEW can take a closer look at specific client needs and tailor analyses to help a client be better informed. These analytical services include: Site Location Analysis, Customer Profiling, Demographic Analysis, Product Usage Analysis, Media Analysis, and Creative Analysis. In addition, EYEVIEW service will offer new and very sophisticated geo-demographic mapping methods and graphical analysis of results.

Out of "cluster-clutter" and into the future.

The wide and comprehensive range of AIM services were created by people who know the problems of direct marketing and the rewards of solving them.

That's why we developed the software to take you out of "cluster-clutter" and give you individuals. That's why we revolutionized targeting-precision to help you see the differences between the Smiths and Johnsons. And that's why, when you're working with Advanced Information Marketing, you'll know you're working with the best.

So call us today. Find out how a little individual thinking can get you out of the cluster, and get your products to so many more of the right people.

Ad Sizes/Specifications
Directorio Telefónico
Las Páginas Amarillas de Pacific Bell
The who, what, why, when & where of Pacific Bell's new
Spanish Yellow Pages
and how they translate into extra business for you.
LOS ANGELES
Published by PacTel Directory, a Pacific Telesis Group Company
RATES
LOS ANGELES SPANISH YELLOW PAGES
WHEN
HOW to create an ad.
WHAT your ads cost.
WHY your ads will reach them.
WHERE they live.
WHO these directories reach.
YOUR PROFIT GUIDE TO THE
Los Angeles Hispanic Market
THE LOCATION OF L.A. HISPANICS
L.A. HISPANICS REPRESENT YOUR LARGEST AND FASTEST GROWING MARKET.
Hispanics are a majority in the Spanish Yellow Pages coverage areas.
Almost 3/5 of these residents are Hispanic.
They're fast becoming an even bigger majority.
The L.A. Hispanic population is increasing much faster than any other ethnic group.
They have money to spend.
Los Angeles Hispanics have $6 billion collective spending power.
They want to spend it in your market.
84% of L.A. Hispanics prefer to shop in a Spanish community or surrounding area.

NAME THE MOVIE† ON THE PRECEDING PAGE AND OWN IT (OR ANY ONE OF 40 OTHERS) FOR ONLY $4.95

WITH MEMBERSHIP IN THE LARGEST HOME VIDEO CLUB IN AMERICA.

THE HAD FAY WRAY IN THE PALM OF HIS HAND.

WALT DISNEY PRESENTS...
RCA SelectaVision VideoDiscs
DUMBO

ON GOLDEN POND #0523082	PSYCHO #1013032
GREAT EXPECTATIONS #4504032	*STRIPES #1513082
*THE MAN FROM SNOWY RIVER #0788242	*CADDYSHACK #6023002
*THE BLUE LAGOON #1512092	*FUNNY GIRL #1511002
*THE ALAMO #0583052	*HIGH ROAD TO CHINA #6022012

41 TOP HITS TO CHOOSE FROM.
SEE ADDITIONAL CHOICES INSIDE.
*ALSO AVAILABLE ON CED DISC

Courtesy of RKO General Pictures

NAME THIS MOVIE AND GET IT FOR ONLY $4.95

(OR PICK ANY ONE OF 40 OTHERS ON NEXT PAGE)
PLUS MEMBERSHIP IN THE CBS VIDEO CLUB

Title: King Kong
Art Director: Don Baker
Copywriter: Bill Keisler
Design Agency: Wunderman, Ricotta & Kline
Client: CBS Video Library

A guessing game linked to a famous movie was used to generate orders for the CBS Video Library among movie buffs who owned videocassette recorders and were willing to spend $50 or more to buy a movie.

Title: Who, What, Why Sales Kit
Art Director: Jim Huppenthal
Copywriter: Nancy Wahl
Design Agency: Wunderman West
Client: Pacific Telephone Company [PacTel Directory]

When PacTel Directory launched its first Spanish-language telephone directories in the Los Angeles area, this kit was created to help convert leads for directory advertising generated by a separate direct mailing.

A Christian Chevrier
French, born in 1950. Entered the Club in 1970.

Christian is the perfect example of a success story in our company. By virtue of his intelligence and perseverance, he climbed the ranks of the vacation village hierarchy, becoming one of our finest Chefs de Village. His will to succeed manifests itself in a tremendous energy on tap for our guests. Impelled by a profound love of the sea and of nature, he eagerly welcomes our North American guests to his Playa Blanca village, in hopes of guiding them to the discovery of Mexico's magic and the fantastic world of Club Med.

B Michel Saint Jean
French, born in 1954.

A native of the Pyrenee Mountains, Michel spent his childhood living on a sheep farm operated by his parents. His competence and knowledge in this domain were such that he was nicknamed "Berger" (the Shepherd) He derives his strength, stability and vitality from this experience. "This man is the epitome of energy in its purest form," says his entourage. He has devoted a lifetime to the enhancement of human relations and returns regularly to his source of tranquility in the mountains from which he draws his energy that he re-imparts enthusiastically to those captivated guests who join him in the Bahamas.

C Luc Distelmans
Born in Belgium.

No one who meets Luc would imagine that he brings together two exceptional, and often opposing, qualities: science and art. He holds two graduate degrees in both chemical and civil engineering, though modesty keeps him from admitting it. His talent, as both artist and actor, is such that we tend to applaud him more for these gifts than for his diplomas. He shines as an exceptional showman, leaving a lasting impression in the memories of those who surround him. This winter, Luc and his team will incite laughter and ovations that will echo for a long time to come at Buccaneer's Creek.

D Amal Benaissa
Moroccan, son of a noteworthy family of the city of Rabat.

If the Club is able to draw its strength and its unique identity from a multitude of personalities, traditions and cultures from around the world, it's undoubtedly, first and foremost, thanks to men like Amal. He brought with him, to our company, all of the exceptional qualities of his Eastern origins: courage, loyalty, and above all, his princely hospitality. His sensitivity toward others is expressed through his work as a never-ending search for the welfare and happiness of those around him. This winter, Ixtapa will be marked with the royal seal of this master in the "art of welcoming."

E Michel Simon
French, born in 1948

Woody Allen's latest hit, "Zelig," portrays a character thirsting for tenderness, craving for the opportunity to receive or share such warmth. Michel Simon, better known as "Minedieu" by his friends, could easily be the leading man in a counterplot: one which portrays a character overflowing with a tenderness he extends to others. This ability to disseminate his congeniality has made him one of the Club's most treasured Chefs de Village. Michel will open the doors, to all those who join him in Bora Bora, to the unparalleled serenity of the Pacific and the fervor of a remarkable team.

F Sylvio de Bortoli
Born in Switzerland in 1943.

As a company executive, gazing out his office window, contemplating the Alps' snowladen mountainside, Sylvio made the unanticipated decision to join the Club. Ever since that auspicious day in 1968, Sylvio has devoted his life to our organization. A calm and brilliant man, he has many passions: snow-skiing, waterskiing, air piloting, but above all, that of the well-being of others. On the occasion of the Club's 30th anniversary, he was awarded our most prized distinction by the Chairman of the Board: the Golden Trident. Sylvio de Bortoli is the example of the perfect marriage of imagination and precision. Those who join him in Cancún this winter will have that rare chance to share, what is for us, perfection's most concrete example.

G Christian Maille
French. Married to his hometown sweetheart.

Christian grew up, blossomed and nourished himself with the energy and experience of his elders—a veritable offspring of the villages! He incorporated the irreplaceable experience of his contact over the years in this business, sharing it with those who meet him in the villages. A native of an Alpine town where both tradition and love of skiing have produced many champions, Christian, along with his top-notch team in every phase of the village organization, will offer the indispensable experience of a professional to those who select Copper Mountain as their destination.

H Alain Blanc
Born in the South of Married, father of 3 child

His remarkable physical c and innate sense of strateg made him a hero in profe soccer. But, above all, it w radiant personality that wa mental in his nomination French Government as N Coach of their Women's Sw in 1973. A shrewd busine family hotel operation. In after visiting one of our v villages as a G.M., he dec abandon everything and enabling us to reap the be his outstanding leadershi organizational qualities. A welcomes our friends thi in a genial ambiance, to marvelous village of Eleu

SO YOU WANT TO BE A G.O.?

The most frequently heard words when people return from a Club Med vacation are: "I wanted to stay and be a G.O."

For those of us who routinely go to work every day and wish we were somewhere else, the life of a G.O. sounds like heaven. But what is it really like?

Heaven. But only if your idea of heaven is a people-oriented lifestyle that can keep you busy almost around the clock. When you're a G.O., your job and your life are one and the same—you don't go home at 5. Mind and spirit, you are involved with the Club Med way of life 24 hours a day.

A typical G.O., say the sailing instructor, may spend only 6 hours a day teaching sailing—but the rest of the time he or she is interacting with the G.M.'s, making us feel comfortable, and putting on those delightful cabaret shows in the evening.

You still want to be a G.O.? Not surprising. As a matter of fact, about ⅔ of the present G.O.'s come from the ranks of G.M.'s. But what did Club Med look for in hiring them?

Based on recent profiles, G.O.'s are single and between 21-26 years old when they start. Roughly 60% are male, and 40% female. Many speak French, although it's not required to work in the American zone.

Having some expertise in an area—whether it's water-skiing, cooking, accounting, or scuba diving is also a plus, but it's not absolutely required.

What is required is something that Club Med can't teach. It's called many things—kindness, a dedication to people, generosity, the ability to give of yourself—but what it comes down to is personality, with a capital P.

But say you do get hired. Then what? In the American zone, you'll go either to Paradise Island or Eleuthera for intensive training by the G.O. instructors from Paris. They'll make sure that the tennis instructor can teach groups, and that the cook is just as affable as any other G.O. If you need some special certification, you'll have to qualify for it at that time.

Once you're assigned to a village—chosen by Club Med management, not by you—you will serve as an apprentice under an experienced G.O.

If you decide that this life is for you, you can really go far—all over the world, as a matter of fact. Because

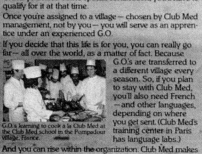

G.O.'s learning to cook a la Club Med at the Club Med school in the Pompadour village, France.

G.O.'s are transferred to a different village every season. So, if you plan to stay with Club Med, you'll also need French—and other languages, depending on where you get sent. (Club Med's training center in Paris has language labs.)

And you can rise within the organization. Club Med makes it a rule to promote from within, and of the entire management of Club Med, all but 3 people started out as G.O.'s.

You still want to go for it? Well, here are the hard numbers. There are approximately 4,000 G.O.'s during the winter season, and 6,000 during the summer. About 2,000 people are hired per year for locations around the world. But, in the U.S. zone alone, Club Med received 20,000 applications—and hired 200 people. Clearly, those who get chosen are outstanding!

And for them, being a G.O. is heaven. They work in exotic locations, meet people from all over the world, and enjoy a wonderful mix of exercise, great food and partying. You want to be a G.O.? Go for it!

I **Jean Viviani**
— French, graduate of the School of Dramatic Arts in Paris.

Even as a youngster, Jean wanted to become an actor. To pay for his studies, he worked in all phases of his chosen field: mime, song, dance, set design, sound and lighting. In the evening, he drove taxis. His energy and audacity were such that he was soon known and admired as the fastest and most competent cabbie in Paris. Jean's hiring with the Club is linked to this little anecdote: One day, his speedy delivery of a Club executive to the airport allowed him to catch an important flight at the last instant. In Haiti this winter, days will start early and finish very late with stunning shows and reviews, that Jean and his team, together, will create in a spectacular environment.

J **Myriam Karahoanessian**
Born in Armenia.

This artist brings to us all of the tranquillity and creative intensity of the East. The artistic sensitivity which give her paintings their dreamlike illusion, is expressed in her villages today as a delicate balance of detail. Everything is fashioned in her organization to offer a harmonious atmosphere to those she welcomes. "My villages," she says "are like my paintings. I use colors and forms which come to life in the light." Drawn together by her radiant enthusiasm, Myriam and her team guarantee a season of contrast and sensitivity at Caravelle.

K **Rod Frankel**
American.

Educated at West Point and U. of Penn., Rod graduated with his degree in engineering. He is gifted with exceptional athletic ability, and ranked 5th, without any special training, at an American athletic championship. Rod first applied to the Club as a waterskiing instructor. Six months later, he was designated as head of our largest waterskiing school, and just a year later as Chief of Sports. Nothing could stop this talented young man on his way to becoming the first American Chef de Village. Taking great interest in psychology and human relations, he today speaks French fluently. We find in him the unique example of the harmonious intertwining of the European and American cultures. This winter, Fort Royal will be the offspring of this rare union.

L **Christian Joujon**
Born in Lyon, France.

Christian's unique experience in the habits and tastes of our American G.M.'s has made him an "expert" in our sector. "To insure the carefree living of others, one must be very involved and attentive," he says. This philosophy, put into action, has been responsible for his many accomplishments. He is able to orchestrate, down to the last detail, the functioning of his village, so as to allow our G.M.'s to fully take advantage of their vacation, in the village's festive environment. At Punta Cana, Christian and his team will have the opportunity to reveal to you their expertise in the "art of living".

CLUB MED

L'Esprit des Villages

Title: L'Esprit des Villages
Art Director: Emily Hirn
Copywriter: Susan Enterline
Design Agency: Ogilvy & Mather Direct
Client: Club Med Resorts

To build loyalty among former visitors to Club Med's resorts, this 12-page newsletter was created. The publication was scheduled to be mailed quarterly. Oversized stock and four-color printing were used to give the piece an upscale appearance, and although the piece was mailed only in North America, a French name was chosen to reflect the international flavor of Club Med's facilities.

Title: Norman Rockwell Remembered
Art Director: Sally Sartorio
Copywriter: Ginger Farry
Design Agency: Doubleday Creative Services
Client: Doubleday Book Clubs

Owning an extensive mailing list of book club members, Doubleday designed this piece to sell other merchandise and to make orders for books above and beyond their scheduled book club purchases.

Celebrating Donald Duck®
The 1984 Christmas Bisqu

Genuine Porcelain Collector Plate

With the passing of Norman Rockwell from the American artistic scene, now, more than ever, we can see and appreciate his genius: the painter who portrayed our nation at work, at play, at prayer. This Special Edition Collector's Plate is produced on fine porcelain and depicts the Norman Rockwell masterwork, "Mother's Love." Measures a full 6¼" diameter, trimmed with 22-karat gold.
81018 $12.95

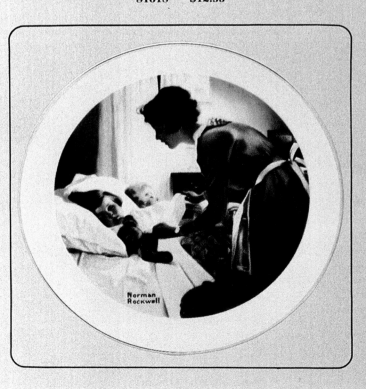

"The Toymaker"

"Lighthouse Keeper's Daughter"

"For a Good Boy"

"The Cobbler"

NORMAN ROCKWELL'S
Four Seasons

George Mendoza

Famous "Classics" Norman Rockwell Porcelain Mugs

Re-creating an enchanting scene from the "classics" of Norman Rockwell, each porcelain mug is elegantly trimmed on handle and rim in pure 24-karat gold. The back of each mug includes a brief description of the scene portrayed and the base bears the Norman Rockwell Museum Seal of Authenticity.
80861
Set of 4 porcelain mugs
$17.95

Norman Rockwell's Four Seasons

Norman Rockwell marked the seasons with his witty, compassionate observations of their effect on our daily lives. Now you can celebrate the year with this superb collection of more than 90 full-color Rockwell paintings, each complemented by verse from the great poets of the world. A treasure! Buy any merchandise from this brochure and get **Four Seasons** for only $14.99*
10421 Book with merchandise purchase $14.99
21881 Book (alone) $17.99
plus shipping and handling

Book Club Associates
501 Franklin Avenue
Garden City, New York 11530

50th Christmas...
Figurine

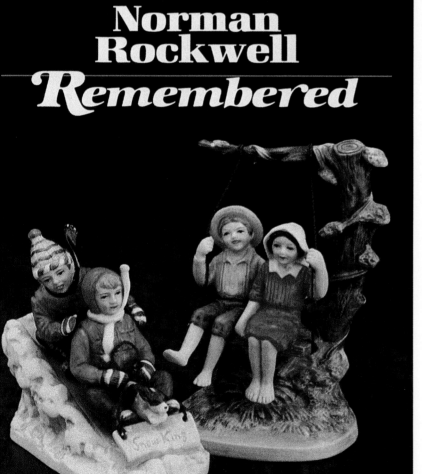

Shown smaller than actual size.

HOLIDAY FUN CAPTURED IN
HAND-PAINTED BISQUE PORCELAIN

This year's colorful figurine commemorates a very special event
... Donald Duck's fiftieth birthday year. In a comical Christmas
scene, Daisy Duck opens her package to find a most unexpected
gift — Donald himself!

You'll delight in your 6″ x 6¼″ figurine, which was created from
original art by Walt Disney Studios. It is beautifully detailed —
right down to the tiny ornaments on the family Christmas tree —
and exquisitely hand-painted in warm, rich colors. Each figurine
is individually numbered as part of a limited edition. You can be
proud to display this unique work of art year after year.

Please note that this edition is strictly limited to just 20,000
hand-numbered figurines. Once the edition is fully subscribed,
these figurines will no longer be available, so send in the attached application as early as possible — to be sure a numbered
figurine will be reserved for you.

RESERVATION APPLICATION
THE DISNEY CHRISTMAS 1984 BISQUE FIGURINE

Please accept my order and reserve a limited edition Disney Christmas 1984 Bisque Figurine for me. I understand
that my figurine will be individually numbered as part of the worldwide limited edition of 20,000.

I need send no money now. I will be notified when my figurine is available for shipment, and I will then be billed for just
$42.50 plus $2.50 shipping and handling (total $45.00*). Or I may choose to make four convenient monthly
payments until the total price is paid in full. THERE IS NO FINANCE CHARGE.

I may examine the figurine for 14 days without obligation to keep it. If not satisfied, I may return it for full refund. As a
subscriber, I will also receive, for free examination, future additions to The Disney Collection Christmas Figurine
series that are offered. I may purchase only those I wish to own. (*N.Y. and Ct. residents please add sales tax.)

I prefer to use my: ☐ VISA ☐ MasterCard

Account No. _____ Card Expires _____
                                                              Month   Year

Name _____
                        (Please print)

Address _____

City _____ State _____ Zip _____

Signature _____

CB

625-1

Norman
Rockwell
Remembered

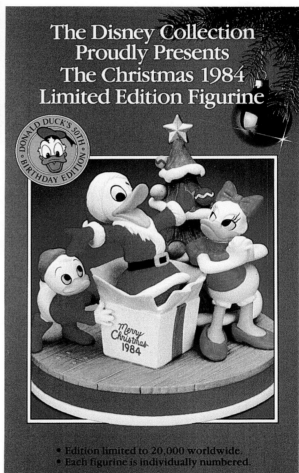

The Disney Collection
Proudly Presents
The Christmas 1984
Limited Edition Figurine

DONALD DUCK'S 50TH BIRTHDAY EDITION

• Edition limited to 20,000 worldwide.
• Each figurine is individually numbered.

Title:	Donald Duck's 50th Christmas
Art Director:	Ed Cotter
Copywriter:	Nancy Brisotti
Design Agency:	Grolier Enterprises
Client:	Grolier Enterprises

Figurines of Donald Duck were displayed in plexiglass
cases throughout the Disney theme parks along with this
brochure. Visitors were encouraged to take a brochure
and order the figurine as a Christmas commemorative item.

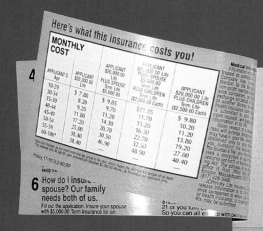

Title: Who Takes Care of Them?
Art Director: Jack O'Neal
Copywriter: Ted Isaac
Design Agency: ConComCo
Client: JC Penney Life Insurance Company

This package was created to accompany invoices to JC Penney charge customers. The four-page brochure and reply card generated leads for the field sales force for Penney's life insurance program. First tested with the man torn out of the photo, it was revised to show the woman torn out, as most Penney's invoices are opened by women. This revised version outperformed the previous control package.

Title: Andrew
Art Director: Terry Sandusky
Copywriter: William H. Stansfield
Design Agency: Circle Advertising
Client: Andrew Corporation

In order to increase sales of its telecommunications products in mainland China, the Andrew Corporation produced this brochure detailing its products and capabilities and soliciting inquiries.

SPEND 2 DAYS BEHIND BARS.

Join the American Lung Associations of Minnesota and Ramsey County on a weekend bicycle trek this summer. All you need is your bike and proper clothing.

We provide guides, meals, lodging and pre-trip instruction. For more information, call Pat McAllister at **227-8014**. Outside the metro area call toll-free: 1-800-642-LUNG.

Title:	Behind Bars
Art Director:	Bob Barrie
Copywriter:	Mike Lescarbean
Design Agency:	Fallon McElligott Rice
Client:	American Lung Association

The campaign was designed to attract participants for a weekend bicycle trip. Profits from the trip went to the American Lung Association.

Result:
The piece was very effective, generating a tremendous phone response.

Four Winds Tours Are Special...

Here's Why ▶

Title:	Four Winds Are Special . . . Here's Why
Art Director:	Abdul Waahid Mansur
Copywriters:	Susan Lasky Meyer, Risa Weinreb
Design Agency:	Sunbeam Advertising
Client:	Four Winds Travel, Inc.

Sent to everyone requesting information on Four Winds Tours, the piece explained the deluxe features that made Four Winds tours more expensive, but a good value.

Result:
Conversions from inquiries increased between 38% and 205% for various tours compared to the previous year.

Four Winds—More Deluxe...More Included...Better Value!

"Absolutely first rate. The itinerary as described was fulfilled and even exceeded. The local guides were superb. Our tour director was a professional in all aspects—it was apparent that he was known and respected by the local people in all areas we visited. Thanks to your entire organization."

Mr. and Mrs. Ralph Thiele, Old Bridge, NJ

26 Years of Four Winds Excellence Deluxe escorted travel is our **only** business. Four Winds is one of the largest deluxe tour operators in the world: we constantly monitor hotels, restaurants, transportation companies, local guides and tour directors to make sure their performance meets our high standards. This tradition of excellence and service has earned Four Winds many prestigious travel awards—plus the respect of satisfied tour members who vacation with us year after year.

Deluxe Hotels Four Winds carefully selects the finest deluxe and first class hotels and resorts available. Our hotels feature central locations, excellent service and plenty of amenities—like restaurants, boutiques, saunas and swimming pools. Each has a unique personality that will enhance the pleasure of your journey. And expect lots of smiles—since the hotels have done business with Four Winds for years, their staffs work especially hard to please our guests.

Enjoy luxury hotel facilities.

Gourmet Dining at Famous Restaurants On Four Winds tours, most—frequently all—meals are included, with many opportunities for a la carte dining. We also feature gala cocktail parties and banquets at some of the world's most celebrated restaurants, offering superb food, memorable surroundings, and attentive service. We choose a wide range of restaurants too—from quaint country inns to sophisticated showplaces. And **you'll always know what a Four Winds tour includes.** Our itineraries state what percentage of meals are included—which ones they are—and which are extra special.

Dine at famous restaurants.

Perfect Planning Meticulous—that's the tour planning you get from Four Winds' staff of travel professionals. We have **product managers** who seek out the most exciting places to visit...**travel counselors** to answer questions...**coordinators** who will send complete pre-tour information (travel tips, mailing addresses, suggested reading lists and a Four Winds flight bag)...plus **operations managers** on call 24 hours a day.

...Winds gives you more...gala entertainment—like fiesta dinners ...Mexico...complete sightseeing, such as Glacier Nat'l Park...and special touches—like a 4th of July celebration in Scandinavia.

Terrific Sightseeing—All Included Compare what other tour operators offer. We think you'll agree that Four Winds includes more sightseeing and more variety. We take travelers to the Taj Mahal by day—then again at night, for a dazzling visit beneath the full moon. Our tour members enjoy the best vantage point for sightseeing: from flightseeing over Africa's Victoria Falls to a jeep ride through Arizona's Red Rocks country. And groups are always accompanied by knowledgeable local guides as well as an experienced Four Winds tour director.

Discover China's Great Wall.

Four Winds Saves Travelers Money A Four Winds deluxe, escorted tour actually costs less than if you make the same arrangements on your own. Since Four Winds is one of the largest deluxe tour operators in the world, we get the lowest possible rates from hotels and other suppliers.

Four Winds holds down prices— For 1984, Four Winds has lowered or maintained tour prices to such popular destinations as Mexico, South America, Scandinavia, Africa, Egypt and Israel. In the U.S. and Canada, our prices have increased by less than 3%.

Seasonal savings— To many areas during the off-season.

Savings for single travelers— For people traveling alone, Four Winds offers a "share alternative" that can save hundreds of dollars over the standard single supplement.

Low air fares— Four Winds works with airlines to assure the lowest fares possible...with the added convenience of direct flights usually available from many cities.

Relax! Our Tours Are All-Inclusive Four Winds' value-packed price is all-inclusive. We tell you in advance exactly what the tour price covers, so there are no "hidden extras." Plus we give you many travel bonuses that make our vacations even more memorable.

Special entertainment included— We give people a real feel for the countries we visit—since Four Winds tours also feature evening activities such as cocktail parties ...Mexico's Ballet Folklorico... Denmark's Benneweis Circus... "Siamese Night" dinner in Thailand... regional theatre...geisha shows... Sound and Light performances.

All entrance fees included— To the historic sites, museums and attractions we visit on tour.

All tips included— Four Winds takes care of all tips on tour to local sightseeing guides and drivers, porters, bellmen and waiters.

See a Las Vegas dinner show.

All airport taxes included— Airport taxes really add up...$15.75 in Bogotá...$18.00 in Australia...these fees are covered in Four Winds' land rate!

Four Winds Tour Directors Handle All the Details All Four Winds tours are fully escorted by a mature, professional tour director who stays with groups from start to finish. (With many other companies, travelers are passed from one escort to another in each new city.) The Four Winds tour director will introduce tourmates...arrange hotel check-ins and baggage transfers...give informal briefings about the places visited...and be available 24 hours a day to make sure vacations run smoothly.

Jens Meyhre (r.) and group in Denmark.

Small Friendly Groups Friendly company but never a crowd— that's what you'll find on a Four Winds tour. Our limited group size is a very important feature, assuring personal attention and plenty of companionship while exploring the world.

Special Arrangements for Groups Your own group can reserve any Four Winds departure—we'll modify the itinerary to suit size and needs. Free land tours may also be available.

Member: USTOA & ASTA Tour Payment Protection Plan Book with even greater confidence—knowing Four Winds is a member of and bonded by the United States Tour Operators Association, and participates in ASTA's (American Society of Travel Agents) Tour Payment Protection Plan.

Varied Transportation— Getting there is half the fun with Four Winds. We choose unusual modes of transportation that show off the world's wonders at their best—like first class accommodations aboard Egypt's Deluxe Sleeping Train or Nile cruise ships...first class seats aboard Norway's Flam Line and Japan's Bullet Train...riding an elephant to Jaipur's Amber Palace...sailing aboard "Maid of the Mist" for an up-close view of Niagara Falls...or a thrilling "snocoach" crossing of Athabasca Glacier.

Travel across Canada aboard Via Rail.

And That's Not All! Yes, Four Winds tours may seem to cost a bit more. But take time to read the "fine print" in other tour brochures. You'll find that Four Winds includes many features that cost extra on other tours. Four Winds gives you day rooms if flights are in the evening...many a la carte meals...gala welcome and farewell parties and banquets...specially arranged regional entertainment. And there's more...lots, lots more to enjoy.

Get Your FREE Tour Brochures— Send the convenient coupon on the back or call Four Winds toll-free: **800-248-4444.** (NYC: 212-505-0901). Do it today!

Title:	The San Francisco Opera Endowment
Art Directors:	Ben Wolf, Edith Lee Shen, and Janet Carpinello
Copywriter:	Henry Goldstein
Design Agency:	Benedict Norbert Wong Marketing Design
Client:	The San Francisco Opera

To inform opera patrons of a new $30,000,000 endowment, this insert was mailed to the most affluent patrons. A unique calligraphic styling of the program's name was printed in metallic silver on coated white stock. To intrigue opera buffs, three unidentified operas were featured by symbols and recipients were invited to identify them.

Result:
The piece was very well received by the opera management.

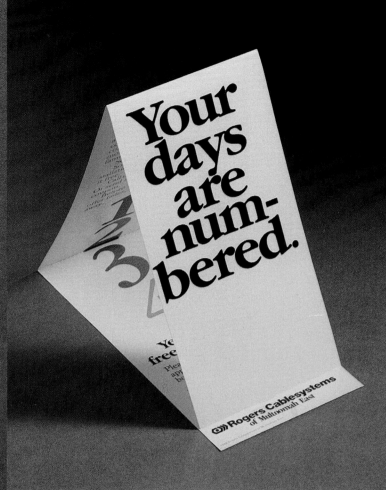

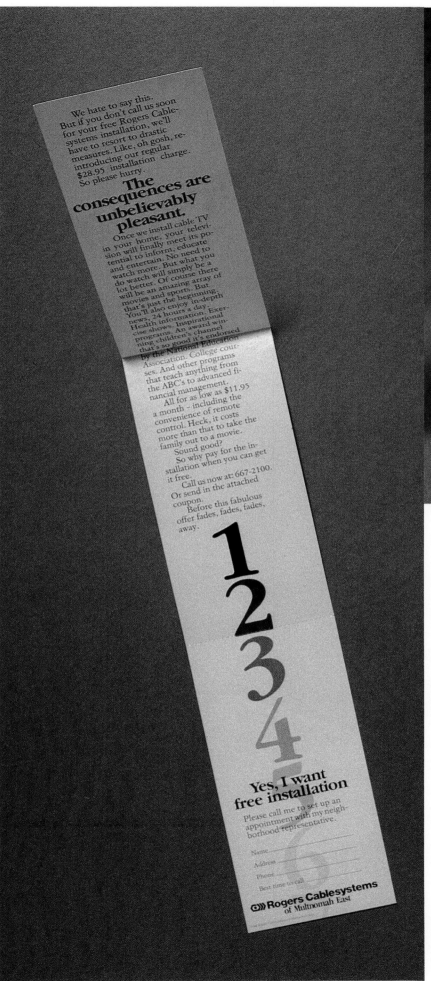

We hate to say this. But if you don't call us soon for your free Rogers Cablesystems installation, we'll have to resort to drastic measures. Like, oh gosh, reintroducing our regular $28.95 installation charge. So please hurry.

The consequences are unbelievably pleasant.

Once we install cable TV in your home, your television will finally meet its potential to inform, educate and entertain. No need to watch more. But what you do watch will simply be a lot better. Of course there will be an amazing array of movies and sports. But that's just the beginning. You'll also enjoy in-depth news, 24 hours a day. Health information. Exercise shows. Inspirational programs. An award winning children's channel that's so good it's endorsed by the National Education Association. College courses. And other programs that teach anything from the ABC's to advanced financial management.

All for as low as $11.95 a month – including the convenience of remote control. Heck, it costs more than that to take the family out to a movie.

Sound good?

So why pay for the installation when you can get it free.

Call us now at: 667-2100. Or send in the attached coupon.

Before this fabulous offer fades, fades, fades, away.

1 2 3 4 5 6

Yes, I want free installation

Please call me to set up an appointment with my neighborhood representative.

Name _____

Address _____

Phone _____

Best time to call _____

Rogers Cablesystems of Multnomah East

Your days are numbered.

1 2 3 4

Ye_ free _

Plea_ app_ bo_

Rogers Cablesystems of Multnomah East

Title: Your Days Are Numbered
Art Director: Lynn Frost Guitteau
Copywriter: Brian Ross
Design Agency: Pihas, Schmidt, Westerdahl
                  Company
Client: Rogers Cablesystem

This piece was one of a series designed to sell cable services to customers in categories with low conversion rates. The fading numbers enhance the concept of "numbered days."

Keep your business moving, even when you're on the road.

Title: Now A Phone In Your Car That
                    Works As Well As The One On
                    Your Desk
Art Director: Dick Capell
Copywriter: Mel Bruck
Design Agency: Wunderman, Ricotta & Kline
Client: NYNEX Mobile Communications

A whole new product category, cellular mobile tele-
phones, had to be sold to business people in a concise
format and in a small space. The piece emphasized how
a cellular mobile phone could increase the client's job
efficiency.

◄

Title: The Spirit of Massachusetts
Client: Donald McKay Festival

Funds were needed to build a wooden sailing vessel that
would carry the name "Spirit of Massachusetts." This
piece was created to solicit donations for the project.

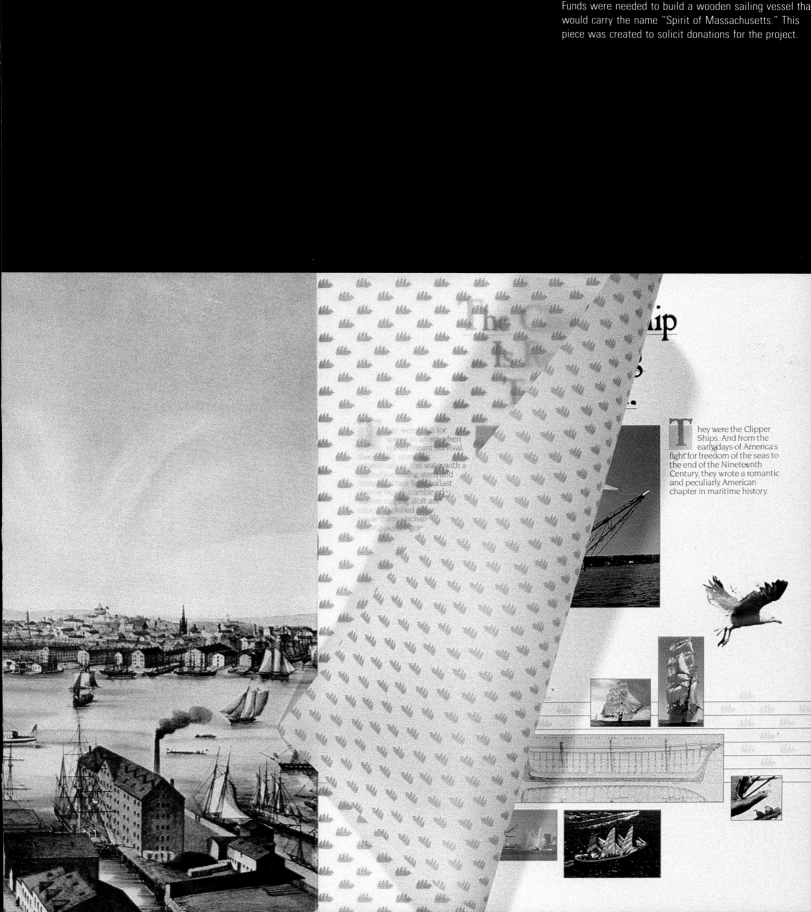

Funds were needed to build a wooden sailing vessel that would carry the name "Spirit of Massachusetts." This piece was created to solicit donations for the project.

The Clipper Ships

T hey were the Clipper Ships. And from the early days of America's fight for freedom of the seas to the end of the Nineteenth Century, they wrote a romantic and peculiarly American chapter in maritime history.

MAKE YOUR IMPRESSION ON A DIFFERENT SURFACE.

EVEN THE TOUCH AD

PHOTOGRAPHY: RYSZARD HOROWITZ

Title: Kimdura
Art Director: Bob Pitt
Copywriter: John Mattingly
Design Agency: Cargill, Wilson & Acree Inc.
                    Advertising
Client: Kimberly-Clark Corporation

To increase sales of a synthetic paper, Kimdura, a display
book was printed on Kimdura and mailed to paper
wholesalers to make them aware of the product's printing
qualities and durability.

ILLUSTRATION: HENRY VIZCARRA & JEFF WACK • GRIBBITT!

Title:	Kimdura
Art Directors:	Bob Pitt
Copywriters:	John Mattingly
Design Agency:	Cargill, Wilson & Ac
	Advertising
Client:	Kimberly-Clark Corpo

6

Campaign / Multimedia

Multi-piece Appeals Produced in More Than One Medium

Consumer advertising has long made use of the multimedia campaign. The campaign is a powerful way to saturate a market with your message, to keep prospects interested, to reinforce the image and the promise of the product you want them to try or buy, and through repetition in as many forms as possible, to increase the probability of recall when a purchase opportunity is at hand.

Yet for many years direct marketers did not believe this strategy was either relevant to their needs or even possible to execute. In fact, it was considered dangerous to assume that the positioning, the message, and the graphics used successfully in, say, a direct response print ad would also work when used for a direct mail piece, a response radio spot or a response television appeal.

Direct marketers traditionally treated each medium as a separate entity.

Once there was no such thing as a direct response "campaign." There were only individual communications. Each communication had just one job to do: Make an immediate sale.

When practitioners found an ad that made sales, it was run until it was gray with fatigue. When a direct mail package that pulled was found, it wasn't embellished or supported. It was just mailed. After all, a truly breakthrough direct mail package might pull for three, five, or even ten years.

The use of multimedia advertising campaigns today parallels a basic change in the business. We used to be in the "mail order" business. Now our business is direct marketing. The reason for the difference is as much a product of cultural changes and technological advances in our society as it is of increased sophistication and risk-taking in our disciplines.

When we were in "mail order" we contacted our prospects at home or through publication. We got our responses and checks in the mail. With the advent of the credit card and the toll-free 800 number, we could attract customers through television, radio, or the telephone—even if they are away from home or their check-books.

With the help of the computer's increased efficiency in accessing and cross-referencing data, new prospects can be identified more easily. But often, they must be found and sold in new places and in new ways.

Moreover, the uses of direct marketing have broadened. Today it is not uncommon for a direct marketing program to include simultaneous communication to the cus-

tomer at home and at work, and also to the wholesale distributor and the retail dealer—giving each the same basic positioning for the product, but different reasons to order, stock, and promote. In addition, the product must be supported with highly visible advertising in other media. The distributor must be supported through personal communications to the retailer. And the retailer must be supported with point-of-purchase materials, take-ones, hand-outs, and brochures for walk-in customers.

There is at least one more reason for the rise in multimedia communication. Through an increase in entertainment vehicles—cable television, home video, sprawling shopping malls open seven days a week, multi-film movie theaters—competition for the consumer's attention has increased. Meanwhile, the two-income

family of the 1980s has given prospects discretionary income but eroded discretionary time.

It all adds up to one thing. Today's direct marketer must take advantage of every available medium of communication to get sales messages read, recognized, and acted upon.

The multimedia campaigns that follow will give you some idea of how these challenges are being met.

Title:	ChemLawn CarpetClean
Art Director:	Mitch Achiron
Copywriter:	Leila Vuorenmaa
Design Agency:	Ogilvy & Mather Direct
Client:	ChemLawn Corporation

YOUR CARPET'S NOT CLEAN TILL YOU SAY IT'S CLEAN–EVEN THE HEAVY TRAFFIC AREAS.

YOUR CARPET'S NOT CLEAN TILL YOU SAY IT'S CLEAN–EVEN THE TOUGH SPOTS. GUARANTEED.

Some carpet spots are tough—very tough.
To get them all out you need ChemLawn CarpetClean.
With CarpetClean, you won't

under other pieces of furniture. Wherever they hide, your Specialist will find them. He'll carefully move furniture. And after cleaning, he'll move everything back and place

So why put up with tough carpet spots? Call ChemLawn CarpetClean today. And we'll get your whole carpet clean—or you don't pay. Guaranteed.

YOUR CARPET'S NOT CLEAN TILL YOU SAY IT'S CLEAN–EVEN UNDER THE FURNITURE. GUARANTEED.

WE'LL GET 'EM OUT OF YOUR CARPET OR YOU DON'T PAY. GUARANTEED.

Dirt. Grime. Spots. They're just some of the culprits responsible for dulling, matting and eating away at your carpet.
To get them all out you need

GET TRAFFIC AREAS THOROUGHLY CLEAN
Ground-in dirt, grime and spots love to congregate in your carpet's heavy traffic areas. Using state-of-

So why put up with dirt, grime and spots? Call CarpetClean today. And we'll get 'em out— or you don't pay. Guaranteed.

ChemLawn, primarily a gardening service, wanted to establish a leadership position for its carpet cleaning service. Humorous drawings and a single-minded theme revolving around a guarantee to get customers' carpets clean proved memorable and effective.

Result:
Total inquiries increased 186% and service appointments increased 218% over the previous year totals.

Title: ChemLawn PestFree
Art Director: Mitch Achiron
Copywriter: Leila Vuorenmaa
Design Agency: Ogilvy & Mather Direct
Client: ChemLawn Corporation

The PestFree guarantee—total satisfaction or full refund—was used to solicit new customers for a new and unknown service line of this established lawn service company.

Result:
Inquiries about PestFree were 150% more than had been projected.

Title: Prudent Buyer Campaign
Art Directors: Chris Quillen, John Coll
Copywriter: John Weil
Design Agency: Allen and Dorward
Client: Blue Cross

The Prudent Buyer campaign was developed to tell corporate health plan buyers that Blue Cross was concerned about the rising costs of health care, and had done something about it. The campaign was also intended to show buyers that the Prudent Buyer plan could save their company money and that employees would like the plan.

ANNOUNCING A NEW DIRECTION IN HEALTH CARE COSTS.

The Prudent Buyer Plan™ from Blue Cross.

Blue Cross is doing something few people thought possible. We're bringing down the skyrocketing cost of health care. Contracting with many of California's leading hospitals and physicians, we can now lower your hospital and doctor costs with the new Prudent Buyer Plan.

Lower costs for the same coverage. We're not just promising to reduce costs. We already have. The Prudent Buyer Plan offers an immediate and substantial reduction in coverage costs. With no reduction in benefits.

Costs are dropping but the quality of care isn't. The Prudent Buyer Plan network extends statewide, including major hospitals, both private and teaching, with long established reputations. The doctors are general practitioners as well as specialists with private practices in their own offices. You may actually find your own doctor is a member of the Prudent Buyer network.

You keep your freedom of choice. Below is a partial list of hospitals participating in the Prudent Buyer Plan network. You aren't limited to these but frankly,

you can realize considerable financial savings when you choose from the Prudent Buyer network. If you obtain medical care outside the network you will be responsible for a larger portion of the medical charges.

Find out more about coverage that costs less. The Prudent Buyer Plan is now available virtually everywhere in California for groups of 10 or more members. Ask about it at work.

Blue Cross of California

No one is doing more to protect your health.

CHEMLAWN GUARANTEES

We guarantee your satisfaction.
We'll keep working until you are satisfied,
or we'll refund your money.

THERE ARE NO BUGS IN OUR GUARANTEE.

CHEMLAWN
PESTFREE
INDOOR PEST ELIMINATION

BULK RATE
U.S. POSTAGE
PAID
CHEMLAWN
CORPORATION

IF THE LITTLE THINGS BUG YOU

"Nobody ever asked what good I did. They only asked how many people I killed."

A Vietnam Veteran remembers his homecoming.

Only now can we

They were outcasts. Soldiers fighting a war that nobod... wanted. Blamed for policies they did not create.

It was a time of turmoil. America was too emoti... ally divided to understand what was really going on.

Now, ten years later, you have an oppo... tunity... step...

Crying out a warnin... his buddies, a Marine fir... M79 grenade launcher at a... near Khe Sanh.

and take a fresh look a... war as TIME-LIFE BOOKS a... BOSTON PUBLISHING COMPANY... bring you THE VIETNAM EXPERIENC... The first series of its kind tha... takes an objective look at... war, putting it into historical perspective.

Your first book *America Takes Over*, takes you back... forth from the action in the jungle to secret meetings at... White House. It seeks new answers. Could we have bee... North Vietnam in the early stages if LBJ hadn't halted th... bombings? Did McNamara accept false information a... manufacture some of his own? And who was behind th... "Forty-Four Battalion request" that escalated the war?

For the men who fought in Vietnam this book is a scra... book of memories, filled with familiar faces, places an... award-winning photos capturing the real story.

For others it's an insight into the realities of Vietnam.

Putting you onto the bat... fields. Mapping out the... strategies. Showing you... reasons behind the vic... tories like Operation... Starlite, and embarrassing... defeats like O... ation Piranha.

Chicken Plo... Dustoff, MAF... LOC. You'll lea... whole new vo... ulary of war. Y... discover Ame... firepower and... the AC-47... ship, know... Puff the M... Dragon, w... the fightin... man's trie...

© 1983 Time-Life Books Inc.

The Vietnam Experience
Raising the Stakes
The Vietnam Experience
Setting the Stage
The Vietnam Experience
Passing the Torch
The Vietnam Experience
America Takes Over

TIME LIFE BOOKS   **The Vietna...**

If order card is... write to: THE VI... EXPERIENCE. T... LIFE BOOKS. T... Life Building. C... IL 60611.

Title:	Jet Support
Art Director:	Dianne Stassi
Copywriter:	Lewis Dana
Design Agency:	Wunderman, Ricotta & Kline
Client:	Time-Life Books

This new Time-Life Book series was considered risky because its subject matter, the VietNam War, is still controversial. The campaign had to effectively sell the books to both veterans and non-veterans without taking a position on the issues covered in the books.

Result:
The annual sales goal was met within the first four weeks of the campaign.

Title: Opportunity Knocking
Art Director: Jean Lehman
Copywriter: Richard Fisher
Design Agency: Wunderman, Ricotta & Kline
Client: Merrill Lynch, Pierce, Fenner & Smith

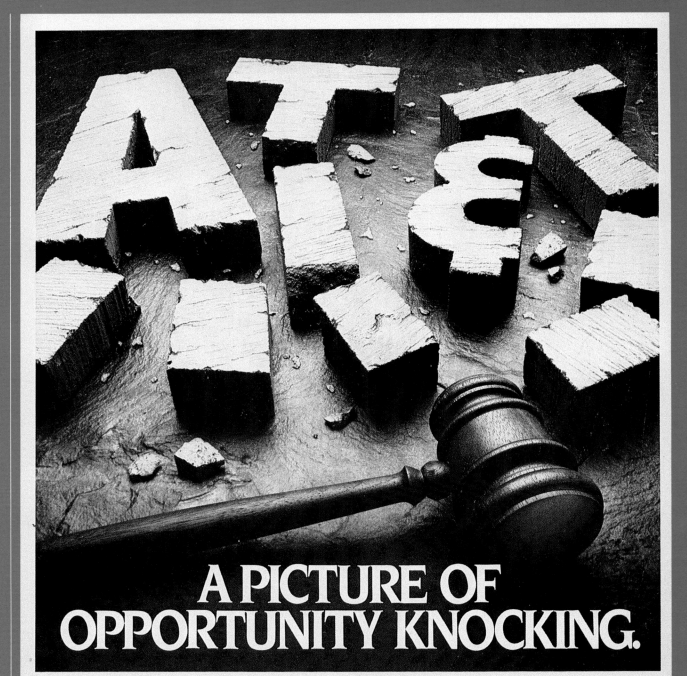

A PICTURE OF OPPORTUNITY KNOCKING.

Introducing the Merrill Lynch Unit Trust for AT&T Shares.

The people who thought it could never happen better think again. Because on January 1, 1984, it's happening. But the coming break-up of AT&T is really opportunity knocking right now. Because now you can invest in a unit trust for AT&T shares created by Merrill Lynch.

This Merrill Lynch unit trust is an excellent opportunity for you to capitalize on the potential of the eight new companies as a result of deregulation. And it's one convenient investment just like AT&T always was. You can exchange each share of your AT&T stock for one unit of this trust. Each unit will represent all eight of the companies in the same proportion as the break-up. And this exchange is generally tax-free.*

Plus you'll have liquidity because Merrill Lynch plans to maintain a secondary market to buy back your units at any time at the then prevailing market value.** Or you can get back your AT&T shares in any combination of the eight new companies until six months after the divestiture. Either of these options is available without any additional fee.

So get the facts about this unit trust for AT&T shares. Call the toll-free number listed below or fill out the coupon. Because now that opportunity is knocking, Merrill Lynch can open the door for you.

YES. I hear opportunity knocking.
Please send me the facts about this new unit trust for AT&T shares.
Mail to: Merrill Lynch, Pierce, Fenner & Smith, Inc
P.O. Box 2021, Jersey City, New Jersey 07303

A Prospectus containing more complete information about the Equity Income Fund, First Exchange Series—AT&T Shares, including all sales charges and expenses, will be sent upon receipt of this coupon. Read it carefully before you invest or send money.

Name _____
Address _____
City _____ State _____ Zip _____
Business Phone _____
Home Phone _____
Note: If you already have an account with Merrill Lynch, please give name and office address of Account Executive.

1 800 637-7455 EXT. 1173

Merrill Lynch
Merrill Lynch Pierce Fenner & Smith Inc
A breed apart.

Title: Who'll Put AT&T Back Together Again?
Art Director: Don Baker
Copywriter: Norma Friedman
Design Agency: Wunderman, Ricotta & Kline
Client: Merrill Lynch, Pierce, Fenner & Smith

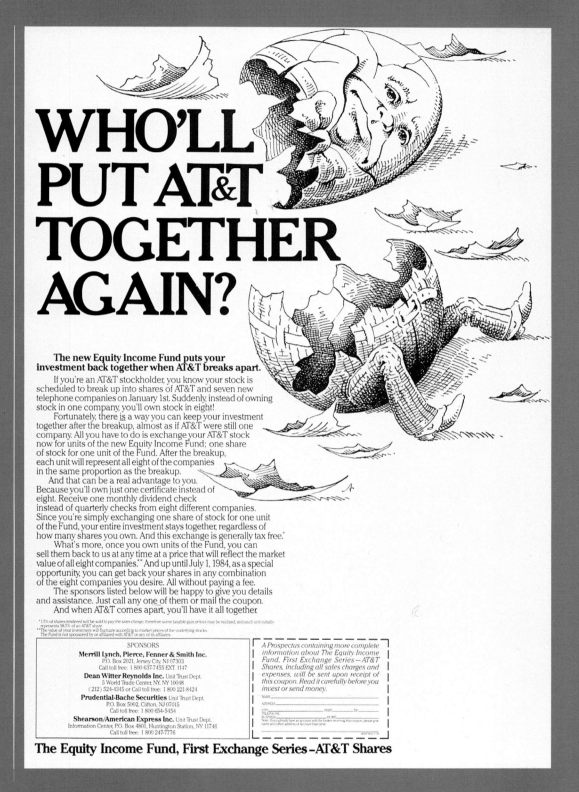

When AT&T was broken up, its stockholders were given shares in AT&T plus the seven regional holding companies created by the breakup agreement. This meant a lot of extra worry for holders of one of the most popular stocks. A group of investment companies created the AT&T Stock Fund, allowing AT&T stockholders to exchange their shares of the pre-breakup AT&T for shares in the Stock Fund. In effect, this kept their investment in all of AT&T—as represented by the holding companies plus AT&T itself—intact, simplifying the investor's financial dealings.

Result:
After only a few insertions of this campaign, the AT&T Stock Fund had reached more than a half-billion dollars in assets.

Campaign / Single Medium

Multi-piece Appeals Produced in One Medium

With the cost of personal sales calls escalating rapidly, direct marketing has become an indispensable tool for business of all types, but especially those that sell to other businesses. The potential value of each sale is high for those advertisers, so they are often willing to invest more heavily in concentrated direct marketing efforts than the average consumer-oriented advertiser.

For this reason, many of the winning entries in the category of campaigns run in a single medium were directed to other businesses.

Many of the most successful business campaigns offer the reader useful business information as an inducement to read the ad.

One of these, created for Bendix Corporation by Hanson Advertising Group (page 237), was even added to the permanent collection of the National Air Museum. The piece offers managers who buy electronics for commercial airliners a basic course in avionics. Bendix has a 60% share of the avionics market in the U.S. They offered the campaign as a service to the managers, some of whom are young, and don't have a deep understanding of the avionics field. One-fifth of those who received the piece wrote unsolicited letters of appreciation, presumably bolstering Bendix's image as the leader in commercial avionics.

These campaigns were designed with all of the limitations inherent in producing a group of ads that are at once consistent and yet varied enough for each to stand on its own. They were, as well, limited to one medium, without benefit of the cross support of other types of advertising vehicles.

The inventiveness shown in creating fresh and original ideas for not one, but a series of executions, reflects both the level of expertise being applied in direct response marketing and the emphasis placed on it by both clients and agencies.

Control Data Corporation took a similar tack in its series of magazine ads on small business (page 238-241). Control Data sells consulting services to small businesses, and the ads focused on the elements needed for these organizations to succeed.

Information, again, was the commodity being sold in the Fallon, McElligott Rice mall campaign for Interline, a telecommunications service company (page 243). With the break-up of AT&T, corporate telecommunications managers no longer have a single source of assistance in solving their telecommunications problems. Interline wanted these professionals to know that the company was capable and willing to help with support, service and information.

The breakup of AT&T enriched a number of advertising agencies this year, as the regional operating companies began advertising heavily to establish their own identities and to compete with other telecommunications companies allowed into the market by deregulation.

One of the most innovative campaigns was a series of newspaper ads created for U.S. West by Fallon, McElligott Rice (page 230-234). U.S. West was created as a holding company for the eight regional telephone companies in the western U.S. The ads used evocative photos of "Old West" subjects to link U.S. West to the tradition of service established by the western Bell companies.

Perhaps the most unusual campaign was the one created for Phoenix House, a drug rehabilitation organization, by Wunderman, Ricotta and Kline. Rather than simply hand over finished materials, the Wunderman, Ricotta & Kline team worked with Phoenix House residents in the rehabilitation program, teaching them how to write and produce the ads themselves.

We're out to win

We're not AT&T anymore. We're the 73,000 men and women who work for the companies of US WEST. We're Mountain Bell, Northwestern Bell, Pacific Northwest Bell and a growing number of unregulated companies, continuing a legacy of strength and a tradition of character.

We have reduced bureaucracy so that each of us has a very real stake in making our company grow and prosper. We serve more customers now than ever before, yet through re-organization, advanced technology and our own hard work, we have reduced our total work force by a third since 1981.

Start thinking
you haven't alread
utility. And we are
For a 32 page
write US WEST R
Englewood, Colo

Title:	Old West
Art Director:	Pat Burnham
Copywriter:	Bill Miller
Design Agency:	Fallon·McElligott Rice
Client:	U.S. West

After the breakup of AT&T, U.S. West was created. The new corporation needed to establish an image among investors and attract new stockholders. This campaign introduced U.S. West and let investors know the new company was willing and eager to compete on an equal footing with other telecommunications suppliers.

our spurs.

us as a growth company. If ou will soon. We are not a acting like one. ort, call 1-800-828-2400 or t, 7800 East Orchard Road, 80111.

USWEST

Mountain Bell. Northwestern Bell. Pacific Northwest Bell.
And a growing number of unregulated companies.

Bring on the

We are not AT&T anymore. The rules have changed. And so have we.

As the holding company for Mountain Bell, Northwestern Bell and Pacific Northwest Bell, we welcome our new competitive environment with a new and competitive organization.

We have learned from our past that regulation cannot shelter us from competition. So, today, whenever we find competition, we advocate deregulation. It is our belief that our customers and our share owners are best served by the laws of the marketplace.

Start thinking of us as a growth company. If you

PHOTOGRAPHED ON THE NATIONAL BISON RANGE, MOIESE, MONTANA BY HARLEY HETTICK

e competition.

haven't already, you will soon. We are not a utility. And we are not acting like one.

Find out how we're different than the other companies created by divestiture. For a 32 page report, call 1-800-828-2400 or write US WEST Report, 7800 East Orchard Road, Englewood, Colorado 80111.

USWEST

Mountain Bell. Northwestern Bell. Pacific Northwest Bell. And a growing number of unregulated companies.

We have been around these parts for over 100 years. You have known us as Mountain Bell, Northwestern Bell and Pacific Northwest Bell. But we're not AT&T anymore. We're US WEST. And we're blazing new trails.

As one of the largest corporations in America, we manage $17 billion in assets. Yet, uncharacteristic of a company our size, we are staffed lean and uniquely organized to take full advantage of the opportunities created by divestiture. Our decentralized structure makes us more responsive to our customers and to our new opportunities for growth.

Start thinking of us as a growth company. If you haven't already, you will soon. We are not a utility. And we are not acting like one.

For a 32 page report, call 1-800-828-2400 or write US WEST Report, 7800 East Orchard Road, Englewood, Colorado 80111.

USWEST

Mountain Bell. Northwestern Bell. Pacific Northwest Bell. And a growing number of unregulated companies.

Title:	Old West
Art Director:	Pat Burnham
Copywriter:	Bill Miller
Design Agency:	Fallon McElligott Rice
Client:	U.S. West

After the breakup of AT&T, U.S. West was created. The new corporation needed to establish an image among investors and attract new stockholders. This campaign introduced U.S. West and let investors know the new company was willing and eager to compete on an equal footing with other telecommunications suppliers.

NEXT YEAR, SHE COULD BE PLAYING WITH DRUGS.

At ten I had a toy firetruck. At eleven I sold it for a five dollar bag of pot.

Using drugs that young was unusual when I was eleven. It's not anymore. These days, in just about any sixth grade classroom there are kids using drugs. That's why people from Phoenix House are talking to kids in classrooms all over the country...trying to stop them before they start.

It's one part of a program of drug prevention and cure started by five ex-addicts almost twenty years ago. Since then, Phoenix House has kept thousands of kids from getting hooked. It's cured thousands more who're already hooked. Over 70% of the drug abusers who complete one year of a Phoenix House program come out drug free and stay that way.

I know...I'm one of them.

Now, due to government cutbacks and increasing costs, we need your help. Phoenix House can beat drug abuse, but not without your support.

Please give whatever you can and help keep more kids from trading in their toys on dope.

I WANT TO HELP STOP DRUG ABUSE.

☐ Enclosed is my donation of $_____ to the Phoenix House Development Fund.
☐ Please send me more information about Phoenix House drug abuse prevention, education and treatment programs.

Name_____
Address_____
City_____
State_____
Zip_____

PHOENIX HOUSE
164 West 74th Street, New York, N.Y. 10023   3
Contributions tax deductible to extent permitted by law.

THE PEOPLE WE SAVE MAY BE PEOPLE YOU LOVE
This message created by the drug-free people of Phoenix House

---

5 OUT OF 10 OF THESE BABIES WILL BE USING DRUGS BY THE TIME THEY'RE 15

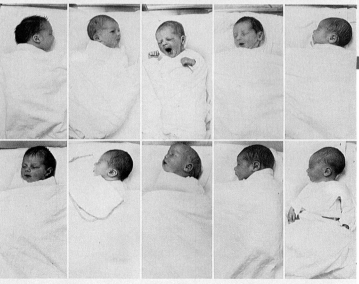

They will unless they learn the truth. It won't matter whether they live in a ghetto or a nice suburban home. Drugs don't care where you live, or who you are. I know. I got hooked when I was in fifth grade. By the time I was 14, I was selling the stuff to younger kids in the school yard to support my habit.

Drugs are a disease crippling our youth in every way there is. I know that too. I hit rock bottom in my own drugged lifestyle.

Then, on January 24th, 1983, I entered Phoenix House. When I did I quit drugs cold. They were replaced with counseling, residential therapy, vocational training and self-respect. There's no way to describe the way I am compared to the way I was except to say I'm drug free. Phoenix House worked for me. It's worked for more than 90% of the drug abusers who've completed the program. It's working in classrooms all over the country, keeping thousands of kids from getting hooked by telling them the truth about drugs.

We need your help to maintain that success rate. Because of government cutbacks, we have to rely more and more on private funding. With your help, Phoenix House can continue its winning fight against drug abuse. Without it, I don't know. There are a whole lot of kids out there going through what I went through. There are more being born every day who might. Please give what you can.

I WANT TO HELP STOP DRUG ABUSE.

☐ Enclosed is my donation of $_____ to the Phoenix House Development Fund.
☐ Please send me more information about Phoenix House drug abuse prevention, education and treatment programs.

Name_____
Address_____
City_____
State_____
Zip_____

PHOENIX HOUSE
164 West 74th Street, New York, N.Y. 10023   2
Contributions tax deductible to extent permitted by law.

THE PEOPLE WE SAVE MAY BE PEOPLE YOU LOVE
This message created by the drug-free people of Phoenix House

---

Title: Phoenix House
Art Directors: D. Stasi, B. Pasternak
Copywriter: C. Blood
Design Agency: Phoenix House Residents and
                  Wunderman Ricotta & Kline
Client: Phoenix House

Phoenix House is a drug rehabilitation and education organization in New York. The agency created a multi-media awareness and fund raising campaign by teaching residents of Phoenix House, who were currently in drug treatment programs, how to generate the advertising themselves.

Title: Phoenix House
Art Directors: D. Stasi, B. Pasternak
Copywriter: C. Blood
Design Agency: Phoenix House Residents and
                  Wunderman Ricotta & Kline
Client: Phoneix House

IS YOUR CHILD USING DRUGS?

HERE ARE TEN SIGNS TO LOOK FOR:

1. Change of Friends
2. Lack of Motivation
3. Abrupt Mood Changes
4. Redness in Eyes or Dilation of Pupils
5. Change in Sleeping Habits
6. Secrecy
7. Sudden Change in Weight
8. Decline in Personal Hygiene
9. Failing School Grades
10. Marks or Swelling on the Body

If you think you know your child like my parents thought they knew me, take my advice. Look into what your child has been doing lately. Drugs are wrecking more young lives than anything else today. They were wrecking mine before I got help from Phoenix House.

Phoenix House has been turning drug abusers into former drug abusers for almost 20 years. In all that time, more than 90% of their graduates have gone on to live drug-free lives.

Thousands more who might have become hooked, didn't get hooked because they learned the facts about drugs in prevention sessions held by Phoenix House in classrooms all over the country.

But due to government cutbacks, the success rates of our programs are threatened.

We can't keep going without your support. By helping us fight the war against drug abuse, you can help win it.

Please give what you can.

I WANT TO HELP STOP DRUG ABUSE.

☐ Enclosed is my donation of $_____ to the Phoenix House Development Fund.
☐ Please send me more information about Phoenix House drug abuse prevention, education and treatment programs.

Name _____
Address _____
City _____
State _____
Zip _____

PHOENIX HOUSE
164 West 74th Street, New York, N.Y. 10023
Contributions tax deductible to extent permitted by law.

THE PEOPLE WE SAVE MAY BE PEOPLE YOU LOVE

This message created by the drug-free people of Phoenix House

---

IS THIS THE KIND OF JUNK THAT'S PASSING FOR LUNCH IN YOUR CHILD'S SCHOOL?

In my school drugs were as common as cookies and milk. I started off using my lunch money for drugs. I wanted to be accepted by the rest of the kids. After a while, lunch money wasn't enough. I started stealing from home and it was all downhill until I entered Phoenix House and learned to deal with my problems instead of using drugs to run away from them.

Phoenix House was started by five ex-heroin addicts who believed they could prevent and cure drug abuse. They did and Phoenix works. It keeps thousands of kids off drugs with classroom prevention sessions all over the country. It has cured over 90% of the drug abusers who've completed its rehabilitation programs. Including me.

If Phoenix House is going to keep on working, we need your help. Government cutbacks are one reason. Higher costs are another. Please give what you can. Help Phoenix House keep on helping the kids of today... and tomorrow.

I WANT TO HELP STOP DRUG ABUSE.

☐ Enclosed is my donation of $_____ to the Phoenix House Development Fund.
☐ Please send me more information about Phoenix House drug abuse prevention, education and treatment programs.

Name _____
Address _____
City _____
State _____
Zip _____

PHOENIX HOUSE
164 West 74th Street, New York, N.Y. 10023
Contributions tax deductible to extent permitted by law.

THE PEOPLE WE SAVE MAY BE PEOPLE YOU LOVE

This message created by the drug-free students of Phoenix House

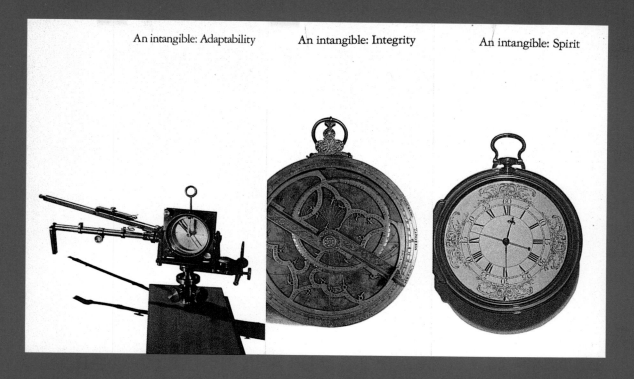

An intangible: Adaptability   An intangible: Integrity   An intangible: Spirit

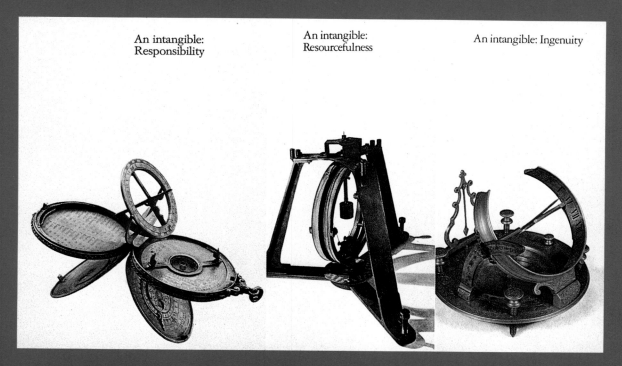

An intangible: An intangible: An intangible: Ingenuity
Responsibility   Resourcefulness

Title:	Intangibles of Leadership
Art Director:	Mike Faulkner
Copywriters:	Maryellen Horgan, Chuck Hanson
Design Agency:	Hanson Advertising Group
Client:	Bendix Air Transport Avionics Div., Bendix Corporation

With a 60% share of market, Bendix is the traditional leader in electronic equipment for commercial airlines. A new generation of airline managers who are unfamiliar with avionics technology are now making decisions at these airlines. A six-part campaign was created to generate high-level inquiries and to strengthen Bendix's leadership position by providing the managers useful information on the basics of aircraft electronics.

Result:
Of those receiving the series, 48% responded, including 20% who sent unsolicited letters of appreciation. Bendix also received requests to reprint the pieces in the airlines' own publications, and the corporation was accepted into the National Air Museum.

The Small Business's Three Worst Enemies.

Most small business ventures don't fail in the marketplace.

Nor do they succumb to cash flow problems and government regulations.

In truth, most small business ventures fail even before they begin.

In the hearts and minds of the very people responsible for their success.

Thinking too big.

Enthusiasm and energy are what make a small business tick.

But sometimes all this energy can cloud our ability to assess opportunities realistically.

To be sure, the opportunity may exist.

But in our excitement, we fail to study it. Measure it. Set our goals. Plan our strategies.

Instead, we blindly charge ahead. Scrambling up mountains, which in reality may only be molehills.

Costly adventures are these.

Thinking too small.

While some throw caution to the wind, others will proceed too carefully.

They'll underestimate sales. They'll underestimate production. They'll underestimate costs.

They'll underestimate everything.

Thinking Too Small.

Thinking Too Big.

including themselves.

And, ironically, what may have been a great opportunity, both financially and personally, never amounts to anything.

Thinking too much.

Fear of failure can paralyze even the most brilliant and talented small business operators.

They'll tediously examine, re-examine, cross-examine, analyze and trivialize every detail. Endlessly meeting and discussing every possible option with all its ramifications.

Ultimately, what may have been a simple and exciting idea becomes lost in a dull, intellectual maze.

Thinking straight.

Control Data has, of course, experienced these very same human conditions with all their derivative problems.

But in its search for ways to correct them, Control Data has discovered a unique approach.

An approach that gives its managers the tools to approach problems systematically and intelligently. And, consequently, take full advantage of business opportunities as they arise.

Delusion, fear and indecision are, thankfully, replaced by intelligence, confidence and authority.

It is in this spirit that Control Data our parent company, gave the breath of life to Control Data Business Advisors.

Practical advice. Predictable results.

Our charter is simple. To bring to you the excitement and challenge of making your business run your way.

Our technique is equally simple.

We give you the tools. And let you use them.

Unlike most traditional consultants, the people you will work with have experienced the very same problems you are experiencing now.

Thinking Too Much.

Unlike most traditional consultants, the techniques for solving these problems are the techniques we ourselves have used successfully. In real business situations.

At Control Data Business Advisors, we don't propose to solve your problems for you.

But, rather, teach you to take control and solve them yourself. Confidently. Intelligently. Efficiently.

And, most importantly, correctly.

Mail the coupon for an invitation to our free, introductory seminar.

Or, if you prefer, a free personal consultation, including program recommendation and costs.

Better yet, call 800-382-7070 toll free right now.

It may be the most courageous business decision you'll ever make.

Help. I have seen the enemy. And he is me.

☐ Please have one of your staff call to make an appointment for a free consultation.
☐ I'd like to attend your free seminar.

Name
Company
Address
City   State   Zip
Phone (   )

CONTROL DATA BUSINESS ADVISORS
Box 0-MNB07S, Minneapolis, MN 55440

Title: Small Business Consultation
Art Director: Bob Barrie
Copywriter: Phil Hanft
Design Agency: Fallon McElligott Rice
Client: Control Data Business Advisors

Control Data ran this series of ads examining the causes of small business failures, and offering its consulting services as a solution to the small business owner's lack of experience.

You aren't born with a good business head.
You have to develop it.

Lack of confidence is, generally speaking, not a problem for most people running a small business.

But, without question, lack of business acumen is.

"Ninety percent of small business failures are caused by lack of general and managerial experience." Dun & Bradstreet

Unfortunately, one can run a business for years and still never acquire the knowledge and expertise required to do it successfully.

Bad business habits, like bad personal habits, are hard to recognize. And equally difficult to let go of.

The small business or entrepreneurial personality often operates on a purely instinctual level.

Emotions dictate who is hired. And fired.

Gut feelings determine how resources are allocated.

Products and services develop from personal taste. Not marketplace reality.

Day-to-day operation is left to whim. Long range strategy, if there is one, is essentially intuitive.

"One of the greatest failings of today's executive is his inability to do what he's supposed to do." Malcolm Kent

Or as Pogo once wryly observed, "I have seen the enemy. And he is us."

At Control Data Business Advisors, we, too, have seen the enemy.

Unlike most traditional business consultants, many of us grew out of entrepreneurial experiences like yours.

We, too, have worked 48 hour days and 14 day weeks, running on adrenalin and dreams.

We, too, have known the intoxicating thrill of success in the face of impossible odds.

And we, too, have felt the specter of failure breathing down our necks.

Our experience isn't intellectual. It is practical.

Therefore, unlike most traditional consultants, we have no magic solutions, no special panaceas.

Instead, we offer a program that allows *you* to solve problems and take advantage of opportunities.

A program that gives you access to techniques and tools that have proven successful in situations very similar to yours.

A program that gives you continuous feedback while you practice what you learn.

So you see what's working and what's not. And can make appropriate adjustments.

The program revolves around regular strategy sessions between you and a Control Data Business Advisors staff member.

Sessions focus on assessing your needs. Where you want your business to go. What's going well. What isn't.

At the conclusion of each strategy session, you agree on an Action Plan, including a written summary for one or more specific problems.

"Management by objectives works if you know the objectives. Ninety percent of the time you don't." Peter Drucker

The areas you can choose to focus on are things like how to hire the right people. And how to get rid of the wrong people.

How to train your people for more responsibility. And how to get them to accept it willingly.

How to improve your cash flow and allocate resources.

How to improve your knowledge of your customer and use that knowledge to your advantage.

How to manage your time and delegate responsibility.

How to improve the day-to-day operation of your business. And how to plan long range strategies.

Most importantly, how to get your business running your way.

What kind of program you need and how much it'll cost is, of course, critical to someone operating a small business enterprise.

The answers are surprisingly accessible.

"To make headway, use your head." B. C. Forbes

Simply mail the coupon for an invitation to our free introductory seminar. Or, if you prefer, a free personal consultation, including program recommendations and costs.

Better yet, call 800-382-7070 toll free right now.

Help. I, too, have seen the enemy. And he is me.
☐ Please have one of your staff call me to make an appointment for a free consultation.
☐ I'd like to attend your free seminar.

Name

Company

Address

City   State   Zip

Phone (   )

CONTROL DATA BUSINESS ADVISORS
Box 0-MNB07S, Minneapolis, MN 55440

Most small businesses go
not the capital, is

Most operators of small businesses don't run into trouble because they have a shortage of cash.

On the contrary, they almost always run into trouble because they have a shortage of time.

The person who sells the product is the person who makes the product.

And the person who makes the product is the person who keeps the books, takes the calls, does the billing, types the letters and cleans the toilets.

That is as it should be.

But as the business grows, enthusiasm and entrepreneurial spirit aren't enough.

There are too many jobs. And not enough time to do any of them well.

Business stagnates, falters and often fails.

Unfortunately, the idea of giving up control in order to gain control is not an acceptable alternative to most entrepreneurial types.

For most small business owners, more frenzied activity is the only solution.

So the bigger the problem, the harder they work at getting nowhere. As Pogo once wryly observed,

"I have seen the enemy. And he is us." At Control Data Business Advisors, we, too, have seen the enemy.

Unlike most traditional business consultants, many of us grew out of entrepreneurial experiences like yours.

We, too, have worked 48 hour days and 14 day weeks, running on adrenalin and dreams.

We, too, have known the intoxicating thrill of success in the face of impossible odds.

And we, too, have felt the specter of failure breathing down our necks.

Our experience isn't intellectual. It is practical.

Therefore, unlike most traditional consultants, we have no magic solutions, no special panaceas.

Instead, we offer a program that allows *you* to solve problems and take advantage of opportunities.

A program that gives you access to techniques and tools that have proven successful in situations very similar to yours.

A program that gives you continuous feedback while you practice what you learn. So you see what's working and what's not.

under because the owner, stretched too thin.

And can make appropriate adjustments.
The program revolves around regular strategy sessions between you and a Control Data Business Advisors staff member.
Sessions focus on assessing your needs. Where you want your business to go.

What's going well. What isn't.
At the conclusion of each strategy session, you agree on an Action Plan, including a written summary for one or more specific problems.

The areas you can choose to focus on are things like how to hire the right people. And how to get rid of the wrong people.

How to improve your cash flow and allocate resources.

How to improve your knowledge of your customer and use that knowledge to your best advantage.

How to allocate your time and delegate responsibility.

How to improve the day-to-day operation of your business.

And how to plan long range strategies.

Most importantly, how to get your business running your way.

What kind of program you need and how much it'll cost is, of course, critical to someone operating a small business enterprise.

The answers are surprisingly accessible.

Simply mail the coupon for an invitation to our free introductory seminar. Or, if you prefer, a free personal consultation, including program recommendations and costs.

Better yet, call 800-382-7070 toll free.

But do it today. Tomorrow you'll be too busy.

Title: Capture a Maryland Memory
Art Director: Phil Pope
Copywriter: Susan Daugherty
Design Agency: Earle Palmer Brown
Client: Maryland Tourism

As a vacation destination, Maryland had very low awareness among potential travelers and was being outspent by other state tourism boards by a large margin. The goal of this campaign was to increase market share to 3% of total domestic and 20% of the regional travel market. The campaign was designed so that it would be supported by counties and private businesses, to help the state stretch its limited media budget.

Result:
Maryland Tourism received 60,692 coupon responses; 19,364 toll-free telephone responses; and 34,760 written responses requesting information on Maryland travel. The number of tourists visiting Maryland increased 20% over the total for the previous year.

Title: Hats
Art Director: Dean Hanson
Copywriter: Rod Kilpatrick
Design Agency: Fallon McElligott Rice
Client: Interline Communication Services

Corporate communications managers were faced with a problem after the breakup of AT&T. They no longer had one single organization which could handle all of their business or act as a telecommunications resource. Interline wanted these managers to know they could rely on Interline to answer questions and supply necessary services. This light approach emphasized how complicated the managers' jobs had become by referring to the number of hats they now had to wear—how many different jobs they had to perform.

Since January 1st, You Might Have To Do It By Plane.

Until now, you could solve any problem, anywhere, with a single call to your phone company representative. No matter how widespread your office network was.

But these days, a single call to your travel agent might be more appropriate. Because the only way to keep tabs on your distant offices could be to barnstorm the country and visit them in person.

Fortunately, there is a more down-to-earth alternative. Interline can take full responsibility for the service and maintenance of your communications equipment. Locally or nationwide.

Just ask, and we'll send you a free booklet with all the details. The next time you're flying a rescue mission, it'll give you something to read on the plane.

How To Wear Your New Hats Without Losing Your Head.

☐ Please send your free booklet detailing the full range of In communications support services.
☐ Please call me to arrange a m

Art Directors

Copywriters

Design Agencies

Clients